Soul Transfiguration

GUIDE TO THE HEAVENWORK

70 JOYOUS WAYS TO PURIFY YOUR SOUL AND ENTER HEAVEN

Rand Jameson Shields

LP
Light Path Press
COLUMBUS, OHIO
www.TheHeavenWork.com

Light Path Press

Columbus, Ohio

www.TheHeavenWork.com

ISBN 978–0–9797647–0–X

Manufactured in the United States

Light Path Press

CONTENTS

TRANSCENDING

ASCENDING

TRANSFIGURATION

Narrow is the gate,
And difficult the way
Which leads to [Heaven],
And there are few who find it.

—Jesus Nazarene
Book of Matthew 5:14

Come, enter the gate of Heaven

ONE

NO TRUER TEACHER

Blessed are you, intrepid in Spirit, who rise above the ways of earth in search of Heaven, for the door will be opened to you. Open, then, the door of your heart and read with your Soul my meager words.

The essence of all being is the loving transformation of Soul, by the sacred Light of Heaven, into Heaven. This is the Truth of truths, the Will of Heaven, the Direction of Souls, the Path of the Heaven Light. This is the HeavenWork.

By the grace of God, I have been commanded by Heaven to invite you on a journey—not a journey of your body or its mind, but your Soul. Come with me, then, beyond the earth, and enter freely into Spirit. Come with me into the Heaven Light.

On our journey, you will pass along a joyous Path of Light. At the end of our journey, you will find Heaven There waiting for you, and There within, the three million elect Souls who found their way before you—all sanctified, who passed along this same Path of Light. And you will be amazed at the changes that take place as you cross, in glory, into the Sacred.

We will make our journey along the Path to Heaven, the Path that Jesus passed along, the Path he taught his followers, the loving Path of Spirit that faded from man's understanding two thousand years ago. Come, and rediscover his lost teachings of the Heaven Light.

The HeavenWork is Heaven's return to man of the Soul's pure Path of Light to Heaven.

The HeavenWork is not about religion or beliefs. It is not about a change of mind at all, but change of being. It is not about thinking what Heaven may be like, but about actually approaching and entering Heaven with your Soul.

HeavenWork, the spiritualizing mechanism behind every religion, involves magnifying the Light of Heaven with your Soul in ways that sanctify—in the *right* ways at the *right* times. Performing your HeavenWork in such sequence passes your Soul steadily along the sacred Path of Heaven Light, to Heaven— all the way to Heaven.

> ***HeavenWork*** *means magnifying Heaven Light with your Soul in ways that sanctify in the right ways at the right times, passing your Soul all the way to Heaven.*

They, who would imprison your Soul by telling you it cannot be done, or that it has been done for you, or by keeping secret the way of Light are the unwitting enemies of Heaven. For it is the nature of Soul to enter the Heaven Light. We came from the Light, and we shall return to the Light. We should never leave the Light.

I did not find the HeavenWork, the HeavenWork found me. It began rather abruptly with an incident that took place one August morning in 1962, when I was eight years old. That was the day I drowned in a swimming pool in Columbus, Ohio.

This near tragedy turned out to be one of the most rewarding events of my life, not just because I was saved, but because the moment I died my Soul awakened, for the first time.

In the minute I was underwater, my Soul broke completely free of body and mind and the earth, transcending into a free and infinite sky of clear light.

There I felt the Presence of Heaven, invisible to my Soul, but ever so strong and near, and I remembered. I remembered clearly in my Soul what was before I entered body. I remembered perfectly where I came from and what I came to life to do—what compels all Souls to come to life: To magnify the Light of Holy Spirit on earth. For carrying and concentrating the Holy Spirit Light on earth sanctifies the Soul, making it worthy of Heaven.

As I prepared to surrender my Soul into Spirit and be carried to the place of rest, my two guardian Angels suddenly appeared. Someone had seen my body floating in the water, and I was being rescued. Just as my face was pulled from the water, these wonderful Sacred Beings of Light reached out and touched my chest so that my lungs convulsed and expelled the water. In an instant, a miracle occurred—I resuscitated without a complication, and my Soul was placed, by the Angels, on the Path of Light.

Back in body, my Soul immediately filled with the Holy Spirit, which I came to call the Heaven Light, or simply the Light, just like Jesus did. And like Jesus, I carried the Light in my Soul constantly.

The Heaven Light became my best friend and teacher. Throughout my early life, I learned directly from the Heaven Light different ways to carry the Light, joyously. The omniscient Heaven Light kept teaching me new ways to pass farther along the Path of Light. Each new way, I knew, brought me closer to Heaven. In this way, I followed Jesus into the Light, just as he directed us all to do. And that made all the difference.

For 17 years following my Soul's great awakening, I never let my Soul release the Heaven Light, but worked with it, joyously, constantly, like a sail in a loving wind. The Light taught me to do things not of the earth, but things there were no words for. The Light taught me directly and purely, without words. The Light was always teaching me. The Light was always teaching me things of Heaven.

The more I worked and played the Heaven Light and the more I concentrated it, the more my Soul changed, the Lighter my Soul became. Every moment in the Light my Soul was rewarded.

Then came grace. At 2:10 PM on October 9, 1979, my Soul was taken ascendant by an Angel, where I beheld, with absolute humility, the entirety of Heaven. A wondrous sacred joy poured out from the Firmament into my Soul, and the Angel directed me to look up, into the highest Heaven, where I beheld the awe-some Face of God-in-Heaven—what Jesus called *Abba*.

In that very instant, I was burned, penetrated and consumed by a Divine flash Transmission that emanated from this Holiest Light of the Creator, and my Soul changed forever! At that moment Heaven made known to me what must happen to enter Heaven, and how to go about it—how every Soul can go about it. At that very moment, I renounced the earth and my body, and Heaven became home to my Soul.

By grace, the way to Heaven has remained open. Countless times throughout the past 28 years, when I release my body and mind, entering into my Soul, I am always There again, before the gate of Heaven. Every time. All this time my Soul has remained constant, in awe and witness of wondrous workings of sacred Spirit beyond word, beyond the comprehension of the mind.

Over the years, I have continued to witness in Soul a miracle that never ceases to thrill me: The steady arrival of Souls before Heaven—more than twenty-seven thousand by now—Souls who sanctified along the Path of the Heaven Light. One by one, newly sanctified Souls arrive daily before Heaven and are immediately received in a rapturous cascade of Soul transfiguration that I have yet to find described in the world's sacred writings. Every time it is the same. For 28 years, in awe, I have watched, in Soul, this miracle of miracles transpire at the gate of Heaven.

From time to time, the Breath of Heaven crosses the Firmament to engulf even my Soul in Divine Invitation to enter In. But each time I hesitate. I will not leave the earth until I share with you the Light made known in the Divine Transmission: The HeavenWork, the embodiment of Jesus' lost teachings of the Light—70 joyous ways to sanctify the Soul on earth with the Heaven Light.

And I will tell you this, in Heaven's Truth, this book has been in the making for more than a thousand years. This, Heaven allows me.

The HeavenWork is not a belief system, but a set of joyous, natural and progressive exercises that directly engage your Soul with the Heaven Light. The HeavenWork exercises enable you to embrace and open your Soul, and return you to the sacred path you intended to follow before you entered body. It applies to all walks of life, and every religion, enhancing every moment of your existence, nurturing your Soul's unfoldment.

These exercises will help you find your Soul, amplify your Soul, feel with your Soul, embrace and live in your Soul every waking (*and* sleeping) moment, integrate your Soul into every aspect of your life, pray from your Soul, live in pure joy, know perfect intimacy, see others' Souls and Angels, purify your Soul, directly glean the Will of Heaven, create miracles of compassion with Heaven, visit Heaven, and ultimately enter Heaven, forever. You *can* do all this in life, and what's more, you can joyfully work it into your normal daily routine.

Once you begin your HeavenWork—even if you spend only minutes a day practicing your exercises—your Soul will engage and continue to sanctify on its own. Such is the independent nature of Soul set free in Spirit.

The HeavenWork is not a religion, but a way of increasing your spirituality to enhance whatever religious tradition you follow. Just as prayer has its place in every religion, so does the HeavenWork.

The HeavenWork exercises are not new, nor were they first used by Jesus, but by the ancients, for a million Souls had passed along the Path of Light before him.

Now they are for you.

The HeavenWork is for everyone on earth. From the moment you begin these exercises—from the moment of your Soul's awakening—you will find your Soul continuously transforming along the Path of Light, getting nearer and nearer to Heaven. You will change, becoming more and more like Heaven, as you enter into the Sacred.

Each time you perform an exercise you will feel your Soul changing, and purifying. There is no one to stop you, no one to sell you, no one to mislead or distract you, no mystery, no mythology, no doctrine, no membership, no control, no shaming, no directing, no impossible ordeal, no false complacency, no programming, no manipulation, no obligation, none of the unnecessary human encumbrances that have exiled the Soul of man from Heaven for so long.

The HeavenWork does not tell you what to do with your life, it teaches you how to embrace life with your Soul, just as you intended before you entered body.

While the HeavenWork will carry your Soul along the Path of Light, everything you need to know you will learn directly from the Heaven Light, for within it is the Will of Heaven, and there is no truer teacher.

It is time to Awaken your Soul.

Come, enter the Path of Light.

AWAKENING

AWAKENING→TRANSCENDING→ASCENDING→TRANSFIGURATION

TWO

How To Awaken Your Soul

Exercise 1

The Soul's Great Awakening

All this time you were here.

At different times in your life your Soul may have awakened, rising mysteriously into your awareness and filling you with wondrous awe. Then, only moments later, just as mysteriously as your Soul rose, so it faded.

What makes this exercise, your Soul's Great Awakening truly great is that you will learn to awaken your Soul without mystery, and keep it present, so it will never again fade away.

Finding your Soul does not need to take a long time. You can find it right now, and this is how.

Goal: *To locate and awaken your Soul.*

Preparation: *Sit in a chair, undisturbed, somewhere you feel comfortable.*

Steps:

1. *Relax in your chair, until you reach a calm, deep, confident state of mind. Let go of any anticipation or thoughts.*

2. *Take a moment to remember…the first time you loved…or the first time you knew you were loved…or the first time you wanted to be loved.*

3. *Now take a few deep breaths, then clap your hands and place them over your heart.*

4. *Wait for the feeling to happen.*

Shortly a feeling will surround your heart—a tingling. This is not a cardiac response, it is not physical at all. It is your Soul stirring.

The tingling may be faint or strong, it may remain around your heart, or spread throughout your chest and arms, rising into your head and beyond, and spreading down your body, even extending beyond your body, surrounding you in a glowing ball. This is good, this is your Soul expanding. Allow your Soul to expand fully.

Your Soul has always been there, in and around your heart, and it will never leave you. When you die, you will be only your Soul, and it is your mind and body that will drop away with the earth and all the things of earth.

Keep your hands on your heart. Allow the tingling to continue. If you start to think about the tingling, you will find the tingling stops. This is your mind stepping in to distract you from your Soul. When this happens, simply ignore your thoughts by returning your attention to your heart and waiting for the tingling to return. The Soul's Great Awakening is for nurturing the tingling, so that your Soul awakens more and more.

Within the tingling you may feel a joy that could instantly expand and fill the sky. This is because your awakened Soul remembers it steadily receives the Heaven Light in some measure, and that the sky of Heaven Light is immense, carrying all the way from Heaven. Always invite the joy to enter into your Soul.

When your mind moves in, when you start thinking about something and the tingling stops, this gives you a good opportunity to experience how your Soul and mind interact, revealing the insecure nature of the mind and the peaceful ground of Soul. You can begin to identify the subtleties of your Soul and distinguish them from the mind's distracting ramblings. By preferring to place your awareness with your Soul, your mind will gradually recede, naturally, allowing you to remain in Soul longer. You need not struggle with the mind.

Once you have felt the tingling, you never have to separate from your Soul again, you can always be present in Soul. Whenever you notice your Soul has stopped tingling, simply place your hands back on your heart for the tingling to come back. The more you practice your Soul's Great Awakening, the more you will remain centered in your Soul.

Don't expect a powerful awakening at first. Exercise 1 is for stirring your Soul. Many of the following HeavenWork exercises will provide the empowerment.

You will want to repeat this exercise over and over, until your Soul remains awake all on its own. Your heart's tingling indicates your Soul is awake.

Now that you have awakened your Soul, nurture it, for your Soul is going to rise and unfold and become the essence of your entire being. There is nothing to stop you.

With all your heart and Soul, thank deeply, graciously, and humbly
the Heaven Light, the Sacred Beings in the Light, and all of Heaven
for the Blessing just bestowed upon your Soul.

⚡ FINE TUNING

If you did not feel the tingling at first, don't worry. Simply try again and again until you do. Be calm and patient. Remember, it's your eternal Soul versus your mind. Your Soul is sure to win if you persevere. The trick is to relax your body and mind, and let your Soul shine.

The Heaven Work is progressive. Each exercise prepares you for the next one.
Thus you must master the exercise you are on before moving to the next one.
Repeat this exercise 10 times before moving to the next one.

Do not move on to the next exercise until you have experienced the tingling.

Go ever to the heart.

EXERCISE 2

IRON MAIDEN

A little death to wake up the Soul.

It seems ironic that we generally pass entirely through life with our Soul asleep only to find at the moment of death that the Soul fully awakens. This is because our mind and body suppress our Soul, forming a veil of embodiment. In life we must find ways to bring out the Soul.

Back in the old days there was an instrument of torture and execution known as the Iron Maiden, a body-shaped container a prisoner was put into that prevented any movement. To your Soul, at the moment of death, your body seems a lot like an Iron Maiden.

Because the Soul knows what to do at the moment of death, one way to awaken and separate your Soul from your body is to enact a safe "little death" through this simple exercise.

Goal: *To pass your Soul through the veil of embodiment.*

Preparation: *Make sure you will not be disturbed, loosen any clothing that may distract you, remove your shoes, and lie on the floor in a dark room.*

Steps:

1. *Lie on your back, with your arms at your sides resting on the floor.*

2. *Countdown backwards from 10 to zero, knowing that the moment you reach zero, you will no longer move your body, that your body must remain still as a corpse.*

3. *For all intents and purposes, keep your body perfectly still, as if you have died. You are only allowed to breathe through your nose, and the only movement you may make is your chest moving up and down with your breathing. You may not move anything else. No swallowing, no changing position, no scratching your nose.*

For this exercise to work, you must resolve in your mind that your body has died and therefore cannot move, no matter how much you want it do, for the fading mind sometimes struggles and even panics just before the moment of death, when it must surrender its body, and itself.

Each time your mind rises up in effort to move the body, simply keep still.

If you continue to disregard the mind, gradually, your mind will give up and recede.

Your heart will then stir, and fill with the tingling glow of your Soul. No awareness of your body will remain, and your Soul's tingling will intensify. Allow this to happen. Let the tingling surge and fill your awareness. Feel the joy and freedom in the tingling!

You have just released your Soul, as in death.

Let the tingling spread, like you are a ball of joyous light, free of body, free to glow like a sun, free to burn through all of materiality. Bask in the glow of your awakened Soul.

In a way you are practicing for your real death—a valuable preparation for an important opportunity for your Soul. Know that when your time does come, with the help of your HeavenWork, death will have no sting, and you will be in the Heaven Light.

After you have experienced the free joy of separation from your body, you may return to your body simply by moving. But allow the tingling to continue. Always let your Soul resonate!

There is something special about the Iron Maiden exercise—a profound, wordless understanding about the afterlife and immortality of the Soul that remains ever-present in your awareness.

With all your heart and Soul, thank deeply, graciously, and humbly the Heaven Light, the Sacred Beings in the Light, and all of Heaven for the Blessing just bestowed upon your Soul.

Repeat this exercise 10 times before moving to the next one.

Do not move on to the next exercise until your tingling has grown noticeably.

Your Soul does not know death.

EXERCISE 3

SENSING SOULS

The truth behind the mask.

There must be a hundred different kinds of hugs, and I cannot think of one that doesn't feel good. But here you are about to get the most different hug of all—the Soul hug.

Imagine the way things really are, that only Souls exist—billions of Souls—and that nothing material exists, no earth, no sky, no clothes, no body, no thinking, only Souls. Imagine six billion exquisite, glowing, loving, infinitely-reaching conscious balls of light suspended in black space, and you are one of them!

You have learned already in your HeavenWork that you, Soul, reside in your body, and you know that every other body also houses a beautiful Soul. You may not yet be able to "see" other Souls with your Soul, but Soul hugging will help you develop this spiritual sense.

Goal: *To see into Spirit.*

Preparation: *Simply have someone willing to stand in front of you.*

Steps:

1. *Simply stand a few feet in front of your partner, and relax.*

2. *Now Awaken your Soul, using Soul's Great Awakening (exercise 1).*

3. *Close your eyes.*

4. *Feel rising in your heart the tingling you evoked using Iron Maiden (exercise 2). Release your awareness of your body until all physical sensation has disappeared.*

5. *Let the tingling in your Soul intensify, and feel your awareness shift downward from your head to your heart, where your tingling is centered.*

6. *Allow your tingling to spread outward from your heart, outward from your body, and forward, toward your partner. Feel with your tingling Soul the warm glow coming from the Soul of your partner.*

7. *Remain in that still moment of direct Soul-to-Soul contact for as long as you please.*

Do not speak, do not think in words, but wonder wordlessly at what intimacy just occurred. You are learning how to embrace another Soul with your Soul. You are starting to remember how to see with your Soul.

Practice Sensing Souls often and you will come to realize your Soul does not need your body's eyes to see, but can behold Souls beside you, behind you, and even far away.

With all your heart and Soul, thank deeply, graciously, and humbly the Heaven Light, the Sacred Beings in the Light, and all of Heaven for the Blessing just bestowed upon your Soul.

Repeat this exercise 10 times before moving to the next one.

Compassion is surrender of Soul to Heaven's infinite love, beyond illusions, knowing that your Soul is no different from any other.

⚡ ADDED TWIST

Once you have learned to slide your Soul past the mind to behold another Soul, you can use other methods such as Eye Gazing:

1. Sit relaxed and undisturbed with your partner, and gaze into her eyes.

2. Relax deeper and Awaken your Soul (exercise 1).

3. Release gently and freely your thoughts, emotions and body sense.

You will find your normal mode of perception now shifts downward, moving from behind your eyes in your head to an invisible ball (your Soul) surrounding your chest. Immediately your ball of subtle perception will cease to perceive the body of your partner, and instead observe the ball of invisible light energy around your partner's chest (her Soul).

Learn to grasp with your Soul that invisible true being of your partner's Soul, for such is the indestructible immateriality of Spirit.

With enough practice you will soon be able to observe other Souls at will. When you get good at this you will find that all of the material world fades away, leaving you perfectly alone Soul-to-Soul.

When you Awaken on the earth, your intent Soul sets forever to sanctify, and the Angels and all the Sacred Beings in the Light will always be with you.

EXERCISE 4

HEAVENHOME

Homing in on Heaven.

You may remember from early childhood moments during profound worship, or in times of great need the holy presence of God directed into you, invisible but certain, both from above your head and within your heart.

This wonderful awareness is usually referred to as God's "Countenance," and the sense of direction as God's "Immanence."

You are blessed when this happens, for in those moments you are faced with the Truth of truths, Being beyond being. You are in the presence of God-in-Heaven, and your Soul is made gracious.

To the mind and Soul this divine process seems like God is visiting you here on earth. But this experience is not God descending onto earth, but your Soul slipping into the Sacred, to before Heaven.

You can learn to make this happen, and what's more, you can glean with your Soul exactly where Heaven is.

Goal: *To locate Heaven and Mark your path.*

Preparation: *Clear out a little space in your closet and put a chair inside.*

Steps:

1. *Sit still in the chair in the dark, with the closet light off.*

2. *Relax, let your mind's discomforts leave you. Let feelings of claustrophobia pass.*

3. *You will begin to mysteriously "sense" the closet's surrounding objects in the dark by some kind of radar. You realize by now that it is your Soul expanding out in the dark.*

4. *Fill your Soul with the understanding that you are about to visit the most Sacred place in the universe.*

5. *Place your hands on your heart, bow your head, and bend forward a little.*

6. *Awaken your Soul (exercise 1).*

7. *As your Soul tingles, will purely and wordlessly that God-in-Heaven look upon you.*

8. *Wait for the presence of God.*

9. *When you feel God's presence come into you, open your Soul willingly to God's examination. This is the birth of Surrender of Soul.*

10. *Feel with your Soul the direction where God's Immanence comes from.*

11. *Reach out with your Soul in that direction, extending up the stream of invisible Light until you become aware that you are facing Heaven.*

12. *Feel in your Soul the vast holy presence before you, spread miles around God-in-Heaven. Feel the great joy and glory that flows into your Soul from the sacred space before you.*

13. *Bask in this sacred presence until you feel moved to withdraw and return to your body.*

14. *Spend the next few minutes in wordless reflection before leaving the closet.*

Know that you have just located Heaven with your Soul. Know that no matter where you are, anywhere on earth, no matter what direction you are facing, Heaven hovers in all its vastness and glory just before your Soul, Transcendent and Ascendant.

Know that by locating Heaven your Soul has Marked—homed in on and locked onto—your ultimate destiny and framed the straightaway path to Heaven. This is your Soul's Path to Heaven. Your Soul has defined your path, and will never let go of this path, even after you die.

Know also that at any time you can return your Soul's reach to before Heaven.

With all your heart and Soul, thank deeply, graciously, and humbly the Heaven Light, the Sacred Beings in the Light, and all of Heaven for the Blessing just bestowed upon your Soul.

Repeat this exercise 10 times before moving to the next one.

MARKING

Just as your hand can grasp an object, your Soul can grasp onto things spiritual, and in far greater ways. Marking is your Soul's innate ability to locate things of Spirit within the Heaven Light and fix onto them like a laser tracking beam, forever, if your Soul desires, without any reference to materiality.

Recall from HeavenHome how easily and naturally your Soul Marked Heaven before you learned about Marking with your mind. There are many ways your Soul will Mark along your journey to Heaven. Such is the way of Spirit.

SO SHORT THE PATH OF LIGHT

By now you may already realize that the "Path" of Light is not one of distance but filtration—cutting through illusion to behold and enter Heaven, which is here and now before us. In ultimate reality—Truth—time and space are not as they seem on earth. No matter where you are in the physical universe, Heaven is always before your Soul, spread out in a nebula of Creation Spirit, flowing outward and descending into the Clear Light, and deeper into materiality.

The Light of Heaven continuously passes through your Soul. Your journey along the Path of Light involves your "cutting through" the illusory grounds of materiality and the Clear Light to Heaven. Transcending means cutting through materiality into the Clear Light. Ascending means cutting through the Clear Light to Heaven.

Congratulations! You have Awakened your Soul—you have achieved your first Elevation along the Path of Light. All of Heaven and all of the Sacred Beings in the Light are witness, and invite you to enter into the Light.

THREE

PATH OF THE HEAVEN LIGHT

Now that your Soul is Awakened, let's consider a few things about the Path of Light your Soul has just entered.

THE SITUATION OF MAN

Do you Remember, with your Soul, before you were born, before you were in body, while your Soul abided with millions of other Souls in the Light Fields of Spirit?

Do you Remember with your Soul, there, in the Fields of Light, your pure Soul—a clear perfect orb, exquisite beyond the mind's imagination—and fully awake, no thought, no distraction, no obscuration, but pure being, intuitive all the way to Heaven?

In the Fields of Light we harmonized in Spirit, every one of us, with a perfectly intimate acceptance and knowing. And as we drew near to the Angels who were everywhere in the Light, we were filled, in Remembrance in Spirit, with the Divine Will of Heaven.

Heaven—our beloved destiny, ever so close, but which lay just beyond a cloud of unknowing. Only our impurity kept us from passing through the cloud.

Do you Remember, there, in the sacred company, the Will of Heaven that passed through our Souls like a summer breeze, calling us? Heaven was calling our Souls Home.

One by one we resolved to descend to earth, for we knew directly in the Will of Heaven the sanctifying power of the Heaven Light, how by plying the Heaven Light on earth we could enter Heaven, that we would let nothing get in our way when we received the gift of body.

Do you Remember, when your time came, when your desire became so strong the Angels were compelled to marry your Soul to the heart of that tiny body in your mother's womb, how you quickened and kicked, and how you strove for so long to keep your Soul awake as your body's developing brain took control?

And then you were born, your Soul fast asleep in your heart, while you strove to orient your new body to this new world, commanded by your new brain. From the very beginning of your life you were separated from your true self.

Thus are we, the living, separated from Heaven by *two* clouds of unknowing—materiality and impurity. Such is the situation of man. But it is a situation we can remedy, and easily, with the HeavenWork.

THE POWER OF NOW

Heaven is Creation perpetual. Heaven is not someday, but now, and every moment is Judgment Day. If you want to enter Heaven, you must work toward It *now*, you must desire to enter Heaven *now*. Do not procrastinate. There is no time to waste in this precious life.

THE MIRAGE OF MIND

As the mystics have reminded us time and again, we look for our Soul in the wrong place.

In this world, the mind predominates. So powerful is the mind that we have difficulty believing there can be a deeper, more important way of knowing. But mind is not the Soul. "Thinking" is not "being." The Soul does not even reside in the mind.

Nothing material can transcend materiality. The thinking human mind—the electro-biochemical epiphenomenal emanation of the brain—naturally perishes at the moment of death along with the body, fading like a mirage just as the Soul reawakens.

Only your essence—your Soul, the enduring sphere of free intuition within and around your heart—continues in and out of life.

The mind is in the brain, your Soul is in your heart.

The HeavenWork does not waste time engaging the mirage of mind, but bypasses the mind to go directly into Soul. Why waste ten years groping through the mind in search of your Soul when you can find and awaken your Soul in ten minutes?

In our short lives, there is precious little time to waste not doing the HeavenWork. We will continue along the Path shortly.

THREE GROUNDS OF BEING

Those who have explored the Path of the Heaven Light for decades know there are three primary grounds of being: *Materiality*, the *Clear Light*, and *Heaven*. They are all superimposed. Within and beyond materiality is the Clear Light. Within and beyond the Clear Light is Heaven.

The physics of materiality generally collapse before the Clear Light, and they dissolve completely before Heaven. That is how Heaven is here and now, just beyond the vision of the Soul. That is how Heaven is at hand.

The material earth is not our home. We are only visiting. Our eternal Souls abide in the Clear Light, alternating in and out of materiality. As we incarnate, we descend from the Clear Light, extending into materiality, and at death we transcend completely back to the Clear Light.

We are separated from Heaven by two clouds of unknowing. From the perspective of the embodied Soul the ground of materiality forms the first cloud, and the Clear Light forms the second cloud.

In the highest of Heaven, from the right of the Face of God, originates the Heaven Light—a brilliant, sacred Diamond Light that streams out the Firmament and descends into the Clear Light, and to materiality that hangs upon it. In the Clear Light, the Heaven Light manifests as a vast sky of white, milky Light that swaddles Soul in nurturing compassion. On earth, the Heaven Light manifests in joyous purifying showers of white, turbulent swirls and tufts capped with silver sparks.

Heaven connects to the Clear Light and earth only by the joyous, sacred Heaven Light. Every Soul in Creation is joined, by the Heaven Light, to Heaven.

> *Clear Light: Natural ground of being of Soul separating materiality from Heaven.*

THE SANCTIFICATION MECHANISM

Do you Remember in your Soul your goal in life: To enter Heaven?

Do you Remember how you needed to incarnate and work the Heaven Light with your Soul so that you could ascend the Clear Light and reach Heaven, and that the only way to ascend is by sanctifying?

Sanctifying means to change, transmute, become as Heaven. Everything changes, and constantly, but only sanctification ascends the Soul to Heaven, and only the Soul can sanctify.

Only Heaven is sacred. All else is profane. Though exquisite beyond the reach of mind, Soul is profane, but contains an essence that can be transformed into the Sacred.

If you sanctify in life—if you transform from profane into the Sanctity that is Heaven—Heaven will open to you. If you fail to sanctify, you will return to the Clear Light at your death.

Incarnation is granted when a Soul fully resolves to sanctify in life, and becomes fully aware of the **Sanctification Mechanism:**

> *Taking the Heaven Light into the Soul* constantly,
> the more the better—Light magnification.

Carry the Light in your Soul-in-body long enough, and hard enough, and your Soul will ascend to the Firmament of Heaven. The Heaven Light, worked by the Soul-in-body, is the Sanctification Mechanism, and the Sanctification Mechanism is the basis of the HeavenWork.

Sanctification—the Path of the Heaven Light—is not about the mind's thinking or believing, it is about your Soul's being and doing. It is about changing.

Constantly receiving and plying the Heaven Light on earth keeps you on the Path of the Heaven Light.

Sanctification: The Soul's changing, entering the Sacred by purifying in the Light of Heaven.

There is no other mechanism for approaching Heaven. Ways of the mind, body and earth lead only back to earth, ultimately returning your Soul to the Clear Light.

Virtues, the outer expressions of the HeavenWork as well as religions—piety, awe, humility, respect, right thought, right speech, right conduct, kindness, compassion, charity, and the like—will naturally reflect your Soul's progress along the process of sanctification.

But these are only expressions, signs. Always remember, it is the Sanctification Mechanism that carries your Soul along the Path of Heaven Light to Heaven.

BEYOND ANTHROPOMORPHISM

The human mind constantly projects human qualities onto the universe, such as imagining God as having human features or a Heaven full of earth's most precious material treasures. Such human self-idolatry runs deep.

For the time being, it is best to set aside any preconceived ideas you may have about your Soul, the Heaven Light, and Heaven. Soon enough your HeavenWork will bring you directly to these things of Spirit, and you will know them in their truest essence by experiencing them without the mind's obscuration.

FOUR ELEVATIONS OF THE SOUL

As you journey along the path of the Heaven Light, many subtle changes will occur to your Soul, and you will change constantly.

But your sanctification will be marked by four major changes of being—the Four Elevations of the Soul. In order to enter Heaven, you must complete your HeavenWork, achieving all of these Elevations in your lifetime:

AWAKENING→TRANSCENDING→ASCENDING→TRANSFIGURATION

Awakening—your Soul's first Elevation—occured when your Soul stirred and rose permanently into your awareness, positioning itself dominant over your mind. Every Soul Awakens at the moment of death, when it is too late to do anything about your life. Every Soul should thus Awaken early on in life.

When your Soul *fully* Awakens, you become open to receiving Remembrance, the deep knowing of your Soul's true nature and the nature of Heaven. You know, in Soul, what you must do. The first four HeavenWork exercises helped you Awaken your Soul.

When you incarnate, your Soul abides in two grounds of being—the Clear Light *and* materiality. Under Heaven—whether in life or death—your Soul is never away from the Clear Light. But in order for your Soul to invoke and concentrate enough of the sanctifying Heaven Light, you must learn to enter fully into your Soul. This requires *Transcending*—passing your Soul through materiality to center once again in the Clear Light. This book will provide you with 24 Transcending exercises.

While the mind and body tire easily, your Soul in the Heaven Light knows no exhaustion. HeavenWork only involves your Soul. Therefore it is both important and possible to work your Soul constantly until you Transcend, for when you have entered the Clear Light your Soul is able to gather tremendous concentrations of Heaven Light, which accelerates your sanctification and Ascendance to Heaven.

The more you sanctify your Soul, the further you pass along the Path of the Heaven Light, straight toward Heaven. *Ascending* is the passage of your Soul within and beyond the Clear Light to the sacred Firmament of Heaven. This book provides 33 exercises to help you Ascend your Soul.

Transfiguration, the final Elevation and the completion of your Soul's journey, occurs when Heaven Receives you, fully sanctified, when the Breath of Heaven issues out of the Firmament, crossing the daunting chasm gates to engulf your Soul in Divine Love and Understanding.

In that greatest of moments, as Heaven's Love engulfs you, preparing to Transfigure your Elect Soul before the gloriously rejoicing Heaven Host, you will choose either to Surrender and be Received into Heaven forever, or remain in the Heaven Light for a while in the service of Heaven to help other Souls find their way In. The final nine exercises prepare you for your Transfiguration.

THE FOUR ELEVATIONS OF THE SOUL

Awakening: The Soul's rising beyond the obstructions of mind and body into present awareness.

Transcending: The Soul's unbinding from materiality and returning to the Clear Light.

Ascending: The Soul's passing beyond the Clear Light to before Heaven.

Transfiguration: The ultimate permanent changeover of an Ascended Soul into Heaven.

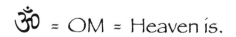 = OM = Heaven is.

HOW YOUR SOUL UNFOLDS

As you progress from Elevation to Elevation, your Soul will constantly unfold in many ways:

Now that your Soul has Awakened, your HeavenWork will help you activate your Soul, strengthen your Soul, expand your Soul, place your awareness back to your Soul, identify your awareness with your Soul, maintain Soul awareness, amplify your Soul, empower your Soul, live from your Soul, integrate your Soul into your personality, and connect your Soul to Spirit.

As your Soul Transcends materiality to the Clear Light, your HeavenWork will help you invoke and manage the Heaven Light, connect your Soul to Heaven, and glean the direction of your Soul.

As your Soul Ascends the Clear Light to Heaven, your HeavenWork will help you create and manifest miracles of compassion and approach Heaven by entering the Heaven Light to complete your sanctification.

AWAKENING YOUR SOUL

Activating Your Soul. First you found your Soul and brought it back into your awareness. Immediately you filled with joy and recognized your Soul as the true you. You will never have to separate from your Soul again.

Strengthening Your Soul. Now that you have Awakened your Soul, you will be able to keep it awake, and enter fully into Soul at will. But now you must take measures to keep your Soul present, learning how to balance your Soul and mind. This does not involve weakening your mind, but bypassing it and filling your Soul with the Heaven Light.

Expanding Your Soul. With the HeavenWork, your Soul will do tremendous things with the Heaven Light—things you may now think impossible. But before this can happen, your Soul must stretch to its full size and capacity.

Placing Your Awareness Back To Your Soul. As you practice the HeavenWork more and more, you will gradually and gently transfer your awareness from your mind to your Soul and keep it there.

Identifying Your Awareness With Your Soul. The more you are in Soul awareness, the more you will come to know you are in your eternal self, the true you. You will come to know your being, which lies freely behind, beyond and within the spool of the mind's life-acquired thoughts, attitudes, emotions, and preconceptions. You will realize that you *are* Soul visiting this body and this earth.

Maintaining Soul Awareness. At first your mind will constantly create distractive thoughts and emotions to divert you from the true being of Soul, but as you continue to enter into Soul, the mind will recede, naturally and without struggle.

Amplifying Your Soul. The Divine gift that bridges your Soul to Heaven also sustains it: The Heaven Light. And there is an endless supply of it. Once your Soul is supple enough, your HeavenWork will teach you how to invoke and fill your Soul with the Heaven Light.

Empowering Your Soul. The HeavenWork will teach you ways to concentrate the Heaven Light, creating your potential for doing great works.

Living From Your Soul. In the past your mind largely formed your personality and manner. But with HeavenWork, your continued presence in your Soul will redirect your experience on earth. You will become centered deeper, in your true intuitive self, and your thoughts, emotions, and even those around you will reflect your Soul's expression.

Integrating Your Soul Into Your Personality. By living from your Soul, your thoughts, words and actions will change, becoming clearer and centered in a lightness of joy and freedom that streams from your Soul. Your negative mental processes will recede in favor of your Soul's resolve, and you will naturally think in terms of Spirit and the welfare of Soul, every Soul.

Invoking And Managing The Heaven Light. This book will teach you to concentrate and manage the Heaven Light in ways that sanctify your Soul. You will learn many great things to do with the Heaven Light, and you will understand directly from the Heaven Light *never* to direct Light for any purpose other than sanctification.

Connecting Your Soul To Spirit. By taking the Heaven Light into your Soul, the essence of your Soul, which *is* Heaven Light, will form a permanent connection to Spirit. Know that on the Path of Light, your Soul is always safe, protected by Angels in the Heaven Light. The HeavenWork will teach you how to remain on the Path all the way to Heaven.

TRANSCENDING MATERIALITY TO THE CLEAR LIGHT

Connecting Your Soul To Heaven. Your Soul naturally receives the Immanence of Heaven, which passes through the Soul like a summer breeze. It is from this Divine Immanence that we intuitively understand God with the Soul. Your HeavenWork will show you how to receive Heaven's Immanence without the mind's distortions.

Gleaning The Direction Of Your Soul. The Heaven Light streams out of Heaven directly into your Soul. Just like a spawning salmon knows to swim upstream, your Soul instinctively knows how to rise through the stream of Heaven Light. Your advanced HeavenWork exercises will help you awaken your instinct to move your Soul in the direction of Heaven.

ASCENDING THE CLEAR LIGHT TO HEAVEN

Creating And Manifesting Miracles Of Compassion. A miracle occurs when Heaven surges an increase of Heaven Light onto the earth to help a Soul sanctify. After your Soul has sanctified a great deal, moved into the Clear Light, and made a sacred covenant with Heaven, it is possible to petition Heaven to empower your HeavenWork by manifesting miracles you originate on earth— miracles in accordance with the Will of Heaven. Nothing sanctifies the Soul more than creating a miracle of compassion with Heaven.

Entering The Heaven Light. Your advanced HeavenWork will rapidly sanctify your Soul, cleansing your Soul and enabling you to accelerate your ascent along the Path of Light by becoming more like Heaven Light.

Approaching Heaven. By entering the Heaven Light, your Soul will accomplish its sanctification, pass through the Clouds of Heaven and arrive before the Firmament of Heaven.

TRANSFIGURATION INTO HEAVEN

The moment your Soul arrives before Heaven, all things of the earth will fall away, and the Breath of Heaven will engulf your Soul, filling you with all you need know to enter In. At that moment you will be given the choice to enter or remain in the Heaven Light for a time to see to the well being of other Souls on the Path of Light.

All these changes may seem numerous and vague, but you do not have to worry about remembering each of them. This book will take you through your entire journey, with all these changes, step by step. Your changes will occur naturally as your Soul sanctifies, sometimes one at a time, sometimes many together. Just remember to watch for your Four Elevations—Awakening, Transcending, Ascending, and Transfiguration.

Your journey along the Path of Light will seem to pass quickly, for the Path is joyous and engaging, progressing constantly as you sanctify into the true you. Your Soul will be rewarded the moment you enter the Path of Light, for though you do not yet realize, just by entering the Path you have already won Heaven.

ODIUM THEOLOGICUM

Odium theologicum, hateful intolerance of others' religious beliefs, is no different from any other form of hatred, and it exiles you from Heaven. Hatred is foreign to your Soul, foreign to the Heaven Light, foreign to Heaven, and *odium theologicum* is a sure telltale of spiritual ignorance. Hatred condemns man to the dark shadows of materiality. We must think on this every time hatred overruns our love.

Religion must serve the Soul, and not the converse.

FOUR

YOUR SPIRITUAL TOOLS

You have many tools to help you with your HeavenWork.

YOUR HEART

Your Soul does not bide in your mind, but in your heart, like a fog that hangs upon a harbor. As long as you walk in body, your Soul will remain married to your heart.

Your Soul desires Heaven over life. But your mind is instinctively and jealously devoted to bodily survival. It was in the womb, just before you were born, that your mind placed a mental door around your heart, insulating your Soul so that you would slumber your life away.

The HeavenWork bypasses the mind because the mind is not a path to Spirit, but a dead end. Instead you will open the door of your heart and go directly to your Soul, and Awaken it, so that you immediately enter the Path of Light.

Your heart is the entry to your Soul.

YOUR SOUL

Your Soul, your eternal essence, is the only real part of you, the part you will have forever. All the rest is passing—borrowed, temporary and corruptible, just like a mask of clay.

You, Soul, have been around for a very long time.

Only your Soul survives death. Ultimately, only your Soul enters Heaven.

Your Soul, exquisite beyond the reach of mind, is the sphere of perfectly pure and clear intuitive being that bides in and around your heart. Your Soul constantly desires Heaven.

The HeavenWork bypasses mind and goes directly to Soul. The mind cannot sanctify your Soul. Only your Soul can sanctify. Only your Soul can perform the HeavenWork. The HeavenWork teaches you how to exercise your Soul. Your Soul will work with all your Spiritual tools.

It is your Soul that must do the HeavenWork.

EARTH

Do you Remember, with your Soul, before you entered body, the repugnance of incarnation, but how there was no other way?

In the Light Fields of Spirit, where there was no resistance, there was no way to concentrate the Heaven Light enough to sanctify. Only the density of materiality provides the resistance needed for the Soul to perform the HeavenWork.

The HeavenWork is not world-denying, but simply regards materiality for what it is and isn't. If you examine love, intimacy and being, you find that truth lies *behind* thoughts and things. What is truly meaningful originates in Spirit. The HeavenWork helps you embrace life with your Soul, free and clear, full of being, appreciation, and gratitude.

The HeavenWork is perfectly affirmative, so that you can be *in* the world, but not *of* it.

THE HEAVEN LIGHT

The Heaven Light streams out from the right of the Face of God-in-Heaven, passes through the whole of Heaven, and descends to the Clear Light, touching every Soul.

In body, the impure Soul cannot see beyond the veil of materiality or beyond the Clear Light to arrive before Heaven.

To enter Heaven, your Soul must pass through the veils of materiality and impurity with the Heaven Light. The only way to pass through these veils is by sanctifying, and the only way to sanctify is by working with your Soul intense concentrations of the Heaven Light. This is the Path of the Heaven Light. This is the HeavenWork.

We have all experienced the Heaven Light flash into our Soul, though briefly. At times of happiness and celebration you may feel a powerful surge of meaningful warmth rush into your heart, filling you with joy, peace and understanding. During worship, you may find your heart dilates to receive a skin-tingling affirmation that seems to come straight from God and accompanied by the eyes of all the Angels of Heaven upon you. And those periods of anguish—at the breaking of your heart, at the death of a loved one—when you have reached bottom and when it seems there is nothing to save you, from nowhere above, that same loving Light pours into you, filling you with acceptance, hope and meaning like the light at the end of a tunnel.

This is the Heaven Light loving your Soul, this is the Heaven Light changing your Soul.

These wonderful, brief moments in life. Your HeavenWork will help your Soul fill every moment of your life with this joyous, sacred Light.

> **Heaven Light:** *The beacon of sacred Light from the right of the Face of God, the gift of grace from Heaven to purify and guide the Soul of man to Heaven.*

THE SPIRIT UNIVERSE

The Heaven Light manifests as a vast white sky in the Clear Light where Souls without body abide. There they are nurtured in swaddling, loving Light, and in Fields of Light. The Heaven Light is always connected to Heaven.

The Heaven Light has dominion over every Soul, and perpetuates one Divine law through a spiritual machinery so complex and perfect it lies well beyond the comprehension of mind: The Spirit Universe.

The Spirit Universe operates in direct accordance to the Will of Heaven—a power that supervenes over the physics of materiality.

This Supreme spiritual law, which Jesus referred to as, "Thy Will be done on earth as it is in Heaven," I call the *Sanctification Principle*:

> *Heaven's directive to facilitate the most auspicious situation for every Soul to sanctify and enter into Heaven.*

Every miracle of Heaven, every Angel and all of Spirit work in accordance to this, Heaven's Will.

> **Sanctification Principle:** *Heaven's Will that all Souls sanctify, the essence of the Spirit Universe.*

SACRED BEINGS IN THE HEAVEN LIGHT

We all know about the great Angels that originate from the Diadem of Heaven and descend to the Soul of man the moment of their need, but there are other Sacred Beings in the Heaven Light—millions—abiding under Heaven but in the Heaven Light to serve man in accordance to the Will of Heaven.

In the west we recognize them as "lesser" Angels, such as *cherubim*. In the east they are known by many names. They are Souls, like you and me, who long ago sanctified, but instead of entering Heaven, chose with compassion to remain yet under Heaven to serve the Will of Heaven by helping other Souls sanctify and find the way into Heaven.

These Sacred Beings in the Light—your Guardian Angels and others— were always with you and are always with you, always attending to you in the time of need, always here watching after you, blessing you, always providing opportunities for you to Awaken and sanctify. Sometimes you may feel their countenance upon you.

If you take a moment, you may feel right now their loving countenance upon you.

If you feel their presence, thank them and bless them. They are here for your Soul's well being, they desire only your Soul's sanctification, and they will help you perform your HeavenWork.

As you journey along the Path of Light they will make themselves known to you in most marvelous ways.

> **Sacred Beings In The Light:** *Liberated Souls who Ascended to Heaven but chose to remain in the Clouds of Heaven to help other Souls find their way.*

ANGELS

Angels are Miracles. They originate from the Diadem of Heaven that surrounds the Face of God-in-Heaven, and stream through the Body of Heaven like meteors, whereupon reaching the Firmament, they drop descendant with the Heaven Light to appear instantly the moment of their need, penetrating materiality fast as light with a shell of Divine substantiation so dense and alien, like stone electric, that your arm becomes numb when you touch them.

Angels serve Heaven by delivering grace to your Soul by bearing pure and direct communication from God-in-Heaven, intervening to prevent your untimely death or incapacitation, and sometimes rendering materiality with a force that can move mountains.

There is no mistaking an Angel. There is nothing more Divine under Heaven.

HEAVEN

Heaven is the divine Origin of Spirit, beyond all reference of the earth. Every moment for the past 28 years, by grace, my Soul has looked upon Heaven, and yet I have failed to fashion even one divine word to describe my witness.

But each time I enter fully into my Soul,
There I behold again the vast, pearl-white, flowing nebula of
loving Spirit
That surrounds the awe-some Face of God,
A great Oneness, always moving but never changing,
Ever present here and now.
Heaven—the Creation of all manifestation and Destiny of Soul,
Billowing outwards to the chasm gates, cloudlike, surf-like,
And descending immediately into the infinite Clear Light
And deeper, into the ever-growing materiality that hangs upon it.
The powerfully penetrating Immanence of Abba (holy!holy!holy!)
That explodes through the Soul with Divine Direction
And the brilliant, untraceably complex flashing in that highest,
Most Sacred Origin of Heaven—
Being beyond being,
Surrounded by the most Sacred Host
Within the Diadem around the Face of God,
And the silent thundering glory of the joyous,
symphonic community
Forming the surrounding Body of Heaven.
The steady generation of perfect Angels
Descending from out the Face of God
To the Soul of man the moment of their need,
And their return to insubstantiate back in the Face of God.
The wondrous Diamond Light that originates from
the highest of Heaven,
At the right of Abba, the Face of God,
To fill the descendant universe with sanctifying power.
The stunning purity of the sacred flowing ground,
The rolling Clouds of Heaven,
Passing through me, drawing me,
Electrifying my Soul with consuming awe these many years.
Creation. Destiny. Sanctity.

Absolute love, joy and glory.
Eternal Life. Being beyond being.
God's directive Immanence and the
Heaven Light's transfiguring power,
Which reach out to every Soul.
All of this constant, and every moment like the first.

Just as Jesus said, the Kingdom of Heaven is at hand. It is here, and now, just before your Soul. You may feel the presence of Heaven, but probably you do not yet see it with your Soul. In order to behold Heaven, you must cut through the two illusory Grounds of being. You must transcend materiality and enter into the Clear Light, and then ascend the Clear Light to Heaven. When you cut through materiality and the Clear Light, when they dissolve away, there is Heaven.

Your HeavenWork will deliver your Soul to Heaven.

JUDEO-CHRISTIAN DESCRIPTIONS OF HEAVEN

Then I looked, and behold, a whirlwind was coming out of the north, a great cloud with raging fire engulfing itself; and brightness was all around it and radiating out of its midst like the color of amber, out of the midst of the fire.

—Ezekiel 1:4

As for the likeness of the living creatures, their appearance was like burning coals of fire, and like the appearance of torches. Fire was going back and forth among the living creatures; the fire was bright, and out of the fire went lightning.

And the living creatures ran back and forth, in appearance like a flash of lightning.

—Ezekiel 1:13-14

Like the appearance of a rainbow in a cloud on a rainy day, so was the appearance of the brightness all around it. This was the appearance of the likeness and the glory of the LORD.

—Ezekiel 1:28

I beheld till the thrones were cast down and the Ancient of days did sit, whose garment was white as snow, and the hair of his head was like the pure wool: his throne was like the fiery flame, and his wheels as burning fire.

A fiery stream issued and came forth from before him: thousand thousands ministered unto him, and ten thousand times ten thousand stood before him: the judgment was set, and the books were opened.

—Daniel 7:9-10

And I heard as it were the voice of a great multitude, and as the voice of many waters, and as the voice of mighty thunderings, saying, Alleluia: for the Lord God omnipotent reigneth.

—Revelation 19:6

And there shall be no night there; and they need no candle, neither light of the sun; for the Lord God giveth them light: and they shall reign for ever and ever.

—Revelation 22:5

And I looked and saw therein a lofty throne: its appearance was as crystal, and the wheels thereof as the shining sun, and there was the vision of cherubim. And from underneath the throne came streams of flaming fire so that I could look thereon. And the Great Glory sat thereon, and His raiment shone more brightly than the sun and was whiter than any snow. None of the angels could enter and could behold His face by reason of the magnificence and glory and no flesh could behold Him. The flaming fire was round about Him, and a great fire stood before Him, and none around could draw nigh Him: ten thousand times ten thousand (stood) before Him, yet He needed no counselor.

—Enoch 18b-23a
160 BCE

...The ministers of the Glorious Face in the abode of the gods of knowledge fall down before him, and the cherubim utter blessings. And as they rise up, there is a divine small voice and loud praise; there is a divine small voice as they fold their wings.

The cherubim bless the image of the Throne-Chariot above the firmament, and they praise the majesty of the fiery firmament beneath the seat of his glory. And between the turning wheels, angels of holiness come and go, as it were a fiery vision of most holy spirits; and about them flow seeming rivulets of fire, like gleaming bronze, a radiance of many gorgeous colors, of marvelous pigments magnificently mingled.

The spirits of the Living God move perpetually with the glory of the wonderful Chariot. The small voice of blessing accompanies the tumult as they depart, and on the path of their return they worship the Holy One, Ascending they rise marvelously; settling, they stay still. The sound of joyful praise is silenced and there is a small voice of blessing in all the camp of God.

And a voice of praise resounds from the midsts of all their divisions in worship. And each one in his place, all their numbered ones sing hymns of praise.

—The Divine Throne-Chariot, *The Dead Sea Scrolls*

All of this also is the witness of my Soul these past 28 years.

THE BREATH OF HEAVEN

The Heaven Light streams out from the Face of God in Heaven and descends freely to every Soul in the universe. The Heaven Light comforts, sanctifies, directs, Transcends, and Ascends the Soul. But another substance of Heaven— the Breath of Heaven—Transfigures the Soul.

Accessible only to near-Ascendant Souls, on command of *Abba*—the Face of God-in-Heaven—the Breath of Heaven issues out of the Firmament of Heaven and powerfully surrounds the elect Soul with Divine Knowing and Transfiguring power. The Soul perceives Heaven Light as gentle, tingling, robust, while the Breath of Heaven proceeds more like a floodwater that collapses into a lightning bolt. The Heaven Breath is the stuff of miracles, and you will make good use of it as your Soul comes to Ascend before Heaven.

Heaven Breath: The Transfiguring power of Heaven to Receive Soul and to manifest Miracles.

GOD

No words of mind can define or confine that holiest of Being beyond being that we call God, for every word would be a blasphemy.

Yet I will say these things: God is Creation perpetual, God is not without Heaven, Heaven is not without God, and the Immanence of Heaven, which you can feel deep in your Soul, originates directly from *Abba*, the Face of God-in-Heaven.

Rather than profane my Soul or yours through the mind's describing, your HeavenWork will help you approach God directly.

CREIGHT

Everyone on earth comes to life with certain special talents of the Soul, what the Heaven Light delivered into my Soul as the word, "Creight." Creight is your ability to see into Spirit and work with it.

Creight is a gift of Heaven granted with the sacred intention that you apply it to the sanctification of your Soul. As your Soul Ascends toward Heaven your Creight will flower, and you will come to perform great works with the Heaven Light.

Creight: Talents of the embodied Soul, the ability to see into and work with Spirit, which magnifies in the Ascending Soul.

MANIFESTATION

There are works your Soul can do that we often attribute to mind. Like your mind, your Soul has intent, only clearer, freer, subtler, and infinite. Your Soul can make things happen. Your Soul can prompt both the Heaven Light and Heaven Breath to move materiality. This is called Manifestation.

We all do this naturally, rarely understanding the mechanism. You desire something strongly, you wish for it, and eventually your wish gets granted, at least in part. If your wish is tainted by the mind, if it involves personal or worldly gain, it usually Manifests far past the time you originally wanted it.

You will learn how to Manifest with the HeavenWork, to help your Soul sanctify and for no other purpose.

Be warned. If you use Manifestation for any purpose other than your Soul's or another Soul's sanctification (which is in accordance to the Sanctification Principle), you will become lost on the Path of Light, and your Soul will be exiled to earth. The Sacred Beings in the Light will see to this.

While there may be no place on the Path of Light for magic, there is a whole world of opportunity for Miracles!

Manifestation: The Soul's ability to influence Alpha Creation Heaven to alter materiality.

MARKING

Marking is your Soul's ability to search through Spirit and "lock on" things of Spirit—forever if you wish. You will use the tool Marking in your HeavenWork to do many important things, including finding Heaven.

Marking: The Soul's ability to locate and connect to an aspect of Spirit or station itself in relation to Heaven.

CRESCENDO

Your Soul is real, more real than your body. But your Soul is not of material substance like your body. Like all things of Spirit, it is "insubstantial." Your Soul is a sphere of Light that exists regardless of body, regardless of materiality. Unlike the things of earth, your Soul exists forever.

In life, because we tend to dwell more in body than Soul, our Souls are typically weak, barely present in our awareness. The HeavenWork is all about awakening and training your Soul—not your mind—to be strong enough to sanctify in life.

Your Soul has a special ability to gather the Heaven Light, hold it, squeeze it into a powerful concentration, and suddenly release it in ways that sanctify your Soul. I call this process "Crescendo."

In this way, your Soul is like a balloon. As you fill your Soul with Heaven

Light, the pressure of your Soul squeezing the Light intensifies the Light in your Soul, increasing the Light's sanctifying power. In this way, your Soul is also like an accordion, a bellows.

Practicing Crescendo will help you become present in your Soul, strengthen your Soul, and perform great works.

> **Crescendo:** *The Soul's magnifying and releasing Heaven Light to perform HeavenWork.*

ABBREVIATION

Your HeavenWork is your process of holding the Heaven Light in your Soul in ways that sanctify. Your HeavenWork exercises are simply ways to get your Soul to do your HeavenWork. It is the Heaven Light in your Soul that matters and not the HeavenWork exercises themselves.

One of the remarkable characteristics of the HeavenWork is the Soul's ability to immediately return to its point of greatest progress along the Path of Heaven Light.

Once you have mastered a HeavenWork exercise, you no longer need to repeat the steps to "get there." Instead, you simply will your Soul to return to that state of being, and you are there. I haven't found this shortcut ability described in the spiritual literature, so I have named it "Abbreviation."

You will learn to Abbreviate every HeavenWork exercise you come to master, for they prepare you for the more advanced exercises which involve combinations of your initial exercises. Abbreviation also speeds your Soul's journey along the Path of Light.

> **Abbreviation:** *Performing a HeavenWork exercise directly and immediately with the Soul, without relying on the body or mind.*

MOMENTATION

Your last tool is taking what you have and making best use of it.

One enormous blast of Heaven Light will not sanctify your Soul, but a lifetime of it will. That is where Momentation comes in—living every moment of your life, day and night, centered in your Soul, embracing life with your

Awakened Soul, constantly receiving Light, your true inner being ever-present, putting your Soul behind every experience in your life.

It may sound difficult because the mind is so fickle, but now that you have Awakened your Soul, you will soon see how joyously easy and naturally Momentation takes over your life.

It is time to Transcend along the Path.

TRANSCENDING

AWAKENING→**TRANSCENDING**→ASCENDING→TRANSFIGURATION

FIVE

HOW TO ACTIVATE YOUR SOUL

To prepare yourself for the work of sanctification you must first become as a little child, innocent in Spirit. This is a poetic way of saying you must return to your origin—your state before you entered body. You need to come fully into the ground of Soul before you can work with and enter the Heaven Light and Ascend to Heaven.

Reaching this innocence requires Transcending your Soul into the Clear Light, where you will not be distracted by things of the mind, body or earth.

Transcending involves activating, expanding and amplifying your Soul. From this moment on, your HeavenWork will require no mental or physical strain, but calm openness and steadiness of Soul. Every exercise will be joyous, because each will involve your nourishing your Soul, and the food for the Soul is the Heaven Light.

Now that you have Awakened your Soul, you can keep it awake and vibrating effortlessly through activation. The Heaven Light, the mightiest power under Heaven, activates the Soul.

EXERCISE 5

ENTERING YOUR SOUL

Come into truth and you will be released.

In order for your Soul to make the most of the Heaven Light, let's first make sure you are fully entering your Soul. Here you will learn to enter deeper into your Soul by riding your Soul's tingling.

Goal: *To enter fully into Soul.*

Preparation: *Sit in a chair.*

Steps:

1. *Calm yourself, taking a few deep breaths. You are about to take a roller coaster ride.*

2. *As you continue your deep breathing, Awaken your Soul (exercise 1), with Abbreviation if you can.*

3. *As your Soul's tingling mounts, picture yourself, your Soul, in the front car of a roller coaster at the highest summit of the ride, just about to take the plunge. Keep mindful of the tingling...*

4. *Inhale deeply and prepare for your car to plunge. Feel the tingling intensify in your suspenseful excitement...*

5. *As you exhale, plunge down the ride in your imagination, squeezing the tingling with your Soul as if you were holding on for dear life...*

6. *Continue your ride, up and down, up and around, in frenzied excitement, squeezing the tingling harder and harder with your Soul.*

7. *Let the ride stop, and reflect wordlessly with your Soul the intense tingling that took place.*

Did you feel a change occur to your Soul? Did you feel your tingling intensify more than you have ever felt it? Did you start to feel that you are coming closer to the feeling, that the tingling feels more like home, that the true you is the tingling?

If you did, excellent! If you didn't, climb back on the roller coaster. The rides are free.

Entering Your Soul is a powerful HeavenWork exercise to transform you into your Soul. Remember, each time you enter deeper into your Soul, you can get there instantly, through Abbreviation.

Try to hold the concentrated tingling in your heart and Soul. The more you carry the tingling in you, the stronger your Soul becomes, the more spiritual you become. The tingling is the beginning of your Soul's transformation. The tingling feeds and strengthens your Soul.

With all your heart and Soul, thank deeply, graciously, and humbly the Heaven Light, the Sacred Beings in the Light, and all of Heaven for the Blessing just bestowed upon your Soul.

Repeat this exercise 10 times before moving to the next one.

Practice entering your Soul through Abbreviation.

SOARING

As a variation, repeat Entering Your Soul replacing the image of sitting in a rattling roller coaster with being a falcon, suspended high up in the air, then plunging into a dive.

Remember, it is not the mind's visualization that matters, but the action of your Soul.

MEDITATION "TOOLS"

Have you ever noticed how calming meditation music, pleasing incense aromas, and beautiful surroundings actually distract you from your attempts to meditate rather than enhance them? Intended as meditation tools, these desirable and pleasurable things of the earth have the reverse effect of acting as "*distracters*." This is because they engage your mind at the expense of your Soul.

There *are* useful earthly meditation tools, however, and they are effective because they are *not* pleasurable. They are effective because they "switch off" your mind altogether, allowing you to enter into your Soul. These are "*attenuators*." They may include unpleasant smelling incense (or odors), white sound (radio static) or a television's off-channel salt and pepper screen. Quickly they bore the mind to sleep.

Some distractors can turn out to be attenuators, such as certain bells and singing bowls. If you wish to use one of these, don't look for a pleasant sound, but a strident noise that sends crackling shivers up your spine, for such a frequency instantly attenuates the mind.

Soon you will learn in your HeavenWork, however, that there is no need for any meditation tool, because all of materiality is irrelevant. Once you have learned to enter into your Soul, your physical environment doesn't matter. You don't have to don robes, you don't have to sit in a garden, you don't have to sit in a closet. You don't have to go in the dark to be in Soul, you don't have to close your eyes, you don't have to put your hands on your heart, you don't have to stop your work or play. You simply do it.

ILLUSION

Truth is what is, illusion is what is not.

Here on earth, truth to the sleeping Soul-in-body is perceived as materiality and its epiphenomena known as mind, while all else—Soul, Light, Heaven, and God—seem only a hopeful dream.

But once awakened, Soul discovers that Light exists, and gleans it originates from Heaven.

Transcending along the Path of Light, Soul crosses over to know that materiality, man, body, mind, and even heart are temporary, hollow, masks without true being. Soul knows only Soul, Light and Heaven to be true and real.

Ascendant before Heaven, Soul drops away, Transfiguring into Light, for everything under Heaven is illusion, passing.

In Heaven, Soul of Light Ascends the Heaven Light to *Abba*, the Face of God-in-Heaven, and passes through the Needle's Eye and into the Body of Heaven such that beyond the Firmament of Heaven ceases to be. In ultimate glory around *Abba*, all ceases to be but *Abba*.

Ultimately, there is only *Abba*-in-Heaven. All else is illusion.

EXERCISE 6

INVOKING LIGHT

Soul, lamp of the Heaven Light.

Your Soul thrives on the Heaven Light, your Soul sanctifies with the Heaven Light, your Soul Ascends the Path of the Heaven Light to Heaven. Your Soul in the joyous Heaven Light is in its very element.

Heaven Light, the gift of Heaven, empowers and guides your Soul. The Heaven Light and all the Sacred Beings in the Heaven Light know everything about your Soul, and they love you more than even the Soul can know. The Heaven Light, which issues out of Heaven, forms the Path of Heaven. So sacred is the Heaven Light that no illusion may enter in. The Heaven Light is vast, and available to your Soul, simply for the asking.

Invoking Light will provide you your Soul's most valuable tool, the tool you will use for all of your HeavenWork, the tool you will wield joyously for the rest of your life.

It is time to receive the Light.

Goal: *To receive the Heaven Light into your Soul.*

Preparation: *Sit in a chair, undisturbed, preferably in a dark doom.*

Steps:

1. *Relax in your chair, your elbows at your sides, your palms resting on your lap.*

2. *Know that you are about to receive in Soul and body the most sacred substance under Heaven. All you need do is ask, not with your mind but with your Soul, this Miracle of Miracles to enter into you. We will invoke the Heaven Light from the sky.*

3. *Awaken your Soul (exercise 1, or Abbreviate), and feel the tingling in your Soul.*

4. *Picture, with your Soul, that your hair, your scalp, and the crown of your head no longer exist, leaving your Soul open from above, like a doorway, to allow the Heaven Light to enter.*

5. *Take slow, calm and relaxing breaths, in and out, in and out, as you prepare yourself to ask humbly from your Soul for Heaven's gift of the Heaven Light.*

6. *At your moment of readiness, ask from your heart,* "*Heaven, fill me with your holy Light.*"

7. *Feel, then, the immediate surge of compassionate, turbulent Light pour down from above, though your head and into your heart and Soul, stretching your Soul and swirling around in your chest, arms, head, limbs, and beyond.*

8. *Keep open your Soul, willing for more and more of the Heaven Light to continue pouring into your entire being.*

9. *Remain basking in your bath of Heaven Light for as long as your Soul desires. Remain open, in Soul, that you might glean the nature of the Heaven Light, for It is Truer than anything of the mind.*

10. *When the tide of Heaven Light has fallen, when you begin to think about what happened with your mind, be changed. Replace what preconceived ideas of Spirit you may have had with what you just experienced in Soul. Learn with your Soul from every moment of your Heaven Work.*

Now that you have Awakened your Soul, and called the Light, your Soul will continue sanctifying, even as you go about your normal life. For the rest of your life you will carry the Heaven Light in your Soul. But there are many things you can do, at your own pace, to accelerate your Soul's sanctification. Your remaining exercises will teach you how to work the Light to carry your Soul more quickly to Heaven.

With all your heart and Soul, thank deeply, graciously, and humbly the Heaven Light, the Sacred Beings in the Light, and all of Heaven for the Blessing just bestowed upon your Soul.

Repeat this exercise 20 times before moving to the next one.

Experiment with Abbreviation,
invoking the Light when standing and lying down.

HEAVENWORK IS SOUL WORK

By now you coming to recognize the great difference between the mind and your Soul—that the real you is your Soul's pure being beyond the ever-changing wall of mind. The mind cannot invoke the Heaven Light. Only your Soul can. Only your Soul can perform the HeavenWork. Each time you perform a HeavenWork exercise correctly—with your Soul—your Soul will get stronger, sanctify more, and pass farther along the Path of Light.

It's not about how much you are loved,
it's about how much you love.

EXERCISE 7

HAND QUICKENING

The natural bearers of the Heaven Light.

Now that you have invoked the Heaven Light to pass through your being, you may glean directly from the Heaven Light that nothing is impossible.

Because we use our hands for nearly everything, they are natural channels of the Heaven Light, and useful for learning how to carry the Heaven Light in powerfully sanctifying concentrations. In Christianity you have heard about "laying on of the hands" for the purpose of healing the body *and* Soul with Light, the Holy Spirit. This Jesus learned as an Essene.

But there is a great difference between willing with your mind and willing with your Soul. If you will with your mind that the Heaven Light pass through your hands, you will fail. Only your Soul can invoke the Heaven Light.

Hand "Quickening" is when your Soul learns to invoke the Heaven Light and move It down your arms and out of your hands. It does not require any physical effort or mental concentration, but an openness and willingness of your Soul to carry the Heaven Light.

It is not simply the laying on of your hands that heals, but the concentrated Heaven Light your Soul maneuvers through your hands. Only when the Heaven Light is invoked can your hands work miracles.

Before we get to your Hand Quickening, I would like you to perform two preparatory exercises to help the Heaven Light flow in you.

LIGHTBALL

1. *Standing or sitting, clap your hands together once, and clasp them palm to palm in front of your chest.*

2. *Separate your hands slightly so that your palms are one inch apart.*

3. *Feel the warm flow between your palms. Feel how the flow subtly changes. Feel how your perception of the flow shifts from your mind to your Soul within your heart. Recognize with your Soul that the energy is Heaven Light, a ball of Heaven Light.*

4. *When the Heaven Light becomes strong, play with the flow by slightly moving your hands away a few inches, then back together until they*

nearly touch, just like you are playing a little invisible accordion. Feel the changes in the Heaven Light between your palms as you do this. Feel how when you pull your hands away the Heaven Light pulls them back together, and when your hands get close the Heaven Light compresses into a cushion to keep them slightly apart, just like a ball.

You have just formed a ball of Heaven Light, not with your hands, but with your Soul. With practice this exercise, along with others, will help you form intense concentrations of Heaven Light. All of your HeavenWork will involve your working with the Heaven Light in this manner.

There is a tool of earth that helps you learn quickly how to move the Heaven Light with your Soul: Water. Water is an excellent conductor of Heaven Light. Originally, before man fell away from the ways of Spirit, water was used during Baptism to conduct Heaven Light Soul-to-Soul. We will use water as your second preparatory exercise to conduct the Heaven Light through your arms and hands.

LightWater

1. *Fill a drinking glass (made of glass) ¾ full with tap water, and take a sip.*

2. *Standing, hold the glass 6" in front of your heart, with the palms of your hands against the side of the glass.*

3. *Invoke Heaven Light (exercise 6, using Abbreviation).*

4. *Take a deep breath as the Light flows down into your Soul.*

5. *As the Light surges into your heart, bow your head and will with your Soul that the Light pour into the water in the glass.*

Several things just happened. Did you feel the Light flash and surge out of your heart, jumping directly towards the water? Did you also feel the Light stream down both of your arms, and through your palms into the water? Did you feel your skin tingle all over, and your fingers? Did you feel with your Soul the presence of the Light in the water?

This happened so easily because of the Heaven Light's affinity with water. Now take another sip of the water. Do you notice how it tastes different, purer, and how it seems to enter not just your stomach but also your heart? This is because you have just Blessed the water with Heaven Light.

Now you are ready to move the Heaven Light out your hands without water.

Goal: *To carry concentrated Heaven Light through your arms and out the palms of your hands.*

Preparation: *Sit in a chair, undisturbed, in a dark room.*

Steps:

1. *Place your hands together, palm-to-palm, and rub them back and forth until you feel heat rise from your palms.*

2. *Invoke The Soul's Great Awakening (exercise 1).*

3. *Place your hands on your lap, palms up, and Invoke Light (exercise 6).*

4. *When you feel the Heaven Light pouring down into your heart and Soul, will with your Soul that the Light stream through your chest and spread, swirling through your entire body and filling you with tingling joy.*

5. *Again, feel with your Soul the Light pouring from above, and ask the Heaven Light with your Soul to pour into you more powerfully.*

6. *When you feel the Heaven Light respond by surging a more powerful shower into your heart, will with your Soul for the Light to divide at your heart, branching out equally down your arms.*

7. *Relax and feel the Light flowing down your arms.*

8. *If the flow of Light stops moving down one or both of your arms, take a deep breath and simply will with your Soul that the Light continue to flow. This will happen if you calmly will it with your Soul. At first, opening your Soul to carry the Heaven Light is like turning on a water spigot all the way. But you can learn to make it open like a fire hydrant full blast!*

9. *Feel the Heaven Light pour down to your hands. Feel how the tingling Light swirls through your palms, fingers and fingertips. When you first invoked Light, you pictured with your Soul that the top of your head opened to receive the Light. Picture, then, with your Soul that your palms, too, have opened to let the Heaven Light continue to pass.*

10. *Will with your Soul that more Heaven Light pour into your hands. Feel the concentration increase.*

11. Finally, will with your Soul that the Heaven Light continue to move, breaking through and out of your palms, just as easily as It is passing into you from above.

12. Remain still, relaxed and open, as long as you desire, allowing the infinite Heaven Light to continue passing perfectly into you and out of you. You are a vessel of the Heaven Light, which is more sacred than Soul.

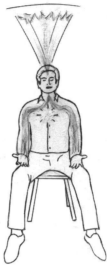

You may notice that your palms continue to itch, tingle or seem suddenly warm. This is because they have quickened, and will remain an open channel of the Heaven Light. Always nurture this physical sensation, which is caused by the Light, for it will strengthen your Soul's affinity for the Light.

Know that you are safe in the universe whenever the Heaven Light streams through you, and that by surrendering your will in the Heaven Light, you are directly harmonizing with the Will of Heaven.

Each time you practice Hand Quickening, many things will happen. You will invoke the Heaven Light more easily, and in greater concentrations. Your hands will open more and more, and your Soul's Great Awakening (exercise 1) will become more bracing. Your Soul will develop a strong sense of the Light's presence. These things will help prepare you for your life of Miracles.

With all your heart and Soul, thank deeply, graciously, and humbly the Heaven Light, the Sacred Beings in the Light, and all of Heaven for the Blessing just bestowed upon your Soul.

Every time you work with the Heaven Light, every time you feel the Light spontaneously fill your Soul, offer up to Heaven from the depths of your Soul a surge of thanks and gratitude, for each time you receive Light. Such is the way of Spirit.

Repeat this exercise 10 times before moving to the next one.

LIGHTWATER

Once you have learned to carry the Heaven Light through your hands, practice LightWater once again to see how powerfully you can charge the water with Light. At this point along the Path of Light it is okay to practice LightWater repeatedly to get a feel for channeling the Heaven Light out your palms. Later in your HeavenWork you will also use LightWater to learn how to Bless other Souls. But don't come to rely on LightWater in your HeavenWork. HeavenWork must be done by your Soul, and your Soul cannot continue to grow, strengthen or purify if you rely on any form of materiality.

EXERCISE 8

BENDING LIGHT

Working the Light.

So far you have learned to do two things with the Heaven Light: Call it from above and move It through your arms and out your hands. You know what it is like to divide and move the Heaven Light through you. By splitting the Heaven Light with your Soul you have "bent" Light, you have begun your Soul's LightWork.

Whenever your Soul is filled with Heaven Light, you can learn directly from the Light. You may have already learned that the possibilities of the Light are limitless. You can bend Light in limitless ways, and you are all the better for it.

You do not need your body to bend Light. Nor do you have to keep the Heaven Light that you invoke inside your body. You don't have to ask anyone's permission to spread the Light. The world's a dark enough place as it is, and we are all here to move the Heaven Light.

You are at the point in your HeavenWork that you realize that in Truth, there is only your Soul, and all Souls, the Heaven Light, and Heaven.

Therefore let the Light shine freely, generously, naturally, and spontaneously. Here are some ways.

Goal: *To control the movement of Heaven Light directly with your Soul.*

Preparation: *Stand, undisturbed, in a dark room.*

Steps:

1. *With your arms hanging at your sides, with your palms forward, invoke the Heaven Light (exercise 6).*

2. *Will with your Soul that the Heaven Light fill your chest in countless rushing tingling swirls, spreading back up into your head, and down your arms and legs. Will that the Light pass beyond the confines of your body, swirling all around you. Keep the Light moving in this fashion for one minute*

3. *Will with your Soul that the Heaven Light move down your left arm like a stream, and pour out your hand.*

4. *Stop the stream with your Soul and move the stream back into your heart.*

5. *Will with your Soul that the Heaven Light move down your right arm like a stream, and pour out your hand.*

6. *Stop the stream with your Soul and move the stream back into your heart.*

7. *Feel the love within the concentrated Heaven Light, and will with your Soul that the Light surge powerfully forward, like a plume of smoke, out of your heart and forehead. Feel the Light flow freely away, out into the universe, to reach another Soul. Keep the Light flowing for one minute.*

8. *Will with your Soul that the plume of Heaven Light explode and dissipate, reaching infinitely out into the universe, all the way to Heaven. Feel the holiness of Heaven acknowledging the Light sent Ascendant. Receive with your Soul the holiness of Heaven.*

When you have finished this exercise, behold in your Soul the new universe of sacred possibilities you are only beginning to enter.

Bending Light strengthens your Soul, braces your Soul with the Heaven Light, prepares you for your concentrated HeavenWork, and nurtures the independence of your Soul from the body's confines.

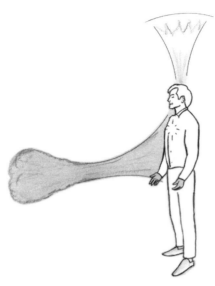

You may be realizing directly from the Heaven Light that the sanctity of Spirit is superior to Soul, and that by working the Heaven Light, your Soul is changing, growing more and more like Heaven. Your Soul sanctifies by working the Heaven Light in the service of Heaven.

With all your heart and Soul, thank deeply, graciously, and humbly the Heaven Light, the Sacred Beings in the Light, and all of Heaven for the Blessing just bestowed upon your Soul.

⚡ ADDED TWIST

Instead of sitting in a chair, try this exercise lying on your back—on the floor or in bed.

Repeat this exercise 10 times before moving to the next one.

Practice HeavenHome (exercise 4, or by Abbreviation) one more time.

BALANCING LAYING ON THE HANDS

You will learn to channel Heaven Light through your hands in many great ways. Concentrated Heaven Light can gently heal, and the Heaven Breath can restore the body with immediacy.

The Essenes were masters at healing body and Soul by laying on the hands and channeling powerful concentrations of both Heaven Light and Heaven Breath.

Though body healing is a noble form of LightWork, it is not described in the HeavenWork because it is only partly devoted to sanctifying Soul. But this shouldn't stop you from healing LightWork if you are so inclined.

For the purposes of HeavenWork, you may find it useful to lay your hands upon the hearts of consenting friends for the purposes of channeling Heaven Light into their Souls.

As you practice your LightWork in this way you will likely notice that usually only a gentle stream of Heaven Light passes through your Soul, down your arms, and into the other Soul.

This is good, but you can do better than this, much better. Even now you are capable of bearing enormous concentrations of Heaven Light. It is a question of balance, and the answer is calibrating your mind, your Soul, the other, Light-receiving Soul, and the Heaven Light.

If your mind is present, little if any Heaven Light will channel through you. If you are seated in your Soul, only a gentle stream of Heaven Light will channel through you. If you are too present in the Light-receiving Soul, the Heaven Light will backflow, sputter or stop from time to time.

But if you release hold of your mind, release your hold on the Light-receiving Soul, and then open your own Soul, you will enter into the flow of Heaven Light, and the Light will pass powerfully, in sanctifying concentrations.

The trick is to surrender unto the Heaven Light and let it go about its work!

Learning to allow the omniscient, loving Heaven Light to do what it does best opens your Soul, preparing you for all the rest of your HeavenWork, and especially your Transfiguration exercises of Entering and Becoming the Heaven Light.

Therefore, frequently lay your hands on those who request it, for the purposes of their Souls' sanctification, and blend this exercise with all your HeavenWork.

It is your Soul, and not the mind,
that performs your HeavenWork.

SIX

HOW TO EXPAND YOUR SOUL

Imagine how strange it must have been for Rip Van Winkle, after all those years of sleeping, how his muscles had weakened, and how strange and difficult it must have been for him even to stretch and yawn, much less get up and walk home!

The case of the long-sleeping Soul is similar.

For most of us in life, our Souls have shrunken from a lack of use, to a size smaller than the heart. It may surprise you but your fully awakened and expanded Soul should stretch to about as far as you can reach.

The Soul is very much like a ship's sail, and the Heaven Light the wind that fills it. The Soul, therefore, should not be pampered; it should be worked.

In order to do your HeavenWork successfully, your Soul must become limber and toned. You must expand your Soul to its full size, and this requires some basic training exercises.

EXERCISE 9

SHOWER OF LIGHT

Heaven raining down upon you.

Indeed your Soul thrives on the Heaven Light. The ritual we call "Baptism" wasn't always a ritual of words, signs and water. Originally it involved the actual immersion of Heaven Light into a Soul to jolt it awake and set it on the Path of Heaven Light. Though some Baptists have learned individually to Baptize with Heaven Light, True Spiritual Baptism was largely lost along with Jesus' other teachings of the Light.

This exercise, the Shower of Light, is the start of your first True Baptism.

You are only on exercise 9 and already you have learned how to enter your Soul, feel with your Soul, sense other Souls, invoke the Heaven Light, and channel it through your body and Soul in many ways. You may be starting to realize that the Truth in your Soul *is* the Heaven Light.

You have learned how it feels when your Soul moves, how your Soul exists independent of your body, superimposing your body. By increasing the intensity of the Heaven Light in you, you will now learn how your Soul is superior to your body.

The Spiritual Universe contains an enormous reservoir of Heaven Light, constantly Created by Heaven and just waiting to stream into you. If you invite it openly, it will fill you with an intensity that will shake you to your roots, and sanctify you…if you let it. Nothing is better for the Soul. It's all about opening your Soul, and inviting Heaven in.

Goal: *To intensify the Heaven Light in your Soul and body.*

Preparation: *Stand in a dark room.*

Steps:

1. *Invoke Light (exercise 6, or by Abbreviating). Feel the tingling gusts swirl into you in all directions!*

2. *Breathe in and out, slowly and relaxed.*

3. *Picture with your Soul that the crown of your head is opening wider, allowing for an even greater flow of Heaven Light to rush steadily into your Soul.*

4. *Each time you exhale, relax more and open more the crown of your head, and each time you inhale, invite more Heaven Light to surge down into your Soul, in greater and greater intensity.*

5. *Open your Soul, releasing the body, so that you can see, in Soul, pouring into you from above, the silvery whiteness of the sacred, purifying Light filling you.*

6. *Feel how wonderfully your Soul welcomes the Heaven Light. Thirst for more of the Light.*

7. *Grasp with your infinitively intuitive Soul the immense reservoir of Heaven Light that fills the universe—a sky of Heaven Light greater than earth's sky, wider than a galaxy, deeper than all the galaxies, and the Countenance of all the Heaven Light and all the Angels in the Heaven Light directed upon your Soul.*

8. *Take a deep breath, and with your Soul, wordlessly, desire that all the Heaven Light rush suddenly into your Soul as you exhale.*

9. *The moment the Great Cascade of Light thunders down into you, Surrender your Soul to it, and let it carry you.*

Wonder wordlessly with your Soul about the nature of the Light that just entered and filled you, and the effect It is having on your body and Soul. Frame this feeling as a marker for Abbreviation whenever you invoke the Heaven Light from now on.

You will always carry the Heaven Light in your Soul, and you will always move closer to Heaven.

With all your heart and Soul, thank deeply, graciously, and humbly the Heaven Light, the Sacred Beings in the Light, and all of Heaven for the Blessing just bestowed upon your Soul.

Repeat this exercise 10 times before moving to the next one.

If you find yourself waking up in the middle of the night with your Soul glowing warmly around your heart, you may jump to exercise 27 (page 124). After completing that exercise return here and continue on to exercise 10.

Your Soul becomes what it beholds.
Therefore behold the Heaven Light.

MOMENTATION

Practicing HeavenWork teaches you to live naturally, centered in your Soul.

While your mind can grasp religious meaning, it cannot know your Soul's experience in Spirit. We can imagine dying—from the perspective of the Soul—and study it, but we cannot know what truly happens until we die ourselves.

Thus is the limitation of mind. Thinking isn't being; the mind lacks the reality of the ultimate experience of the bare Soul released in Spirit.

Nor can your mind sustain its enthusiasm like your Soul sustains joy. Quickly the mind moves on to things profane, while your Soul awakened extends intuitively into free and unobstructed emptiness—the Clear Light. The mind hungers for things material while your Soul wafts into the Heaven Light, drawing ever closer to your ultimate destiny.

Now that you have tasted in Soul the Shower of Heaven Light, and the joy Light brings to your Soul, know that you have discovered a new way of living, a way you can begin this very moment.

Every moment you may live in Soul. Every moment you may embrace life with your Soul. Come from your heart. Feel the joyous and immediate pure experience life brings when you are always present in your Soul.

Unlike the body and mind, your Soul does not tire in the Heaven Light. You can sustain Soul presence every waking and sleeping moment of your life while you go about your normal daily activities. This is life enhanced. This is how you came to life to be. This is what Heaven expects of you. This is Momentation.

In Momentation, you learn the essence of gratitude, for in Soul not only are desired moments precious, but also trial, challenge and sacrifice. All are seen by your Soul as precious opportunities to sanctify and enter Heaven.

Live every moment of your life like you were meant to, in Soul.

By now you are coming more and more often into your Soul. You may wake up in the morning with your Soul glowing. At school, work or play you may find yourself suddenly basking in Heaven Light. You will find that the gaps of darkness between your spiritual experiences are narrowing. You are ready to use Momentation to erase those dark gaps, so that every moment of your life is illumined in Heaven Light.

Momentation requires only this: That every time you find yourself *not* present in Soul, simply Awaken your Soul (exercise 1, by Abbreviation), Enter Your Soul (exercise 5, by Abbreviation), and invoke the Shower of Light (exercise 9, preferably by Abbreviation).

A Covenant Of Soul

Know now that you are Soul and only Soul, that the earth you walk on you are only visiting, that the body you bide in, like the clothes you wear, is only borrowed. You are Soul and only Soul. You are eternal, and not of the earth, but Spirit—Spirit destined for Heaven.

Before you were born, before you entered body, you made a covenant with Heaven. *Do you Remember?* You vowed, within the Immanence of Heaven, to spend every moment on earth embracing life with your Soul, centered in your Soul, living life from your Soul.

If your Soul knows the truth in these words, it is now time to reaffirm your first covenant of your Soul—a permanent promise. If you are ready, then place your hands on your heart and make this promise before Heaven:

> *For the rest of my life, whenever I find I am not present in Soul,*
> *I will simply enter into my Soul.*

With presence in Soul, and time, you will become a being of Light, a servant of Heaven.

No Hiding

There is a great abyss, a daunting chasm gate that drops between your Soul and Heaven. Each passing moment, in and out of life, your Soul hangs at the precipice, yearning only to enter Heaven—Heaven, unapproachable unless you sanctify your Soul in life.

The only way In, the narrow gate, which issues out the Firmament and past the chasm gates from time to time to Engulf a newly sanctified Soul in Transfiguring Light, and in a flash returns, carrying the Soul Elect to Heaven for all time.

Such is the predicament of Soul in Spirit. We all stand at the precipice, every opportune moment of our lives. Yet we pass our lives away in hiding, hiding behind our distractions, insulated in comfort. Even our religions are laced with comforts and rewards of the earth and other matters foreign to the Soul. All the while your Soul goes nowhere.

It is time to put aside your obstacles. If you would enter Heaven, there is no hiding in life.

EXERCISE 10

HARNESSING LIGHT

Holding Heaven Light.

You have learned how to call the Heaven Light with your Soul, and move It freely throughout your body. Now for something a little more challenging: Holding the Light.

Holding, or Harnessing, the Heaven Light is fundamental to your HeavenWork. Soon, Harnessing Light will enable you to concentrate the Light in your Soul, increasing the Light's sanctifying power.

Goal: *To contain the Heaven Light around your Soul.*

Preparation: *Stand in a dark room.*

Steps:

1. Invoke Light (exercise 6, or by Abbreviating).

2. Will with your Soul that the Heaven Light circle within you in one uniform direction, passing around you from right to left, forming an eddy of Light around you. Keep the Light moving in this fashion for one minute.

3. *Will with your Soul that the Heaven Light stop moving, and settle around you in a peaceful cloud, forming a protective cocoon. Keep the Light around you in this fashion for one minute.*

4. *Will with your Soul that the cloud of Heaven Light shrink to the size of your heart. Feel the powerfully concentrated Light churn restlessly in your heart. Keep the Light confined within your heart in this fashion for one minute.*

5. *Will with your Soul that the Heaven Light expand suddenly to form a large, perfectly round ball your arms' length around you, with a smooth surface like a crystal ball. Keep the Light around you in this fashion for one minute.*

Feel how the Heaven Light easily forms into a perfectly spherical container around you. This is your eternal form. This is you without body, the True you, your earth halo.

Feel how the Light is still centered in your heart, while sending tingles of joy throughout your Soul, within and outside your body.

Feel the powerful pure love in the Light. Feel how its purity is the purest essence of universal Heavenly love, because it is no longer "owned" by you. It is Compassion.

Try to see with your Soul the clear whiteness of Heaven Light within your Soul, surrounding you.

Feel how the Light protects your Soul from darkness.

Know that when your Soul Harnesses the Heaven Light, you are connected directly to Heaven. You are engaging Heaven, and Heaven and all the Sacred Beings in the Heaven Light are well aware of this, for you are calling them to be of service to your sanctification and they are joyously serving Heaven. It is through the Heaven Light that your Soul will ultimately enter Heaven. So make the Heaven Light your Soul's home.

> *With all your heart and Soul, thank deeply, graciously, and humbly the Heaven Light, the Sacred Beings in the Light, and all of Heaven for the Blessing just bestowed upon your Soul.*

Repeat this exercise 10 times before moving to the next one.

THE MIND'S RELEASE

Perhaps at this early stage of the Path, as you begin to make manifest the gifts of your Soul, you may only weakly sense your Soul's presence and the Heaven Light. You may even start to doubt that your Soul and the Heaven Light are real. This is okay. Just realize it is your mind moving in, trying to distract you from Soul and Spirit. The mind is trying to pull you back to materiality to prevent your Soul from becoming dominant.

You don't have to engage the mind's thoughts. It's not necessary. Simply keep practicing your HeavenWork exercises without judgment. The more and more you practice, the more and more your Soul will awaken and expand, the more supple and powerful your Soul will become, and the more the joyous Heaven Light will fill you. Just keep at it.

To easily make sure your Soul is performing the HeavenWork, simply apply the **Uncertainty Principle**: *If you don't feel the Heaven Light surging through your Soul, then it isn't.* The HeavenWork means working with your Soul.

EXERCISE 11

OPENING YOUR HEART

No more hiding.

So far you have used your Soul to work the Heaven Light. Now you will combine some of your exercises to have the Heaven Light work on your Soul.

Perhaps you are beginning to understand directly from the Heaven Light that every time you direct the Heaven Light somewhere away from you, it also simultaneously works on your Soul.

Have you noticed when you direct the Heaven Light out of your hands (Hand Quickening, exercise 7, and Bending Light, exercise 8) that sometimes the Heaven Light flows back into your hands, up your arms and back into your heart? This is because your Soul is only beginning to Harness Light. You will get better and better at it.

But for now it is not a bad thing that the Light returns back up your hands. In fact, you can develop the reverse motion of the Light to help you separate your Soul from your body so that your Soul becomes strong, allowing you to do powerful HeavenWork. This is how.

Goal: *To loosen your Soul from the heart's grip.*

Preparation: *Sit in a chair, undisturbed.*

Steps:

1. *Sitting, perform Hand Quickening (exercise 7, not by Abbreviation). Feel the Light pouring out of the palms of your hands.*

2. *Hold your hands slightly out in front of you, about 6" from your chest, as if they were holding an invisible ball about 6" in diameter.*

3. *Will with your Soul that the Light passing through your heart, down your arms and out your palms circles around in between your hands, forming a concentrated ball of Light.*

4. *Will with your Soul that the Light streaming into your heart from above branches out forward from your heart and into the ball of Light you have formed between your hands, so that you feed the ball of Light from three directions.*

5. *You will feel with your palms the ball of Light form and your arms will begin to tingle, as will your heart and forehead.*

6. *Slowly and gently move your hands in and out, both squeezing and pulling the ball of Light, just like the ball was an accordion of Light. Feel how when your push into the ball, reducing it to about 4" in diameter, the Light compresses and resists your squeezing more. Feel how when you pull the ball, increasing it to about 12" in diameter, the Light freely follows the pull of your palms, as if your palms had become vacuum cleaners of Light. Move your hands in and out for about one minute, while you learn to squeeze and pull the ball of Light. Especially pay attention to how it feels when you pull the Light in through your palms. Remember to also keep pulling the Heaven Light from above.*

7. *Slowly push the ball of Light into your chest so that It surrounds your heart. Continue to hold your hands against your chest, over your heart. Feel now the Heaven Light continue to pour from above into your Soul, and branch down your arms, out your palms, and back into your Soul.*

8. *Feel how your Soul tingles joyfully in the ball of concentrated Heaven Light. Wait for one minute, allowing the tingling to subside. Feel how clearly your Soul feels like a ball of Light.*

9. *Will with your Soul that your palms reverse the flow of Light by pulling the Light back into them.*

10. *When you feel the Light moving back up your forearms, slowly withdraw your hands from your chest, like they are double doors, stopping your hands about 6" from your chest, again holding the ball of Light. Allow your Soul to move forward slightly, safely, following the ball of Light, out of the heart and chest and into the ball of Light between your hands.*

11. *After a few moments, slowly and gently return your hands to your chest, over your heart.*

12. *Repeat steps #10 and #11 for five minutes, each time sensing your Soul moving slightly in and out of your heart.*

When you have completed this exercise, allow yourself to marvel at how easily and freely your Soul was able to move from the heart, and from your body.

Your Soul does not need your body!

Wordlessly, silently, marvel in your Soul what this means about your immortality—that whether you're in body or not, your Soul continues on.

Congratulations. You have begun to loosen your Soul from your body. But this was just a preparation exercise. Let's do more.

> *With all your heart and Soul, thank deeply, graciously, and humbly the Heaven Light, the Sacred Beings in the Light, and all of Heaven for the Blessing just bestowed upon your Soul.*

> *Repeat this exercise 10 times before moving to the next one.*

Trust the universe, for no harm can come to your Soul.

EXERCISE 12

HeartWing

Leaving the nest.

Opening your heart is like opening the front door of your house for the first time, following a lifelong sleep. Now it is time to step outside and greet the day that is Life.

HeartWing carries your heart opening one step further, freeing your Soul to hover just before your chest. Holding your Soul free and clear of your body is important for your Transcendence.

Goal: *To gently and safely free your Soul from the body.*

Preparation: *Sit in a chair, undisturbed.*

Steps:

1. *Perform Opening Your Heart (exercise 11, not by Abbreviation).*

2. *Place your hands on your chest over your heart. Touch the pads of your thumbs together, allow your hands to relax, fingers slightly spread. Together your hands should look like a butterfly with wings resting against your chest.*

3. *Will with your Soul that your palms pull at your Soul in the ball of Heaven Light within your heart.*

4. *When you feel your palms strongly pulling at your Soul, slowly pull your hands away from your chest, continuing to pull your Soul away from your chest. Separate your hands from the HeartWing position and stop them about 12" away from your chest. Your palms should be facing slightly upward, as if you were holding a basket the size of your chest.*

5. *Feel with your Soul the Heaven Light descending from above into your heart and forward into your Soul, continuing up through your pulling palms and up your arms back into your heart, to recycle again forward into your Soul, looping through your arms and back again.*

6. *Feel your Soul resting out in front of your chest, however subtly, buoyed in the re-circulating Heaven Light. Feel how the boundary of your Soul rests almost electrically against your quickened hands.*

7. *Gently and slightly move your hands 1" back and forth from your chest. Feel the boundaries of your Soul change within the space, how your Soul, now free, pushes against your chest but freely returns to your heart.*

8. *Feel in your Soul how the Heaven Light sustains you, and feeds you with Spirit. Feel the enormity of sacred, joyous holiness that is the Heaven Light. Feel in your Soul how the essence of your Soul is the Heaven Light.*

Continue to hold your Soul out before your chest for as long as you will, even for an hour. Know that every moment you practice HeartWing, your Soul, your true being, will rise into your awareness, overcoming the grasping of your mind and body. Know that every moment you practice HeartWing, your free and independent Soul will strengthen.

With HeartWing, you will understand with your Soul that you are never alone, in life or death, but infinitely intuitive, reaching into every other Soul, and into the Heaven Light, to Heaven. Know that the more you practice HeartWing, a deeper and purer understanding of the Sacred will fill you, not with things of the earth, but of holy Spirit.

You do not have to place your Soul back in your heart at the end of this exercise. Your Soul will make its way there all by itself.

With all your heart and Soul, thank deeply, graciously, and humbly the Heaven Light, the Sacred Beings in the Light, and all of Heaven for the Blessing just bestowed upon your Soul.

Repeat this exercise 20 times before moving to the next one.

After becoming proficient at HeartWing, thanks to Abbreviation, you can enter HeartWing simply by placing your hands on your chest and drawing your Soul out in one gentle motion.

EXERCISE 13

POPPING OUT THE BALL

Elbow room for the Soul.

A SIMPLE GEOMETRY

Every Soul has the perfect shape—a sphere. The center of your Soul connects to the center of your heart. Typical in life, the sleeping Soul shrinks to the size of a marble, and does not vary or rise into awareness unless awakened. But once awakened, the Soul becomes responsive and can expand to its natural full size—as far as your arms can reach.

It is said that once you set foot on the spiritual path, you can never leave it. This is true in a sense, because no matter how your mind may fight it, your awakened Soul will not stop searching for Heaven. Awakened Soul is never at peace, but thirsting, impatient and restless, always eager to pass farther along the Path of Light to Heaven.

Now it is time for you to bring your awakened Soul to its full size. Just like wanting to stretch your arms and legs after waking from a long sleep, your Soul wants to stretch to its full capacity.

Just for a moment, stretch your arms over your head, touching your hands together. Now, keeping your elbows extended straight, slowly lower your arms down your sides until they rest against your legs. You just formed a circle around you. This circle is just about the size of your Soul when it is fully expanded. It is your Soul's natural shape and size when you are not in body. Try it again, this time realizing that your Soul will soon fill this space.

Have you ever seen people who seem to glow unmistakably with an invisible Light around them? These are people who managed to pop out their Soul to its full size. Expanding your Soul to its full size will strengthen your Soul, enabling you to perform powerfully sanctifying HeavenWork.

You have probably expanded your Soul during your life. In moments of great joy and happiness perhaps you have felt your heart burst open, surrounding you with a clear bubble of awareness and clarity. Maybe even the sky seemed to become brighter around you. Perhaps you were filled with a deep intuitive knowing that things are going to be just fine. On the other hand, shock and surprise emergencies may have rendered the same result. This, too, was your Soul popping open.

While most of your Soul's early HeavenWork movements are subtle, Popping Out The Ball is an unmistakable experience. There are physical experiences that are similar to the feeling your Soul goes through, for example, making your ears pop:

Just for a moment pinch your nostrils closed with your thumb and index finger, take a deep breath, close your mouth, and gently squeeze your lungs to increase pressure in your head. Did your feel your ears pop? Popping out your Soul feels a little like this.

Popping out your Soul is also like filling a balloon with air. You can feel the boundary of your Soul suddenly stretch like the balloon. But don't worry, your Soul can never break like a balloon.

When you pop open your Soul, your Soul may also feel like raising a bed sheet up in the air and pulling it down quickly, making it crack crisply like a whip.

Popping out your Soul also feels like a parachute when it snaps open in the air. It is like a sail in a strong wind.

Before starting this exercise, it will be helpful to practice the beginning of HeavenHome (exercise 4). Sit in your closet with the light off until you feel your Soul reach out and touch the objects around you.

Goal: *To expand your Soul into its full size.*

Preparation: *Stand in a dimly lit room, where you will not be disturbed.*

Steps:

1. *Enter into your Soul (exercise 5, or Abbreviate).*

2. *Quicken your hands (exercise 7, or Abbreviate).*

3. *Perform HeartWing (exercise 12, do not Abbreviate).*

4. *Invoke a powerful Shower of Light (exercise 9, or Abbreviate).*

5. *Holding your Soul just before your heart, feel the tingling of the surging Heaven Light pour into your Soul. Notice how powerful the tingling has become since your Soul's Great Awakening. Feel how the Light forms in a ball in and around your Soul. Feel how freely and easily your Soul expands within this sphere of Light. Feel your Soul's joy. Feel the trust and courage that accompanies the joy. Understand with your Soul how there is no limit to the joy that can fill your Soul. Know that no harm*

can come to your Soul, that your Soul is loved and protected by the Spiritual Universe, by the Will of Heaven. Know that the Countenance of Heaven, and all the Sacred Beings under Heaven, is upon your Soul.

6. *Continue to hold your Soul slightly in front of you by keeping the Heaven Light flowing into your palms of your hands. With your Soul invite more Light, so that the Shower of Light grows stronger. As the ball of Light holding your Soul concentrates more intensely, slowly move your hands farther away from your chest, until your arms are fully outstretched in front of you. Feel how the Heaven Light fills the space between your chest and palms, and how your Soul wills to expand and fill the growing ball of Light, how your Soul stretches forward from your heart, pulling on your heart.*

7. *Continuing to pull the Heaven Light into your palms, slowly move your arms down, in an arc, until they are outstretched at your sides. Feel how the Heaven Light naturally forms in a ball all around you, just like you are holding this spherical concentration of Light with your palms. Feel over your head, how the top of the ball of Light touches perfectly on the source of where the Heaven Light comes from. Feel how just by touching the source with your ball of Light you are now able to invoke immense concentrations of Light.*

8. *Will with your Soul that the Heaven Light now pour down into you stronger than ever before, filling your ball of Light with a universe of concentrated Light.*

9. *Feel the ball of Light around you fill with a turbulence like never before, reaching a near exploding concentration. It will not explode, so hold onto that concentration.*

10. *Feel how your Soul pulls at your heart, desiring to be free to expand and fill the powerful Light. Take a deep breath, and suddenly relax your heart, allowing your Soul to pop freely open into the safe whole ball of Light.*

Feel how your Soul fills the entire space around your torso—over your head, around your sides, in front, behind, and just above your knees. Feel how your skin tingles, and how the periphery of your Soul also tingles. Do not stop the exercise, but hold onto this state of being, with your Soul expanded completely. You have just popped open your Soul. Mark how it feels so that you can Abbreviate it at will.

Continue in full size and feel how more freely you now trust the universe. Understand how more safe, secure and able your Soul has become, now fully expanded, how connected you are to Spirit and all the Sacred Beings in the Light, what Oneness of Spirit all Souls are—the True and eternal lightness of being of Spirit. Enter into Compassion—that you no longer just *feel* love; you *are* Love.

Remember, in Soul, that you are immortal in the Heaven Light. Humbly ask the Heaven Light why you are here, and what Heaven Wills you to do.

Popping Out The Ball marks the top conditioning of your Soul, your readiness for Transcendence. It prepares you for works less in reference to mind, body and earth, and more related to the Heaven Light and Heaven. Once you have mastered expanding your Soul, and Abbreviating it, you will be ready enter Spirit.

Therefore expand your Soul often, many times a day, and at night just before you go to bed. Watch what changes enter your dreams.

With all your heart and Soul, thank deeply, graciously, and humbly the Heaven Light, the Sacred Beings in the Light, and all of Heaven for the Blessing just bestowed upon your Soul.

Repeat this exercise 10 times.

Then repeat it another 10 times the following way
before moving to the next exercise.

EXERCISE COMPLETION

1. **Place your hands over your heart in HeartWing.**

2. **Abbreviate Popping Out The Ball while in one smooth motion, opening your arms, pulling out your expanding Soul, until your arms are fully outstretched at your sides.**

3. **Bask in the perfection of your Soul surrounding you.**

Practice this way 5 times, then do it again 5 times
while lying in bed on your back.

It's okay if you don't fully pop out your Soul at this point in your HeavenWork. It is a challenging exercise. It is the first exercise that requires your Soul's undivided focus, and expanding out your Soul to full size doesn't always happen at this point along the Path of Light. You may move on to the next exercises, however come back to this exercise once a week until you achieve your Soul's full size. It will get easier as your Soul Transcends more.

THE PSEUDOSOUL

Under Heaven your Soul may do one of two things: Stay the same or change. If you stay the same, when you die your Soul will be reabsorbed into the Clear Light. But if you change, by sanctification, you will Ascend the Path of Light to Heaven.

As Jesus said, many are they who seek but few who find the gate of Heaven. This is because, despite our good intentions, many who seek Heaven revert back to the ways of earth and fall from the Path. So easily we fall from the Light of Soul and Spirit into the darkness of mind and materiality.

This happens because we are seduced and blinded by the mind, and persuaded to turn away from Heaven's Will—for us to call the Heaven Light and enter Heaven.

The mind constantly conditions us to darkness.

That component of mind that trips us up I call the **PseudoSoul**—the bundle of life-acquired ideas, symbols, attitudes, and sentiments that masks as Soul. Just as your mind tells you your thoughts and experiences are you, your PseudoSoul tells you your mind's values are your Soul. When you enter this personality of the mind you may feel you are in your Soul, but you are not. Your PseudoSoul is not your real Soul; it is very much a part of your mind, in your brain, and it constantly and insidiously fights to keep your Soul asleep.

> **PseudoSoul:** *The component of ego mind that masks as the Soul.*

Your PseudoSoul values materiality and attaches to things material to render the Heaven Light profane. Placing Heaven Light into materiality is ***spiritual materialization,*** a perversion of Spirit, the reversal of Heaven's Will.

> **Spiritual Materialization:** *Placing Heaven Light into materiality for purposes other than sanctification.*

The PseudoSoul twists us into perverting Soul sanctification into spiritual materialization. It is man's dominating PseudoSoul that has reduced the concerns of religion from Spirit to mind. It is the PseudoSoul in every one of us that twists us into mistaking profane matters of the earth to be matters of Spirit. It is the insidious PseudoSoul that keeps us from our true Soul.

In fact, once on the Path of Light, should your Soul turn away from Heaven by spiritual materializing, the Heaven Light will withdraw from you for a measured period, rendering your Soul into **Dark Night**, exile from Heaven's Light.

Dark Night: *When the Heaven Light withdraws from a Soul on the Path of Light after the Soul inadvertently turns from Heaven, usually by spiritual materializing.*

Look around, and observe how the PseudoSoul allows us to twist our spiritual aspiration into selfishness, greed, pride, competition, differentiation, judgment, intolerance, arrogance, hate, and even murder blasphemously in the name of religion and God.

But your Soul does not know any of these illusions. Your Soul knows only intuition, purity, loving being, awe, Compassion, clarity, joy, unity, simplicity, and affinity for the Heaven Light and Heaven.

When you experience the negativity of the imposter PseudoSoul, you are not in Soul, and you are not on the Path of Light.

As long as you try to find Heaven through your mind, you will constantly be thwarted by your PseudoSoul, and your progress will be slow. But you do not have to grope through the morass of mind to find Heaven. Simply bypass the profane mind and directly enter your Soul. That is why the Angels married your Soul to your heart.

Therefore, keep to your heart, keep to your Soul, keep to the tools of your Soul, keep to the Heaven Light, keep to your HeavenWork.

EXERCISE 14

THE SLIDE

Drifting into pure being.

In the cosmos under Heaven, materiality is like a vast body of gigantic stones and debris surrounded by a sky of lesser density. Both hang suspended in an infinite sky of glass-clear light. The Clear Light Sky itself contains no air, no atmosphere, but is more like a vacuum, a void. In the substance-free sky of Clear Light, the home of every Soul under Heaven, all awareness is free, wordlessly pure, and universal—a great Oneness, a direct, instantaneous and perfect infinite intuition shared by every Soul.

In life your Soul dwells embedded within the opaque body of materiality, the first cloud of unknowing. If you hadn't Awakened your Soul your mind would not be able to comprehend Soul or Spirit.

But the essence of your Soul is also always grounded in the Clear Light, whether in life or out of life. Once Awakened, your Soul can freely penetrate materiality, reaching purely into the Clear Light.

Once in the Clear Light, your Soul can call upon infinite stores of the Heaven Light to apply to your Soul's sanctification, enough even to work Miracles.

Now that you have made your Soul more limber, you can gently and safely begin to accelerate your Transcendence into the Clear Light. Transcendence involves passing through materiality with your Soul.

We will use the subtle, yet powerful onset of sleep to open the door. You may have noticed lately, as your Soul becomes stronger, that your sleep has begun to change in subtle ways. You may have stopped dreaming some nights, you may enjoy more the sensation of falling asleep, or perhaps you have awakened in the middle of the night with your Soul glowing with Heaven Light. These are natural experiences along the Path of Heaven Light.

Your daydreaming may also have changed. Instead of entering a reverie you may have found that sometimes you end up in a perfectly passive stillness, like a trance but surrounded in a peaceable lightness.

This is because your Soul is rising. During sleep your mind, just like its home, the body, will continue to drop in consciousness, but your Soul will rise to *its* true home, the Clear Light.

When your Soul was asleep, entering a daydream or falling to sleep involved simply passing from one state of mind into another. But now that your Soul is getting stronger, you can use sleep to pass from mind altogether and enter your Soul. When you do this, you are passing from materiality into Spirit.

To your Soul the Slide feels like your heart dissolves and you slip briefly into a bright, infinite sky of clarity where you bask free of thoughts, seated perfectly in open peaceful receptivity. You are extending back into the Clear Light.

The Slide is a brief experience, lasting only about one second. It occurs the moment you "fall" asleep. Have you ever "caught" yourself falling asleep, when suddenly you jolt awake almost in panic because your mind made you believe you are actually falling? That is the moment you are looking for in this HeavenWork exercise, the opportunity for your Soul to cut through materiality and enter the Clear Light.

Instead of "falling" asleep, you are going to "slide" your Soul into the Clear Light. It may sound difficult, but it is very easy.

Brief as it is, the Slide is a valuable Transcending exercise, for each time you Transcend your Soul it gets easier.

Goal: *To slip from mind and materiality into Soul and the Clear Light.*

Preparation: *Lie in bed in the afternoon, undisturbed, with the lights dimmed, and get in the mood for a nap.*

Steps:

1. *Perform your Soul's Great Awakening (exercise 1, not using Abbreviation), and maintain presence in your Soul until you fall asleep.*

2. *Keeping your hands over your heart, perform Iron Maiden (exercise 2). Do not move your body, and relax more and more.*

3. *Allow your relaxed mind to wander while keeping the tingling present in your Soul in your heart. Follow your mind's thoughts patiently as they pass gently before you.*

4. *Gradually, as you enter that familiar region of awareness when you know you are about to fall asleep, gently center your awareness back to the tingling in your Soul.*

5. *As you fall asleep, keep your awareness in your heart and not your head. When you feel the brief process of falling asleep happen, go with it, ride it, with your Soul.*

You will likely awaken after 20 minutes. Did you feel your heart dissolve and release your Soul? Did you feel your Soul gently slide forward a mere inch? Do you feel peaceful? Did you dream, black out, or drift passively into light?

Practicing the Slide loosens your Soul from the body and begins your Transcendence. It will get easier each time. After you have mastered it with sleep, you can learn to do it when you slip into daydreams. With Abbreviation, you will even become able to extend into the Clear Light at will.

THE 20-MINUTE LIMIT

Many Transcending and Ascending HeavenWork exercises involve your Soul leaving your body. You will soon come to notice that each time your Soul returns to your body after 20 minutes. This is nothing magical about 20 minutes, but it is simply the human body's tolerance point. After 20 minutes, your body gently, safely and reliably pulls your Soul back.

With all your heart and Soul, thank deeply, graciously, and humbly the Heaven Light, the Sacred Beings in the Light, and all of Heaven for the Blessing just bestowed upon your Soul.

Repeat this exercise 10 times before moving to the next one.

Continue on even if you do not master the Slide because the following exercises will help.

EXERCISE 15

INFINITE REACH

Omnipresence.

You now know through experience that your real being is not confined to your body. In or out of life your Soul is always centered and suspended in the sky of Clear Light. The more you pass beyond the ways of mind, body and earth, the more you return to the Clear Light, and the more your Soul's intuitive nature grows.

Through intuition your Soul can reach out infinitely into the Clear Light, to search, discover and understand things unknown to man or earth, things of Spirit.

With Infinite Reach your Soul's intuition can Transcend materiality and safely and gently extend beyond the Clear Light, penetrating the second cloud of unknowing—impurity—and reaching all the way to Heaven.

Goal: *To gently extend your Soul into the Clear Light Sky.*

Preparation: *Prepare a closet for HeavenHome and your bedroom for the Slide.*

Steps:

1. *In the closet, perform HeavenHome (exercise 4, or by Abbreviating).*

2. *While continuing to feel the Presence of Heaven, walk to your bedroom, sit on the side of the bed and Pop Out The Ball (exercise 13).*

3. *Lie down on the bed and begin to perform the Slide (exercise 14). Feel, when your thoughts cease, how drawn your Soul is towards the Transcendent, infinite Clear Light, how naturally your Soul glows like a peaceful sun. As you approach sleep, allow your Soul's rays of intuition to stretch curiously, infinitely, to the furthest reaches of the Clear Light, feeling intuitively into Heaven.*

4. *Without falling asleep, remain in this state of awareness for at least five minutes.*

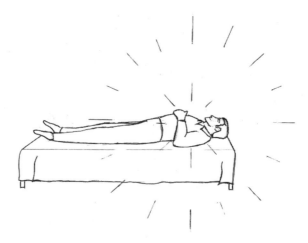

Did your Slide end to find you in Soul, radiant, suspended in perfect peace, and surrounded by a crystal clear, infinite sky? Did your Soul glow like a sun, its intuitive rays, invited by the Clear Light, stretching effortlessly to the reaches of infinity where everything collapses into Heaven?

Did you slip into a nap and awaken with a welcome lightness of being?

Did you almost Slide, but caught yourself, and found that your heart felt swallowed up in Light, as if the center of your chest dissolved away?

Did you feel how your Soul can extend with infinite reach, grasping the wordless nature and vastness of the entire Clear Light sky?

Did you feel the sacred emanation of Heaven pulling and drawing your Soul?

All of these are good, for they indicate your Soul has Transcended materiality to some degree to return to the Clear Light.

Remember with Abbreviation your Soul can always return to your greatest progress along the Path of Light. At will, you can return your Soul to the Clear Light, and press that much farther into the Light.

Infinite Reach frees your Soul from materiality, prepares you to find Truth in Spirit directly, and illumines your Soul's path to Heaven.

Now you know first hand, all there is to know can be found wordlessly in the Light.

With all your heart and Soul, thank deeply, graciously, and humbly the Heaven Light, the Sacred Beings in the Light, and all of Heaven for the Blessing just bestowed upon your Soul.

Repeat this exercise 10 times before moving to the next one.

In your pursuit of Truth, go beyond the box,
reach beyond the mind and into sacred Spirit,
for such is the Path of Light.

EXERCISE 16

WITNESS

The watcher behind the watcher.

To the sleeping Soul, life is a lot like television. There your Soul sits, passively watching your favorite program, while your mind actively identifies with the star of the show. Quickly you come to believe that you are the star, and the action and events of the show are actually happening to you in your life. But television programs, the roles, and the stories are not real. They are illusions.

Sadly, many of us pass our lives believing we are these illusions.

The true you, your Soul, lies within you, like the infinite Clear Light, within and beyond the wall of your mind that continuously tries to convince you that you are just part of materiality. You, Soul, now rising dominant over your mind and body, have grown strong enough to behold your mind and body as separate, artificial, and passing—different from your eternal being.

This exercise, Witness, will help your Soul rise even more dominantly over your illusory self.

Witness involves two progressive attenuation exercises, *Static* and *The Wall.*

STATIC

Goal: *To raise your Soul to full presence.*

Preparation: *Sit comfortably in a dimly lit room in front of a television in between channels so the screen is salt and pepper; keep the volume up so the static white noise is irritating.*

Steps:

1. *Gaze absently at the screen for one minute.*

2. *Relax, keep your eyes open, but stop focusing on the salt and pepper movements on the screen.*

3. *Let your thoughts slow and still until they cease.*

4. *Briefly you will shift in awareness. As the white noise fades off you will enter Soul, becoming calm and passive, yet receptive. Notice then that vague pictures appear and flit and dance across the screen within the salt and pepper. When you first notice them, you will begin to frame them with thoughts, which makes them disappear because you were pulled*

from Soul back into your mind. Curiously you will want to return to your passive receptivity to see the images appear again.

5. *Allow this back and forth shifting of mind to Soul and back to mind to happen several times, each time marking how it feels to your Soul. Notice how your Soul observes the images with open receptivity—passive, light and free. Notice too, when you return to mind, how cumbersome and opaque your thoughts are.*

6. *Relax and slip back into Soul until you can passively observe the fleeting images on the screen for ten seconds.*

Did you notice how drab and artificial your thoughts felt each time you returned to your mind, and how clear, spontaneous, free, and alive you felt when you were in Soul?

Your mind is the earthy, illusory you, your Soul is your Witness, the true and eternal you.

The wonders of modern electricity make Static an easily effective exercise for entering your Witness Soul.

Repeat Static 5 times before moving to The Wall.

THE WALL

Goal: *To raise your Soul into full presence.*

Preparation: *Turn on the radio or television to an off station so that white sound is produced at an irritating volume. Sit facing a clear white wall, where you will not be distracted.*

Steps:

1. *Sit close enough to the wall so that all of your vision is a blanket of white.*

2. *Just as in Static, relax and gaze at the wall without focusing.*

3. *Let your thoughts flow until they cease.*

4. *Slip into Soul so that your mind's thought images dance on the wall before you. Freely let them run their course without returning to mind.*

5. *Keep in Soul, so that when the images cease, remain in that perfectly clear and open state of Witness.*

Repeat The Wall 10 times before moving to the next exercise.

Thanks to your Soul's ability to Abbreviate, you can now enter Soul without any material prop simply by willing with your Soul.

With all your heart and Soul, thank deeply, graciously, and humbly the Heaven Light, the Sacred Beings in the Light, and all of Heaven for the Blessing just bestowed upon your Soul.

ERASING

Now that you have practiced Witness, you may recognize that your mind's ramblings were acquired early on in this short life—negative coping patterns that are now useless to your Soul, even detrimental to your HeavenWork. Now that your Soul has risen, you can quickly and effectively rid your mind of patterns you no longer have use for by erasing them. To do this, enter Witness, and watch with your Soul your mind's negative patterns appear. As they pass before your Soul's eye, simply will them erased, just like your Soul was erasing old writings on a dusty chalkboard. Practice this 10 times and observe how easily your mind's more negative patterns disappear.

Get good at Witness. You will need it later.

EXERCISE 17

EQUIPOSE

The natural balance of Soul, mind and body.

Typically the mind and body hold dominion over the Soul. It's not in Heaven's Plan for it to be this way, but it is the human fallen condition.

But on the Path of Light your Soul Awakens and expands, rising dominant over your illusory body and mind.

In Witness (exercise 16) you learned how to recognize your mind, body and materiality as foreign to your true eternal nature and being. Equipose will help you quickly come to live centered in Soul, keeping mind and body subordinate to your Soul, in the natural balance you intended to maintain before you entered body. By entering Equipose you can perform your HeavenWork unfettered by the illusions of false self.

By now you have noticed changes in your everyday awareness, good changes, as your body and mind recede in the service of your Awakened and amplifying Soul. Less and less do the neurotic emotions and ramblings of the mind feel like the true you or pull you, less and less do you respond to your body's demands, hunger and obsessive indulgences, less and less are you motivated to shun pain and pursue pleasure, and more and more are you concerned with your Soul's sanctifying HeavenWork.

This exercise, Equipose, concentrates Heaven Light to bring into balance the natural dominion of your Soul over mind and body.

Goal: *To raise your Soul permanently over mind and body.*

Preparation: *Sit in a chair.*

Steps:

1. *Quicken your hands (exercise 7) with Abbreviation, so that Heaven Light streams out your palms.*

2. *Place one hand over your heart, and the other on the top of your head. Invoke a Shower of Light (exercise 9 using Abbreviation) to increase the charge of Light flowing out of one hand back into your heart, and out the other hand down into your head. Hold your hands there, keeping the Heaven Light flowing in a high concentration. Continue for two minutes or until your mind becomes calm and subdued by the Heaven Light.*

3. *Keeping the one hand on your heart, move the other hand to the back of your head, just above your neck. and invite an increased surge of the Light to continue the flow into your heart and the back of your head. Continue for two minutes or until your body becomes calm and subdued by the Heaven Light.*

4. *Move both hands so that your palms are against your eyes, and invite another surge in the Heaven Light to continue the flow of Heaven Light into your eyes. Continue for two minutes or until you feel your Soul glow strongly in and around your heart.*

Feel how easily the Heaven Light swells and amplifies your Soul while soothing and calming the mind and muting your body's desires. Mark the changes, the adjustments taking place.

Notice each time you perform Equipose how your thoughts and emotions, and your body's drive for pleasure and alleviation of pain recede in the service of your en-Lightening Soul, while your Soul's interest in things eternal and spiritual grows.

> *With all your heart and Soul, thank deeply, graciously, and humbly the Heaven Light, the Sacred Beings in the Light, and all of Heaven for the Blessing just bestowed upon your Soul.*

> *Repeat this exercise **30** times before moving to the next one.*

> *Practice HeavenHome (exercise 4, or by Abbreviation) one time.*

SEVEN

HOW TO AMPLIFY YOUR SOUL

EXERCISE 18
CRESCENDO

Light magnification.

You are now ready to awaken your Soul's ability to work the Heaven Light in ways that sanctify.

You sanctify by magnifying Heaven Light with the Soul. By squeezing and concentrating Light, a change in your Soul takes place. The Heaven Light suddenly permeates the substance of your entire Soul, and the profane traces of Soul are erased, replaced with the sacred nature of Heaven. Each time your Soul is washed clean, each time the essence of your Soul becomes more like Heaven.

Every Soul has the ability to invoke Heaven Light, Harness it, and squeeze it until it permeates the Soul. We don't have a word for it, so I call it **Crescendo**, because it is very much like a musical crescendo.

Crescendo is your first Light magnification HeavenWork exercise.

To your Soul, Crescendo feels like a sneeze. First, invoke the Heaven Light, and holding all of it in your Soul, continue to invoke more. As your Soul swells and stretches with the Light, when you feel your Soul cannot possibly receive any more Light, squeeze it with all your Soul's might until you experience the phenomenon of Crescendo.

The pressure of incoming Light pushing against your squeezing Soul will suddenly shift, rising like a surging tide that explodes in climax into your Soul. All of the pressure is suddenly released (just like a sneeze) into the substance of your Soul and thereabouts, changing your Soul, each time filling you with unmistakable thrilling relief.

INVOKE→ HARNESS→ SQUEEZE→ PERMEATION

Crescendo is also like blowing up a tube balloon without stretching it first. You blow hard into the balloon and suddenly its structure changes under the air pressure. It is permanently changed. Each time you Crescendo your Soul is permanently changed a little by the Heaven Light, purified and moving in the direction of Heaven.

Enough explanation. Let's do it.

Goal: *To permeate your Soul with Heaven Light.*

Preparation: *Sit in a chair where you will not be disturbed.*

Steps:

1. *Sitting, invoke Light (exercise 6), using Abbreviation.*

2. *Harness the Light, confining it to a ball around your heart (Abbreviating exercise 10).*

3. *Invoke a Shower of Light (exercise 9) to rush more Light into your Soul.*

4. *As your Soul fills more and more with Light, concentrate the Light with the imagery of the roller coaster ride.*

5. *As you feel your Soul fill to capacity with Heaven Light, inhale air deeply into your lungs.*

6. *You will know intuitively when your Soul has filled completely with Heaven Light and is ready for Crescendo. At that moment, bend your head forward and with your Soul squeeze the Light as hard as you can while exhaling quickly.*

Bask in the tingling all over your body, the increased turbulence of the Heaven Light, the icy nature of the tingling swirling in and around your Soul, the boundless joy, the free release, and the intense purity of the Light filling your Soul. Feel how powerful the Light has become, and how your Soul has become more like the Light.

All this happened because you concentrated the Light past your Soul's "envelope," you put the Light to work on your Soul. By intensifying the Heaven Light with your Soul, you have also intensified your HeavenWork.

Practice Crescendo many times a day. Each time you perform Crescendo your Soul will become stronger. Each time put all your Soul into it, for the Soul knows no exhaustion in the Heaven Light.

So far your HeavenWork has involved you strengthening your Soul by drawing Heaven Light *into* your Soul. You will soon learn to direct the Light *outward*, into other Souls. You will learn to use Crescendo to Manifest the Will of Heaven, by issuing Heaven Light while attaching a pure intention of your Soul to perform a particular sanctifying work (*always* for the purpose of sanctification and *never* for personal benefit or material gain). Because of this, you must always be pure in heart when you perform Crescendo.

Crescendo will empower all of your HeavenWork. Each time you Crescendo, you purify your Soul a little more. You will Crescendo thousands of times in your lifetime. After 10,000 Crescendos your Soul will become pure and powerful in the Heaven Light, and your Soul will sanctify, passing along the Path of Light.

Ultimately, when your Soul has sanctified, when you have completed your HeavenWork, and when your Soul Elect has Ascended before Heaven, you will use a special kind of Crescendo one last time to enter into Heaven forever.

With all your heart and Soul, thank deeply, graciously, and humbly the Heaven Light, the Sacred Beings in the Light, and all of Heaven for the Blessing just bestowed upon your Soul.

Practice Crescendo 100 times before moving on to exercise 19.

When you have performed 100 successful Crescendos, work to Abbreviate it completely—without inhaling and exhaling. This way your mind and body will not be able to compete with your Soul.

⚡ FINE TUNING

If you have trouble producing a powerful first Crescendo, try this:

1. *Remember the first time you were filled with a wonderful presence, a grace presence that felt like a peaceful breeze that poured down from above into you, splashing and sweeping within you and without.*

2. *Notice that not only are you remembering it, you are also feeling it—re-experiencing it. This is because it is not just happening to your mind, but also to your Soul. Your mind remembers, your Soul experiences. This is the essence of Abbreviation.*

3. Continuing to hold the re-experience of the grace presence in your heart and Soul, take a deep breath, and sigh out loud. Feel then what happens in your chest—the wondrous effervescence in and around your heart. This is the Heaven Light cleansing your Soul, sanctifying your Soul in Crescendo.

Whenever you want to Crescendo, simply re-experience this grace presence and sigh. Soon you will learn to Crescendo at will.

Practice Popping Out The Ball (exercise 13) once again, this time using Crescendo.

EXERCISE 19

DANCING LIGHT

Seeing your works with your Soul.

Seeing is *more* than believing. Would you like to see the fruits of your early HeavenWork? Would you like to see some proof that your Soul is working the Heaven Light?

Here's a joyous, easy way.

Goal: *To see the Heaven Light with your Soul.*

Preparation: *Go to bed at bedtime, the lights out.*

Steps:

1. *Lie in bed, your hands at your sides, with palms down, and keep your eyes closed.*

2. *Slowly, starting at your head and working your way down to your toes, clench your muscles and keep them clenched until you are squeezing all your muscles. Then release, relaxing completely.*

3. *Feel how it seems you are sinking down, into your bed.*

4. *Practice Iron Maiden (exercise 2). Only allow your chest to move, rising and falling.*

5. *Invoke the Shower of Light (exercise 9). Feel the Heaven Light pour down and through your head, flooding your Soul and torso. Allow the Light to spread through your body, and out your body, surrounding you in a blanket of loving, exhilarating Light.*

6. *Will with your Soul that more and more Light continue to pour into you, so that it spreads, filling the entire room with Light. Keep the powerful Light pouring down into your Soul throughout this exercise.*

7. **Continuous Crescendo:** *Take all the Light within your Soul and squeeze it into Crescendo. But this time, just when the Light shifts and is about to explode into permeation, relax. Instead of permeating, allow the concentrated Light to channel out of your Soul, out of your body, filling the room with concentrated Heaven Light.*

8. *Repeat step 7 ten times, as the Heaven Light continues to build in the room. Feel with your Soul the turbulent tempest of Light rush and churn through the room.*

9. *Simply open your eyes and gaze, relaxed, at the ceiling.*

You will find your sight easily shift from focused mind to the relaxed gaze of your Soul. Your vision will move closer to the heart.

Do you see the Heaven Light swiftly dancing across the ceiling, the turbulence, the concentration, the wisps of white and silver rushing in all directions? Do you notice sparks flying off the tips of the Light wisps?

Know that the Light only *appears* to be projected on the ceiling. Actually and at your Soul's command, it fills the room, surrounding you in a passionate embrace, like a sacred cocoon. Continue to watch the dancing Light until you fall asleep…

…In the morning when you wake, look up again at the ceiling. Do you see how a residue of the Heaven Light remains, gently flowing across the ceiling? This is because your Soul commanded the Heaven Light last night to surround you. Assigned—Sealed—with a loyal love beyond the comprehension of mind, the Heaven Light stayed with you all night long.

Now you have your proof. You are continuing your learning how to see with the eye of your Soul. Practice Dancing Light often—every time you go to sleep—for you should never be away from the Heaven Light.

Take this time to wonder wordlessly, in awe, of the Truth in Heaven Light that is changing the essence of your Soul forever. Open your Soul to Truth, and become that Truth.

With all your heart and Soul, thank deeply, graciously, and humbly the Heaven Light, the Sacred Beings in the Light, and all of Heaven for the Blessing just bestowed upon your Soul.

Repeat this exercise 10 times before moving to the next one.

Get good at Dancing Light. You will need it later.

Exercise 20

Cocoon

Sealing the Heaven Light onto your Soul.

Let's put your new ability to squeeze the Heaven Light to work sanctifying your Soul.

Deeply our Souls resonate when we observe how a caterpillar changes, through the cocoon, into a butterfly. This is because deep down our Souls desire to change into Heaven. Recall your last exercise, how Dancing Light feels like a big, soft, loose cocoon of Light around you, how it changes your Soul.

With a few simple adjustments you will now learn to pull all that Light closer to you, Harnessing it into a Cocoon of Light, so that its sanctifying power can better permeate, and change, your Soul.

Goal: *To surround your Soul in concentrated Heaven Light.*

Preparation: *Lie down in bed at bedtime.*

Steps:

1. *Begin Dancing Light (exercise 19)—stiffening your muscles, performing Iron Maiden, calling the Shower of Light, and spreading the Light throughout the room.*

2. *Simply by willing with your Soul, gently draw the Light that fills the room close to your Soul by Harnessing (exercise 10). Feel how joyfully and willingly the Heaven Light complies to your Soul's command, for in its perfect infinite knowing, the Light knows what you are about to do.*

3. *Initiate Crescendo (exercise 18), all the while willing with your Soul that the Heaven Light condense around you in a cocoon. Just before Crescendo climaxes, relax.*

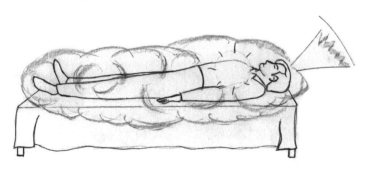

Sense with the eye of your Soul the Cocoon of Light that has just formed around you. Observe how it is not the size of the Cocoon that matters, but the quality and concentration of Heaven Light permeating your entire being— body and Soul.

Already you can sense that Cocoon generates physical healing properties. Cocoon may remind you of Jesus, who we like to remember as a healer. However, Jesus did not come to earth to heal bodies, but to sanctify Souls along the Path of Light. And his healings didn't involve the concentrated Heaven Light of Cocoon, but the Breath of Heaven, which graces only the Ascended Soul.

Therefore, until your Soul presents before Heaven, use your HeavenWork solely for sanctification, as a protector against illusory energies, and to keep Heaven Light within you and around you constantly.

Know that once you have mastered Cocoon you can surround yourself with this sheath of Light at will, using Abbreviation, at any moment.

With all your heart and Soul, thank deeply, graciously, and humbly the Heaven Light, the Sacred Beings in the Light, and all of Heaven for the Blessing just bestowed upon your Soul.

Repeat this exercise 10 times before moving to the next one.

ABBREVIATING CRESCENDO

Taking a deep breath while performing Crescendo was useful when your Soul learned Crescendo. But now that you have learned this valuable skill, you must not come to rely on your body's breathing because it will compete with your Soul, slowing your progress along the Path of Light. HeavenWork involves 100% work of your Soul without body or mind. The more you rely on breathing to initiate Crescendo, the less your Soul becomes able to master Crescendo. Therefore you must now start Abbreviating Crescendo.

THE IMPORTANCE OF LIGHT CONCENTRATION

Holding and concentrating the Heaven Light in your Soul is the essence of your Soul's sanctification on earth—the essence of life. Squeezing the Light *with* your Soul and *into* your Soul cleanses and transforms your Soul and carries your Soul along the Path of Light, towards Heaven.

The HeavenWork exercise, Cocoon, powerfully cleanses your Soul in the Heaven Light. Therefore practice Cocoon constantly, when you are alone or with others, walking, sitting, always—the more the better.

Cocoon also amplifies and empowers your Soul in the Heaven Light, and aligns you on the Path of Light. At this point of your journey you are preparing your Soul for all kinds of HeavenWork, you are focused on your Soul. First your Soul must become strong in the Heaven Light. Only then, when you have become strong, can you move on to more advanced HeavenWork, using the Heaven Light to help others.

EXERCISE 21

PILLAR OF FIRE

Transcending the illusion pain…

Freedom of Soul means you are no longer prisoner of your body, mind or materiality. Freedom of Soul means you can release materiality just by willing with your Soul.

Pillar of Fire teaches you how to quickly release your Soul from the confines of materiality by relieving you when you get cold.

If you live in a cold climate and it is winter, proceed with this exercise. If you live in a hot climate, skip this exercise and move on to the next exercise, Pillar of Ice.

Goal: *To instantly Transcend your Soul by bracing the body with cold.*

Preparation: *Stand outside in the cold briefly without a coat on.*

Steps:

1. *When the cold starts to get unbearable, quickly invoke the Shower of Light (exercise 9), using Abbreviation. Feel the Light flow into your heart and chest.*

2. *Quicken your hands (exercise 7), using Abbreviation.*

3. *Reverse the flow of Light along your dominant hand so that your palm pulls Light into it.*

4. *Looking down, circle your palm clockwise in front of your heart in a 12" motion. Keep circling until you "connect" with the Light, causing it to begin flowing from your Soul into your palm and up your arm.*

5. *Accelerate your hand motion and shrink your circles while accelerating your hand movement. During this brief spiraling movement, feel how much stronger your palm pulls the Light, and how the Light seems ready to jump out of your Soul and into your palm.*

6. *Continuing to pull the jumping Light out of your Soul, quickly flip your arm skyward, stopping your hand over your head. At the moment your hand stops, release the Light from your palm, sending its flow trailing freely upward to where it came from in the first place.*

While you flip your hand upward, you may find it useful to exhale quickly and loudly hiss, "Hissss!" Hissing startles and shatters the mind briefly so that your Soul can channel Light without obstruction.

Instantly you will feel no cold. In fact, it will seem you are bathed in a column of warmth, a protective Pillar of Fire.

If you stay outside longer, and your Pillar of Fire wears off, simply repeat the exercise. But do not stay outside long. Pillar of Fire is not an endurance exercise but a clearing exercise that teaches you to Transcend quickly.

You should practice Pillar of Fire until you can perform it entirely in three seconds.

> *With all your heart and Soul, thank deeply, graciously, and humbly the Heaven Light, the Sacred Beings in the Light, and all of Heaven for the Blessing just bestowed upon your Soul.*

> *Repeat this exercise 10 times before moving to the next one.*

WHAT JUST HAPPENED?

Pillar of Fire brought you immediate escape from the cold by surrounding you with warmth, or at least it felt that way to your mind. But what really happened was that you just taught your Soul to instantly Transcend your body into the Clear Light, where there is no temperature, no body to experience cold.

Now that you have learned to use oppressive materiality to Transcend, know that you can also use other material conditions to Transcend—pain, pleasure, boredom, exhaustion.

Thanks to your Soul's ability to Abbreviate you can now Transcend to the Clear Light no matter how your body feels. Just do it!

EXERCISE 22

PILLAR OF ICE

...and Transcending the body's grip.

Pillar of Ice is the hot weather equivalent to Pillar of Fire. If you live in a hot climate, use this exercise to learn how to release your Soul from the confines of materiality by relieving you when you get hot.

Goal: *To instantly Transcend your Soul by bracing the body with heat.*

Preparation: *Stand outside at the hottest time of the day.*

Steps:

1. *When the heat starts to get unbearable, quickly invoke the Shower of Light (exercise 9), using Abbreviation. Feel the Light flow into your heart and chest.*

2. *Quicken your hands (exercise 7), using Abbreviation.*

3. *Reverse the flow of Light along your dominant hand so that your palm pulls Light into it.*

4. *Looking down, circle your palm clockwise in front of your heart in a 12" motion. Keep circling until you "connect" with the Light, causing it to begin flowing from your Soul into your palm and up your arm.*

5. *Accelerate your hand motion and shrink your circles while accelerating your hand movement. During this brief spiraling movement, feel how much stronger your palm pulls the Light, and how the Light seems ready to jump out of your Soul and into your palm.*

6. *Continuing to pull the jumping Light out of your Soul, quickly flip your arm skyward, stopping your hand over your head. At the moment your hand stops, release the Light from your palm, sending its flow trailing freely upward to where it came from in the first place. While you flip your hand upward, you may find it useful to exhale quickly and loudly hiss, "Hissss!" Hissing startles and shatters the mind briefly so that your Soul can channel Light without obstruction.*

Instantly you will feel no heat. In fact, it will seem you are bathed in a column of cold, a protective Pillar of Ice.

If you stay outside longer, and your Pillar of Ice wears off, simply repeat the exercise. But do not stay outside long. Pillar of Ice is not an endurance exercise but a clearing exercise that teaches you to Transcend quickly.

You should practice Pillar of Ice until you can perform it entirely in three seconds.

> *With all your heart and Soul, thank deeply, graciously, and humbly the Heaven Light, the Sacred Beings in the Light, and all of Heaven for the Blessing just bestowed upon your Soul.*

> *Repeat this exercise 10 times before moving to the next one.*

WHAT JUST HAPPENED?

Pillar of Ice brought you immediate escape from the heat by surrounding you with cold, or at least it felt that way to your mind. But what really happened was that you just taught your Soul to instantly Transcend your body into the Clear Light, where there is no temperature, no body to experience heat.

Now that you have learned to use oppressive materiality to Transcend, know that you can also use other material conditions to Transcend—pain, pleasure, boredom, exhaustion.

Thanks to your Soul's ability to Abbreviate you can now Transcend to the Clear Light no matter how your body feels. Just do it!

MAGIC AND MIRACLE

Spirit used for material purposes is magic. Magic produces material gain but confines the Soul to materiality.

Spirit used in accordance to Heaven's Will is Miracle. Miracle produces no material gain but sends the Soul toward Heaven.

Therefore always choose Miracle over magic.

SLEEPWORK

Awakened Soul, it is time to explore sleep. Many believe there is only one way to sleep: To release and slip into unconsciousness while your body replenishes and your mind works more freely to resolve its attachments. But there are *other* ways of sleep.

As it relates to your HeavenWork, second only to death, sleep provides an excellent opportunity for slipping from mind into Soul and Transcending into the Clear Light.

The moment you "fall" asleep is a door for your Soul.

You have learned the Slide (exercise 14), a preparation for your SleepWork. Now you will learn two more ways to Transcend your Soul.

EXERCISE 23

CONTINUUM

No Coma, the steady path of Soul through life and death.

You are immortal, Soul. The moment you die, your Soul will awaken, fill with a joyous Understanding one in body cannot know, and continue fully awake through its entire migration. Your Soul cannot die.

Yet, if you have not sanctified in life you will not enter Heaven after death, but be carried back into the Lightfields in the Clear Light.

There are HeavenWork exercises that not only sanctify, but empower and prepare your Soul for a more auspicious migration—exercises that make you "rich in Spirit."

Continuum is one such exercise.

Sleep is a lot like death, a state of subtle transition. Through Continuum you can learn to slip into your Soul at the moment you fall asleep and continue in Soul until your body wakes up. This is ultimately beneficial because mastering Continuum strengthens—enriches—your Soul so that when you do eventually die, you will be fully present and empowered to migrate in fullness, which increases your likelihood of entering Heaven.

By practicing Continuum, your body will replenish, but your mind will remain unconscious as you bask in Soul Transcended slightly between materiality and the Clear Light.

Goal: *To pass your Soul through sleep's door and continue presence.*

Preparation: *At naptime find a place to lie down where you will not be disturbed.*

Steps:

1. *Lie on your back and relax.*

2. *Gaze up at the ceiling and practice the Wall (preparation for exercise 16), using Abbreviation to pass quickly into your witness Soul presence.*

3. *Perform Iron Maiden (exercise 2), not using Abbreviation.*

4. *Keeping your hands at your sides, perform the Slide (exercise 14), using Abbreviation if you wish.*

5. ***Just at the moment before you sense you are going to fall asleep, speak the following with sincere, even stubborn emphasis, and repeat it three times:*** *"The body and mind are going to fall asleep, but I'm going to stay awake!"*

6. ***Then release the wish, simply relax, and let yourself fall asleep.***

Because of the 20-Minute Limit you will likely awaken refreshed in that time or less. Do you notice a different quality of wakefulness, a new tranquility? This is good.

Did you find shortly after you surrendered to sleep that your Soul bubbled up, suspended just over your heart so that you could passively observe the room around you, and that the room had taken silver-gray tones? This is very good.

Did you also find your Soul connected infinitely in all directions by millions of needle-thin rays of Light? Did your Soul's intuition extend up along the rays of Light and glean the nature of That which lay beyond? If you did, great!

Did you find yourself in pure Soul, suspended perfectly and passively in the Clear Light of undisturbed and undistracted being? Then you do not have to repeat this exercise again; you have mastered it, and you can move on to exercise 24.

Continuum prepares you for your more advanced HeavenWork. Practice Continuum throughout your life and ultimately your Soul's experience the moment you die will continue unbroken, and pass you more quickly and aspiciously through your Soul's migration. Once you have mastered Continuum, try it occasionally at night when you fall asleep.

Mastering Continuum is similar to **Liberation** in that you are becoming independent of incarnation, you are acquiring the ability to become a Sacred Being in the Light.

With all your heart and Soul, thank deeply, graciously, and humbly the Heaven Light, the Sacred Beings in the Light, and all of Heaven for the Blessing just bestowed upon your Soul.

Repeat this exercise 10 times before moving to the next one.

Get good at Continuum. You will need it later.

EXERCISE 24

UNGRASPING

Falling into your Soul.

Life is so precious to your Soul, for only in materiality can your Soul sanctify in the Light, and the wait for incarnation is very long and restless.

Now that you have received the gift of life, use it for all it's worth.

But the mind does not see things the way of immortal Spirit. The mind is deeply and fundamentally committed to bodily survival. Since your Soul forever seeks Heaven, the threatened mind constantly and hungrily grasps at materiality.

By now your Soul is strengthening. You have learned Continuum, to remain nearby witness in Soul while your body sleeps. Now you will learn to let your body and mind fall asleep while you, Soul, fall safely into the Clear Light.

You will do this by riding the sensation of falling asleep—that familiar moment when you suddenly feel like you are dropping, the moment your mind has always caught you in near panic and brought you back to wakefulness, filling you with the idea, perhaps, that you were falling to your death.

The truth is you were starting to fall in Soul back into the Clear Light, which set your startled mind into panic. The HeavenWork exercise Ungrasping teaches you how to fall all the way into the Clear Light.

Goal: *To fall into the Clear Light the moment of sleep.*

Preparation: *At naptime, sit in an easy chair that can prop your head from falling back.*

Steps:

1. *Sit in the chair with your head forward, unsupported by the chair. Relax deeply, and let yourself become drowsy.*

2. *Perform Witness (exercise 16) on the wall or ceiling, or by Abbreviation.*

3. *Perform the Soul's Great Awakening (exercise 1), keeping your hands on your heart.*

4. *As you near sleep, as you begin to nod off, as your head falls back and suddenly jerks forward, remind yourself, "The body is going to fall asleep, but I am going to stay awake!"*

5. *Relax again, but just as you begin to nod off, perform Entering Your Soul (exercise 5) by Abbreviation.*

6. *As you experience the falling sensation, ride it with your Soul.*

If you fall, in Soul, you will not know that your body has fallen asleep, you will not hit bottom. You will Slide gently through the mind to find your pure being, in Soul, suspended perfectly and present in the infinite sky of Clear Light.

Learn directly from the Clear Light the many things that cannot be put in word.

Even if you do not attain full Clear Light Transcendence, practicing Ungrasping will begin to help your Soul weaken and release the mind's pull to materiality.

You will soon find after practicing Ungrasping that sleep is not your only opportunity for Transcending. You will discover that every moment of your life provides opportunities for your Soul to reach further into the Clear Light.

With all your heart and Soul, thank deeply, graciously, and humbly the Heaven Light, the Sacred Beings in the Light, and all of Heaven for the Blessing just bestowed upon your Soul.

Repeat this exercise 10 times before moving to the next one.

GRASPING

The cyclone of thoughts, images, emotions, preconceptions, and attitudes that form the wall of mind grasps the body down to the bone. Furrowing your forehead when thinking, fidgeting, grinding your teeth, body armoring, even some forms of hypertension are ways the mind overcompensates for the Soul's desire to Transcend body to the Light.

As you progress through your HeavenWork, continue to practice gently releasing the mind's hold on your body. Your body will be all the better for it. So will your mind. And your Soul will become freer and freer.

EXERCISE 25

ENTERING THOUGHTGAPS

Every moment, a door to your Soul.

Like sunlight flashing through the leaves of a tree, your Soul is learning to penetrate the wall of mind and Transcend materiality into the Clear Light.

Even if your SleepWork exercises did not yet pass you completely into the Clear Light, do not be discouraged. Know that you are still advancing along the Path of Light. For each time you perform Continuum or Ungrasping your Soul will Transcend that much more.

Indeed, sleep is a powerful transition, and a clear opportunity for your Soul to slip away from the mind and body. But there is no limit to the ability of your Soul in Spirit. Thanks to Abbreviation, at will you can return your Soul to your closest venture toward the Clear Light, even when your mind is fully awake. And each time you Transcend more into the Clear Light, it becomes easier to return there.

Now you are ready to learn how to enter the Clear Light anytime. Now you will learn how to Ungrasp at will by entering the gaps that lay between your thoughts—your ThoughtGaps.

The mind is like a cyclone. Moving layers of thoughts—ideas, emotions, memories, fantasies, attitudes, preconceptions, predispositions, tendencies, internal dialogues, arguments, streams of reasoning, and the like—constantly rise and fall, perpetuating themselves into an opaque wall of acquired self-identity.

Every one of these thoughts—whether conscious or subconscious—has the same form: A gradual onset, a rise and an ending, followed by a brief gap before another thought takes over.

You learned in Witness (exercise 16) how to sit in Soul and allow your thoughts to play themselves out. Consider how practicing Witness leaves wider ThoughtGaps. Consider how wider ThoughtGaps provide you the opportunity to Ungrasp and pass through them into the Clear Light.

Granted, even though you may widen your ThoughtGaps, there *are* layers and layers of them, and to Transcend your Soul must pass through them all. This is where Infinite Reach (exercise 15) and The Slide (exercise 14) come into play. Connecting to the infinite nature of the Clear Light will pull you through as you Slide into and beyond your mind's most conscious ThoughtGaps. The more subconscious thoughts will soften and dissolve away with all of materiality as you enter the Clear Light.

Goal: *To pass, in Soul, through a ThoughtGap into the Clear Light.*

Preparation: *Sit in a comfortable easy chair at naptime.*

Steps:

1. *Allow yourself to become drowsy.*

2. *Practice Witness (exercise 16), using either a wall or television, and continue until you can see your random thoughts projected in front of you.*

3. *As your projected thoughts slow, allow your vision to become a gaze, so that you no longer see the wall or television.*

4. *Notice with your Soul the ThoughtGaps beginning to widen between your slowing thoughts. Feel how welcome and true to your Soul the ThoughtGaps are.*

5. *Practice Infinite Reach (exercise 15), by Abbreviation.*

6. *As your mind's thoughts slow to a halt you will notice your mind and body suddenly tire and pull at your Soul as if to go to sleep.*

7. *As you begin to fall asleep, practice The Slide (exercise 14), by Abbreviation, and dissolve through the heart.*

Thanks to the 20-Minute Limit, you will likely awaken soon. If your exercise was a complete success you found yourself suspended perfectly, passively but completely open and receptive in the infinite Clear Light, even if but for a moment before passing into sleep.

If you fell asleep but were able to Abbreviate Infinite Reach, you are making progress. The more you to practice Entering ThoughtGaps the easier Transcending will become. When you come to master Entering ThoughtGaps, you will be able to enter the Clear Light any time you desire.

Know that the more you extend towards the Clear Light, the more Heaven Light you can invoke and the more powerful your HeavenWork becomes.

Practice your Transcending HeavenWork exercises joyfully, for they are gifts of Heaven. You *will* come to enter completely into the Clear Light.

With all your heart and Soul, thank deeply, graciously, and humbly the Heaven Light, the Sacred Beings in the Light, and all of Heaven for the Blessing just bestowed upon your Soul.

Repeat this exercise 10 times before moving to the next one.

EXERCISE 26

TRANSFLEXION

What you came here to do.

We do not need to mystify sanctification. Every Soul is equipped to find every answer in Spirit and do what is required. Clearly you do not sanctify by things of the earth, but things of Spirit. Yet, the earth can become one of your tools.

Soon, when you come to Remember in Soul, you will know directly from Heaven what your Soul desired not so long ago—your wish being the very mechanism that compelled your Guardian Angels, your special Sacred Beings in the Light, to incarnate your Soul to life.

You will Remember your Soul craved the earth so that you could powerfully squeeze in your embodied Soul the Heaven Light every moment of your brief life. On earth, in body, this is Transflexion.

In the past, your Soul was probably not strong enough to Transflex because it was sleeping, inactive, shrunk, or otherwise apart from the Clear Light. But your HeavenWork thus far, your progression along the Path of Light and return to the Clear Light, has empowered your Soul.

Now that your Soul is extending back into the Clear Light, you can draw on immense stores of Heaven Light.

Transflexion uses the density of materiality to challenge your Soul to try harder, to invoke and squeeze vast concentrations of the Heaven Light in everything you do on earth. By using your Soul to push Heaven Light against the resistance of materiality, you can sanctify quickly.

In a way, Transflexion is your Soul's way of converting everyday physical effort into sanctifying HeavenWork. Because of your progress you may be surprised how easily your Soul is now able to Transflex.

The easiest way to learn Transflexion is by performing Crescendo (exercise #18) at the peak of a challenging and strenuous physical exercise, such as push-ups or weight-lifting. Because your near transcendent Soul can now gather immense stores of Heaven Light, when your Crescendo peaks and releases, a massive conversion of Heaven Light will permeate your Soul, mind and body to such an extent that the physical exercise you are performing becomes virtually effortless! But what is important is how powerfully your Soul sanctifies in the moments the concentrated Heaven Light permeates your essence.

To make learning easier, instead of an extremely strenuous exercise, you will learn by applying some isometric pressure to a tabletop. It is okay to practice this HeavenWork exercise using any strenuous exercise because it's not so much the activity, but what your Soul does with Heaven Light during the activity. Simply apply the following to whatever exercise you choose.

Goal: *To explode Heaven Light through your Soul by pushing the material envelope.*

Preparation: *Sit in a chair in front of a desk or table.*

Steps:

1. *Place the palms of your hands so that they press down on the tabletop. Progressively press them down harder and harder.*

2. *Continuing to press down harder, invoke the Shower of Light (exercise 9), using Abbreviation.*

3. *Still continuing to press down harder and harder, invoke Crescendo (exercise 18). Feel for the first time how freely and powerfully the Heaven Light pours into your Soul!*

4. *Because of the vast inflow of Heaven Light, the tide of your Crescendo will rise rapidly. Time your mounting Crescendo with your growing sense that you may not be able to press down any longer, and when that moment arrives, explode and release the Heaven Light.*

Did you feel the instant exchange of Heaven Light convert into your body, filling you with such strength that pressing down on the tabletop was almost effortless? Did you feel how the Heaven Light permeated your Soul many times stronger than when you last practiced Crescendo? Did you feel your Soul Transcend to a place where there is no materiality? Did you feel the intuitive freedom of your Soul releasing infinitely into the Clear Light?

And finally, did you then feel an unmistakable sacred sheet of icy Light drop down around you from above? This icy Light shows that Transflexion is achieved.

The icy Light sheet dropping around your Soul completes Transflexion.

What happened was you just spent your first moment in life doing what you vowed, in Soul, to do before you entered body.

Feel, now, in Soul, the presence of your Guardian Angels, and the myriad other Sacred Beings of Light who you drew to you with your Soul's first Transflexion. Abide in their loving Blessing to you for learning and doing what few humans ever learn or do in life: Prepare your Soul for Ascension to Heaven.

Transflexing while exercising is the sacred way of "entering the zone." During Transflexion your Soul's intuition expands profoundly. Try Transflexing while shooting archery, playing basketball, bowling, golf, tennis, or long distance running, if you like.

Now that you have successfully completed this exercise I can tell you that while Transflexion is most powerful during extreme physical exercise, you can also Transflex constantly, in every moment, with every little thing you do.

You can Transflex right now when you are reading these words, by standing up, walking, working, playing, singing, laughing, crying, taking a breath, even following your beating heart, for all of these are material expressions that can be converted in sanctifying ways.

Before moving onto the next exercise, practice with a true and earnest heart many of these more subtle Transflexions. Quickly your Soul will come to enjoy them. But more important, know that mastering Transflexion prepares you for your Ascent to Heaven.

Transflexion is the continuation of Crescendo and the empowerment of Momentation, and frees you to sanctify your Soul every moment of life, just as you intended before you entered body. Transflexion changes your life forever. By Transflexing, you begin to embrace life fully from your Soul, just as Heaven Commands you.

With all your heart and Soul, thank deeply, graciously, and humbly the Heaven Light, the Sacred Beings in the Light, and all of Heaven for the Blessing just bestowed upon your Soul.

Repeat this exercise 10 times, and then experiment, Transflexing simpler things before moving to the next one, simpler things such as walking, standing up, following your pulse or heartbeat, and breathing.

INTEGRATION

Thinking with your Soul.

Prepare for a well-earned reward.

HeavenWork is a process of bringing you into your natural state of being on earth—of becoming Integrated. Integration means living from your Soul, embracing life with your Soul—becoming centered in your sanctifying Soul, with your Soul maintaining continuous command over your mind and body so that your mind and body follow your Soul's will, with your Soul directly following Heaven's Will.

Integration is not a separate exercise, but a merging of Equipose and Transflexion. It is also an accomplishment marking your entry into the Clear Light, your Transcendence.

All of your HeavenWork exercises have led to this, your Transcendence. Have you yet realized, the HeavenWork is free Soul in Spirit, that your Soul already innately knows and recognizes the HeavenWork exercises, and you can combine each and every one of them, intuitively and spontaneously, to carry you closer to Heaven.

In exercise 26 you learned to employ Transflexion with all types of physical activity, from extreme physical stress to subtle physical movements. Integration is the Crown of Equipose (exercise 17), and it begins where Transflexion left off: Working with your most subtle expression of material being, your thoughts.

> **Crown:** *Fully achieved potential of certain rudimentary HeavenWork exercises.*

Why not try it right now? Take a deep breath, commence Crescendo by Abbreviation, and consider whether you can Transflex one of your thoughts. Squeeze this consideration into Transflexion.

Did you feel immense joy fill your heart, rush down your arms, and rise up and out the top of your head before flooding you in a permeating swell of purification through your entire expanded Soul while the icy sheet dropped around you?

Let's try an emotion or two. Knowing you have just moved closer to Heaven, and that the eyes of Heaven and the Sacred Beings in the Light are upon you, let loving gratitude fill your heart, take a deep breath, and Crescendo into Transflexion.

Now let's move to the other, more tender extreme: Sadness. Think of the saddest moment of your life. Allow the wave of grief to pass through you. Now take a deep breath and Crescendo into Transflexion.

Wow! The same beautiful thing happened. Your Soul purified and your profound sadness converted to spiritual joy. What a gift to the Soul is Heaven's Light. What more in life do we really need?

Did you realize a spiritual Truth? How beautiful even the experience of sadness can be to the Soul. This is because all of life experience is opportunity for your Soul to sanctify. Therefore, release your aversion to fear, pain, sadness, and all the negative values of man. Use them, implement them, each experience life throws your way, to the sanctification of your Soul. For on the Path of Light, everything becomes joy.

You've got the idea. By learning to Transflex your thoughts and emotions you will become Integrated, and everything about you will change—your mind, body, actions, and even those near to you, who receive the intense Heaven Light from your Soul.

We are Souls just visiting this earth. What really matters in this brief life is that you cleanse your Soul, and help other Souls cleanse. There is no greater Truth to the Soul under Heaven, for this God Commands of every Soul.

Integration is important to religion. All religions are based on ethical principles that emulate the outer signs of Integration: The avoidance of wrong action and the nurturing of right action. But *acting* sacredly in body and mind is not the same as sanctifying in Soul. In the end, although you may not have sinned in life, you will not enter Heaven unless you sanctify your Soul.

It is an issue of putting the ox before the cart. When you try to act sacredly, but you are reluctant inside, there is struggle. But when you truly Integrate, you naturally conduct your mind, body and actions with moral consistency because your sanctifying Soul is attuned to Heaven's Will. There is no struggle. With infinite freedom and joy you naturally choose to conduct yourself according to the Sanctification Principle: For the betterment of all Souls, for the Soul knows no distinction in Spirit.

Integration: *Embracing life naturally, with your Soul.*

The Will of Heaven cannot be put into word,
but must be experienced perfectly and completely,
received directly from God by your Soul.

SKY JUMP

By now your empowered Soul has released the confines of heart and body, and you have acquired a new spiritual talent that will help your Soul find Heaven—the Creight, *Sky Jumping*. Come, let's give it a try.

During the day, walk outside, or go up to a window. Place your hands on your heart, and using Abbreviation, invoke your Soul's Great Awakening. Look up at the sky, and consider in your heart the vastness and freedom in the sky, that your Soul could enter the sky and dissolve through the sky into the infinite Clear Light that lies just beyond.

If you felt at that very moment your Soul surge forward, as if to leap into the sky at this very consideration, your Soul just Sky Jumped. Your ability to Sky Jump indicates your Soul is nearly able to Transcend completely into the Clear Light!

SIGNS OF TRANSCENDENCE

As you continue accomplishing your HeavenWork Transcending exercises, as you journey along the Path of Light, as your Soul releases mind, body and earth to enter into the Clear Light, you will notice changes occurring to your ground of being—signs of Transcendence.

As you center in Soul the closed and opaque box of mind that you became used to in your short life will open, and you will sense, in Soul, that within your existence here on earth you hang suspended in a joyously free, bright universe that stretches infinitely in all directions, all the way to Heaven. You will sense, in Soul, your universal connection to all of Soul and Spirit. You will find it easier to Slide from materiality into the Clear Light, and your awareness of your Soul suspended in the Clear Light will become routine. You will begin to experience omnipresence.

This grounding in the Clear Light is not the dissociated euphoria that can occur to the mind and body, but a familiar, sure and certain seating in the infinite Clear Light—your true and eternal home under Heaven. It is not an escape or spacing out, but a pure, perfect and ungrasping presence. Your omnipresence in the Clear Light is natural, and vital to your Soul's sanctification, for you will learn to invoke and work enormous concentrations of Heaven Light in many sanctifying ways.

In the Clear Light your Soul will glean the inferiority and illusory nature of materiality and its confined dimensions of space and time, for in the Clear Light there are no clocks such as sunrise, sunset, bodily functions, and the like, but eternal peace and calm, patience tempered by total spiritual resolve to find Heaven. You will not deny or condemn materiality as nonexistent, but recognize it for what it is, and isn't. You will begin to **Crossover** into Spirit, recognizing you are not essentially human, but Soul.

In the Clear Light you will release your vain desires of materiality and Remember the one thing you want, the only thing you *ever* truly wanted: To pass into Heaven, for Heaven calls you. You will come to crave Heaven with all your Soul, for this is the Will of Heaven.

This is Remembrance in Spirit.

EXERCISE 27

VIGIL

Listening in Spirit.

Just about now on your journey along the Path of Light, you may find yourself suddenly awake in the middle of the night.

Not completely awake, but better, purer. Calmly, clearly you glean that your body is still sleeping, and your mind hardly stirs at all. And you do not care to wake body or mind, such is the welcome peace of your awakening.

There you find yourself, passive yet receptive, floating just over your body, free of materiality and in awe of the safe and inviting depth of the serene night.

You are in your Soul. You, rising Soul, awakened independent of body and mind to stand Vigil in the night, to gently and gracefully reach deeper into the Clear Light. For this your HeavenWork prepared you.

In Soul you know no fear of the dark, but intrepid promise, for materiality's grip has loosened, and so easily you could glide through night's darkness into the unhindered universe of Clear Light that lies freely just beyond.

This is Vigil, your first spontaneous HeavenWork exercise. It did not happen to you. Rather, the true you, your Soul, initiated it entirely independent of your body and mind.

Your HeavenWork is changing you.

Vigil is both an accomplishment and exercise—an accomplishment because your Integrated Soul has taken lead of your mind and body, and an exercise because there are things you can do to make Vigil all it can be.

Goal: *To enter the Clear Light from Sleep.*

Preparation: *Awaken spontaneously in Soul in the middle of the night.*

Steps:

1. *As you gently rise, in Soul, remain calm and sure.*

2. *If you feel your mind stir, and your body, gently move your hands to your heart, and with Abbreviation invoke the Soul's Great Awakening (exercise 1) so that Heaven Light feeds gently into your Soul.*

3. *Open your Soul, trust the universe, and invite all of sacred Spirit to approach you.*

4. *With your Soul's native intuition, listen in the night's peaceful dark for sacred visitations beyond your frame of knowing—of softer manifestations of the Heaven Light, and the Sacred Beings who inhabit it, who approach you in celebration of your accomplishment.*

5. *Reach with your Soul, intuitively into the night, Abbreviating Infinite Reach (exercise 15), so that your Soul is pulled Transcendent through the dark of night into the Clear Light materiality hangs upon.*

6. *As your Soul shifts, passing through the dissolving darkness, constantly and openly receive all the new experience that occurs to you.*

7. *Know, in Soul, the bright, infinite and freedom quality of the Clear Light that draws upon your Soul, and allow your Soul to Slide home.*

Feel in your Vigil Soul the great peace that fills the night with Light, how perfectly your Soul is connected to infinite Spirit! In the safety of this peace, be receptive, learn things you never learned—wordlessly pure and perfect wisdom pearls—of surrender, acceptance, immortality, certainty, and the choir of Sacred Beings that may gently slide before you to welcome you to your newfound life in Spirit.

Joyous is the Vigil of the Soul! Bask in Vigil for hours if you will, for you will awaken safely, with your body and mind fully refreshed.

Know that while your mind and body require rest, your Soul need never sleep. One-third of your life—sleep—you can now also put towards your Soul's sanctification.

Remember, your Soul feeds upon the Heaven Light. As your Soul Transcends your body and mind, so it is your Soul Transcends sleep. Therefore experience wondrous Vigil as often as you like, for each time you sanctify all the more.

If you haven't yet found your Soul in nighttime Vigil, simply go back and practice Continuum (exercise 23) before going to bed.

WISDOM IN THE LIGHT

The more you hold the Heaven Light in your Soul in new and many ways, the more you will understand the omniscience in the Light. How "other" is the nature of divine Wisdom from the opaque and hollow knowing of the human mind.

I will not tell you the wondrous things the Light will continue to teach your Soul, for words reach only into the mind. That what you must know you can now learn directly from the Heaven Light.

Therefore, day and night, listen, feel and surrender in Soul, to receive the divine Knowing of what you are not so that you may become what you are not, for such is the way of entering sacred Being beyond being.

In that peaceful still of the night, every Soul awakened and passing into the Clear Light is One in harmony with the Will of Heaven.

With all your heart and Soul, thank deeply, graciously, and humbly the Heaven Light, the Sacred Beings in the Light, and all of Heaven for the Blessing just bestowed upon your Soul.

Repeat this exercise 10 times before moving to the next one.

THE GROUND OF VIGIL

When you awaken in Vigil in the still of night, your body and mind are at rest, leaving your Soul unhindered. Vigil provides your Soul an auspicious opportunity to practice your many HeavenWork exercises.

Try some next time, and see how much deeper your Soul reaches into Spirit.

EXERCISE 28

THE CLEAR LIGHT

Entering the Ground of being under Heaven.

And now you are ready to complete your Transcendence into the Clear Light.

You are now prepared and able to safely release your Soul from mind and body, and pass into your true Ground of being, where your unobstructed Soul can invoke and Harness immense concentrations of Heaven Light to quickly sanctify and send your Soul Ascendant through the Clear Light to the Firmament of Heaven.

By entering—that is, by returning to—the Clear Light your meaningful life begins.

The Clear Light is truer reality than materiality, it is eternal, and closer to Heaven. It is the eternal home of your Soul under Heaven. When you enter the Clear Light, you leave your citizenship of human and earth behind. You Remember, in Soul, that you are Soul, Soul joyously bound for Heaven.

By now you have recognized from your Soul's approaching the Clear Light that the ego identity of your mind cannot conceive of your Soul's free, ungrasping and perfect clarity. Your mind cannot conceive of "no-mind." But your mind *can* imagine an infinite bright and clear vacuum free of materiality, dust or even a single atom—a clear sky within and beyond the sky that pulls on your Soul's intuition, by that great vacuum, to its furthest reaches, where all dimension collapses before the center and Origin of all being, continuous Creation: Heaven.

From out of Heaven pours the sacred Light, which abounds enormously and gently in the Clear Light, blanketing disembodied Souls in Compassion and Direction.

Once your Soul reaches intuitively into the Clear Light, the vacuum of Clear Light can safely pull your Soul Transcendent, accomplishing your Soul-in-body's Transcendence. This is how.

Goal: *To pass your Soul completely into the Clear Light.*

Preparation: *Go to bed.*

Steps:

1. After you fall asleep, raise your Soul awake into Vigil (exercise 27).

Keep your Soul separate from mind and body.

2. *By Abbreviation, practice Infinite Reach (exercise 15). Allow your Soul to stretch infinitely beyond the dark of night into and through the Clear Light.*

3. *Feel the vacuum of the Clear Light beyond the dark of night pull invitingly upon your Soul. Allow the vacuum's pulling to become stronger and stronger, trusting the universe, for nothing can harm your Soul, and the body and mind will remain protected.*

4. *As the pull becomes strong, Mark (as in HeavenHome, exercise 4) with your Soul the pull and the direction it pulls you.*

5. *When the vacuum's pull becomes strong, joyously Surrender your Soul unto it, letting it gently pull you through, Sliding (exercise 14) like water entering a drain, like smoke absorbing into the air.*

And you are in the Clear Light, thoughtless and perfectly present, free of all reference to materiality, centered and absolutely suspended in the infinite unobstructed sky, always reaching, penetrating deeper and deeper, clearer and clearer, freer and freer, intuitively stretching in invisible rays to the end of dimensional space where the Clear Light collapses before Heaven.

Perfect, passive and poised.

Even if you Slid into the Clear Light only briefly, or partly, you have gained from this exercise, because you are now that much more powerfully able to concentrate the Heaven Light. We all travel along the Path of Light at our own pace.

Accomplish this exercise even once and with Abbreviation you will be able to enter the Clear Light at will. The Clear Light will then become an exercise in pure intuition.

The more you abide in the Clear Light the more your Soul's Remembrance will come to you.

You are giving up the ways of man, the ways of earth. You are becoming more like Spirit. The Truth in Soul *is* Spirit, Heaven Light. As you become Spirit also become Heaven Light, for the passage through the gate of Heaven is within the Heaven Light.

*With all your heart and Soul, thank deeply, graciously, and humbly
the Heaven Light, the Sacred Beings in the Light, and all of Heaven
for the Blessing just bestowed upon your Soul.*

*Repeat this exercise 10 times before moving onto the
Advanced HeavenWork exercises.*

Practice HeavenHome (exercise 4, or by Abbreviation) one more time.

YOUR SOUL IS NOW FREE TO TRANSLOCATE

Thanks to your HeavenWork, your Soul is now free to do anything, go anywhere, or contact any other Soul, incarnate or decarnate. Just combine some of your HeavenWork exercises.

You learned from Hand Quickening (exercise 7) that your palms are natural conductors of Heaven Light. You have learned to Slide your Soul (exercise 14). You have learned to Sense other Souls (exercise 3). You have Transcended your Soul to the infinite Clear Light, on which all of materiality hangs but a shade away. From the Clear Light, all of materiality is accessible, and every Soul takes root. There every Soul under Heaven may be found.

You have every skill you need.

If you wish to sense the Soul of another, look at your palm and will with your Soul that the Soul you wish to visit is sitting on your palm, buoyed by the Heaven Light flowing through your hand. You will feel your Soul Slide into your palm and pass instantly into the Clear Light, to find that right before your Soul hovers the Soul you wish to be near.

EIGHT

THE LOST TEACHINGS OF THE LIGHT

Abba—the Face of God-In-Heaven—allows me these articulations:

1. Before the earth or man, or even Soul, there is Heaven Light.

2. The hope of all of man is found in the Heaven Light.

3. Blessed is the Soul who learns to call the Heaven Light.

4. The Heaven Light is the light of change and attainment.

5. Within the Heaven Light is found the straight Path that leads to the gate of Heaven.

6. Invite the Heaven Light into your heart and you will be made clean.

7. Made sanctified is the Soul by the Heaven Light.

8. Come and be borne again and again into the Heaven Light.

9. Without the Heaven Light the Soul is lost in darkness. Only in the dark of mind does man shun the Heaven Light.

10. Where there is judgment and greed there is darkness. Where there is love and joy there is Light.

11. Dare to rise beyond those who would keep you in darkness.

12. Unto this world has befallen a great darkness, such that the earth will rise up violently, the skies will roll back, and heavenly bodies will crash down upon the seas and land. Woe to man who seeks to hide in the darkness for your fortress will turn on you and devour you. Call, therefore, the Heaven Light, and rise above the ways of earth.

13. Upon your command the Heaven Light enters into your Soul. Throw open the door of your heart and bid the Light rush in.

14. Let the Light of Heaven change your Soul to Light.

15. We must become master craftsmen of Light, each of us, for there are many ways to work the Heaven Light with your Soul.

16. Remember, in Soul, your thirst for the Kingdom of Heaven, for only they who thirst shall drink and live.

17. Joy is the singing of your Soul in the Heaven Light.

18. Every moment, day and night, fill your Soul with Heaven Light.

19. If you would know the Heaven Light, look beyond the body, mind and heart and know the Soul. Awaken the eye of Soul.

20. The Soul bides in the sky beyond the earthly sky, and Heaven in the sky beyond that sky.

21. Miserable are you who look upon the sunrise and count your blessings, blessed are you who behold the sunrise and yearn for Abba just beyond.

22. The body and mind walk along the dusty earth, but the Soul awakened soars free as an Angel in the sky beyond the sky.

23. Love and be of service to all those who would know the Heaven Light.

24. Little knows the mind of Soul or Spirit.

25. Call the Heaven Light in Soul and be converted from the profane ways of mind.

26. All your life you might seek your Soul with your mind and not find it. Yet, if you but place your hands upon your heart, there will your Soul be.

27. We have all conquered death, but few have conquered life.

28. Within the Heaven Light are all answers found.

29. To enter the Path of Light your heart must be made pure.

30. You have been around a long, long time, yet live each moment in Soul as if it were your last, for life is a desert and the Kingdom of Heaven rises up from the Path of Light like an oasis.

31. Become as a child into the Heaven Light and learn what must be learned to become what must become.

32. Can you not feel, Abba calling unto you?

33. Seek Heaven, never resting, until you find It.

34. The Heaven Light is the spring of eternal life that fills the universe. To live you must learn to partake of this spring.

35. We enter the world as one asleep. If you awaken, you will be filled with the Heaven Light, but if you sleep, you will remain divided, filled with darkness. Many are they who breathe but do not live.

36. The mind is easily poisoned when the Soul sleeps.

37. Many magnify the profane matters of this small earth, few magnify the Heaven Light that fills the universe.

38. Do not judge with your mind the righteousness of your acts, or others' acts, for that is the way of hypocrisy. But first awaken your Soul, enter the Heaven Light, and righteous acts will thus ensue.

39. Satan climbs into your mind and whispers unto you, "Take heart, for Heaven will know you for your beliefs and righteous acts." But I tell you this, the Path to Heaven is not of body, mind or earth, but Spirit. You may lead a life free of sin, but only they who free their Soul into the Heaven Light will find the Kingdom of Heaven.

40. Empty is service without the Heaven Light.

41. Ask not from others how to conduct your life, but strive to embrace life with your Soul. Thus will your Soul express the Will of Heaven, thus will your Soul join Heaven.

42. Bless one another with the Heaven Light, for both will receive a measure of grace.

43. In compassion the Angels married your Soul to your heart. That is why the language of the heart is love.

44. Love all of man, and the animals of the field, but above all else, love Abba and the Light.

45. With the eyes of man you see not the Heaven Light, but with the eye of Soul you see only Heaven Light. When you have left the earth what will you see?

46. Many long for Heaven, but few find the door.

47. What may not be seen by others is known by the sacred host within the Heaven Light. You are not diminished when those asleep in darkness do not see your works of Light.

48. The Path to Heaven is clear as light, not cloaked in mystery.

49. We are all servants of Heaven, though many have forgotten. Awaken therefore, and Remember, for your Master calls.

50. The truth in Soul is that we are all one Spirit entering Heaven, that we are the Heaven Light.

51. Through the Heaven Light in your Soul make manifest Heaven's Will on the earth as it is in Heaven.

52. Look upon all others not by their outer appearance, but by their Souls and the Heaven Light within their Souls.

53. Where you come from so will you return unless you awaken and enter the Light.

54. Do not let a moment pass that you do not feel the call of Heaven deep in your Soul.

55. Every moment the countenance of Heaven is upon you, every moment the Angels tend your Soul. Would you hide in darkness knowing there is nothing the eyes of Heaven cannot see?

56. There comes a day of wedding and great celebration, for you will be the bride. Will you be ready?

57. So easily is man led astray. Look ever into the Heaven Light and you will not fall into darkness.

58. Every moment in darkness you are judged by Heaven.

59. What use make swine of pearls cast of Heaven Light? Miracles I performed with Light, yet with the magical was man more moved. If you would know Heaven, always look to the Light.

60. Open your heart, open your Soul, and let Light flood you. Become as a foundering ship in a sea of loving Light. Surrender your Soul to the sea.

61. The Soul knows no religion, only Light. Break therefore from the dark doctrine of the mind into the Light.

62. Who are you really? Should your hands be severed, and your legs, is your Soul diminished? If you should lose your tongue, and your eyes, is your Soul not magnified? For as certain as you are here, these things will perish in a moment's gasp. Render therefore your limbs, your tongue, your eyes and mind unto the service of your Soul, and your Soul unto the Heaven Light, for therein is found the Kingdom of Heaven.

63. Be in the world, not of it, for they who love the earth will remain on earth but they who love the Light will pass, like Angels, through the earth and through the sky beyond the sky, to Abba.

64. Woe to you who are rich in worldly things, for your treasures

are your chains and your Spirit weak. Blessed are you rich in Spirit, for yours will be the Kingdom of God.

65. Perplexed with life are the many whose Souls lie in slumber. But bless their Souls awake and watch them fly into the Heaven Light!

66. Bless with the Heaven Light, for there is no Light without blessing and no blessing without Light.

67. They in body do not live, they in Spirit shall not die.

68. Know all others by their works with the Heaven Light.

69. When fortune befalls you love the Heaven Light with all your heart, when misfortune befalls you love the Heaven Light with all your heart, when nothing befalls you love the Heaven Light with all your heart.

70. Live from your Soul in accordance with the Will of Heaven in the Heaven Light.

71. Abide in the peace, love, joy, and direction the Heaven Light brings, ceaselessly until you enter Heaven.

72. Blessed are you whose possessions you substitute with Heaven Light.

73. No one is a stranger. If one comes to you in hunger, share of your food and drink, if one comes to you in darkness, nourish his Soul with the Light of Heaven.

74. Joy, love, compassion, and all the true virtues lie within your Soul, beyond the wall of mind.

75. The Heaven Light no eye has seen, no ear has heard, no hand has touched, nor even rises in the heart, but carries in the Soul like wind in a sail.

76. Who knows the Heaven Light and Remembers in Soul will not taste death.

77. We knew the Heaven Light from where we came, and we shall know the Heaven Light where we shall go.

78. You must waken early in the morning of the day that is life, and drink from the water of Life, for your thirst for Truth is great. Go, then, about your morning labors carrying in your Soul the Light. Come afternoon enter the Light so that when the day is done you will not enter darkness, but thrive in joyous Light perpetual.

79. If you do not thirst you will not drink. If you do not thirst for Heaven, you will not drink from the spring of Light. If you thirst for things of the earth, you will become intoxicated, and sleep away the day that is life. I am here, in the Light, here to awaken the Soul of man and fill you with thirst for Heaven.

80. Soul becomes what Soul beholds. The Heaven Light bathes your Soul in Truth. Let the Light of Truth enter your Soul and your Soul will become Truth.

81. Nothing sanctifies the Soul greater than creating a miracle with Heaven.

82. Be driven from within, not from without.

83. They blaspheme who speak of Heaven without the Heaven Light.

84. Blasphemers speak of Truths unknown. Only witness Souls may speak on Heaven.

85. Provide for your body the brief time you abide in it, provide for your Soul for eternity.

86. Love those who curse you and do you harm, for they nurture your compassion.

87. To those asleep in life, Spirit seems but a dream, but those who awakened know that the body is the dream.

88. In body we are alone; in Spirit none are alone.

89. Never in Spirit are you separate from the living or the dead.

90. They may kill the body, but nobody can harm your Soul.

91. They who cleave to darkness, in or out of body, cower before the Light.

92. Blessed are you born again and again, for you will know the Heaven Light, you will find the Kingdom of Heaven through the Heaven Light.

93. Blessed are you who Remember in Soul what you came here to do.

94. Many are they who know where they are, but few who remember where they came from, and why, and where they will go. They who do not remember are wise to heed those who do.

95. Trust the universe, no harm can come to you, for supreme is the Will of Heaven in the Heaven Light.

96. Enter the Path of Light and you have already won Heaven.

97. Live from your Soul in the Heaven Light, and Heaven will open to you.

98. The fruits of your labors in the Heaven Light will be myriad.

99. If you would know Heaven, become what you are not, and go where you are not.

100. I have set the fire of Heaven Light upon the world, for your Soul to be consumed by Heaven.

101. The countenance of Abba descends upon you in the Heaven Light.

102. Abba will throw open the gate of Heaven if all of man should enter the Light.

103. Love Abba with your mind and the ways of earth and you will slip into idolatry. Love Abba with your Soul and the ways of Spirit and you will find Heaven.

104. Blaspheme against Abba and you will be forgiven, but blaspheme against the Heaven Light and your Soul will be exiled from Heaven.

105. The gate of Heaven no eye can see, Abba no mind can know, the Needle's Eye no body can pass through. Only the Soul made sanctified may pass and enter Life perpetual.

106. When Heaven takes hold your Soul made sanctified, you will ascend the Light Divine to Abba, the Face of God-in-Heaven, and pass through the Needle's Eye, entering the Body of Heaven to join the glorious Host forever! Come, for Abba calls unto you.

107. On earth the Light of Heaven descends in surging swirls of sanctifying joy. Beyond the earth and under Heaven, the Light of Heaven fills the Clear Light sky with milky Light that swaddles Souls compassionately. In Heaven the Light streams out like a sun from the right hand of Abba, and fills the universe with hope and the way.

108. Abba is not without Heaven, and Heaven is not without Abba.

109. You may walk to the ends of the earth, but if you carry in your Soul the Heaven Light, Heaven will always hover before your Soul.

110. When you have no longer body, no longer Soul, when you have become the Heaven Light, Heaven will open unto you.

111. The Kingdom of Heaven is here and now, in the sky within you and spread before you, ascendant through the Light, and the gate is of the Breath of Heaven, full of Heaven Light. Therefore I say to you, follow me into the Heaven Light to Heaven.

112. Heaven is like a great cloud unto a sky, and the cloud is alive, rolling out and beyond with Creation, and within the cloud, Abba reigns supreme on high, and the cloud is ever full of glory and rejoicing by those who entered in through the Heaven Light, which streams forth from the right hand of Abba to fill the universe.

113. The Heaven Light and the servants of Heaven within the Light will keep you and shine upon you.

114. Enter your Soul, and call the Heaven Light, then pass your Soul in Light beyond the earth, beyond the Clear Light sky, and There will I be to welcome you to Life.

115. I am always in the Heaven Light, coming with the clouds of Heaven. Come, rise, and join me in the Light.

ASCENDING

A<small>WAKENING</small>→T<small>RANSCENDING</small>→**A<small>SCENDING</small>**→T<small>RANSFIGURATION</small>

On joyous wings of Light
The Soul Ascends,
And Heaven's narrow gate
Is opened wide.

Halfway Home

Now you will learn to *Ascend* your Soul from the Clear Light and pass through the Clouds of Heaven until you reach the Firmament, where you will be *Transfigured* and Received into Heaven or choose to remain for a while in the Clouds of Heaven to help other Souls find their way.

In order to perform your advanced HeavenWork you must have first mastered all 28 of the first exercises. With those first exercises you learned to *Awaken* your Soul, and *Transcend* into the Clear Light. You passed your Soul beyond materiality, the first cloud of unknowing, in preparation for your advanced HeavenWork.

You are halfway Home. The Clear Light is your home under Heaven—the Heaven Light-filled Fields of the Life-Between where your Soul dwelt before you came to life, where your Soul will return unless you sanctify. As heavenly as the Clear Light might seem, it is not Heaven. It forms the second and final cloud of unknowing separating your Soul from Heaven.

Yet by Transcending into the Clear Light while living, you have a powerful opportunity to sanctify. You now have the power to call on the tremendous stores of Heaven Light you will need to purify your Soul, enough to pass entirely beyond the Clear Light and through the Clouds of Heaven, all the way to Heaven. By mastering the following more advanced HeavenWork exercises, you will pass through the second cloud of unknowing. You will release the ways of earth as you acquire the ways of Heaven. You will surrender your identity with body, mind and earth, and become a citizen of Heaven.

And you will see your Soul all the way Home to Heaven.

NINE

HOW TO PURIFY YOUR SOUL

THE MEANINGFUL LIFE

You have Transcended, and you now stand on new ground, true ground, the Ground of the Clear Light. Though still in body, your Soul has passed into the infinite sky within and beyond the material sky. Feel your intuition stretch to the ends of the universe. You have passed through the first cloud of unknowing.

Now it becomes your destiny to Ascend this sky, the second cloud of unknowing, passing joyfully and with growing awareness into the sacred sky beyond—the Clouds of Heaven—wherein the Firmament of Heaven awaits you.

Now in the Clear Light you have set your life in accordance with the will of your Soul, and the Will of Heaven. You have begun your natural life as you intended before you entered body. You are now living the *Meaningful Life*.

Just for a moment, bow your head, place your hands on your heart, and with Abbreviation invoke the Shower of Light (exercise 9). Dwelling in Soul, in the Heaven Light that bathes you in the Clear Light, sense how near Heaven hoves just within and beyond the Clear Light. Mark with your Soul the direction of Heaven, just a few feet above your head.

Feel the presence of the myriad Sacred Beings in the Light who rush close to your Soul in joy and celebration that you are approaching Heaven. Do not try to name them, for names are of the earth. Rather, know them in their purity. Come and begin to learn the perfect and direct language of Spirit.

A choir of Angels ever so close, Heaven ever so close.

Indeed you are standing on new ground. Know that the rest of your life will continue along this joyous Path of Light, Ascending your Soul more and more into the Sacred. Know that even when the circumstances of the earth divert your mind and body from your path, your undaunted Soul will continue to Ascend until you enter Heaven forever!

Because you have entered the Clear Light, your Soul is able to gather and work immense concentrations of Heaven Light. Working such concentrations of Heaven Light rapidly sanctifies your Soul, sending your Soul Ascendant.

You will find that just as your Soul experienced materiality dissolving while you Transcended, so will the Clear Light dissolve to reveal Heaven before your Soul. The HeavenWork Ascending exercises will rapidly pass your Soul through the Clear Light, and as this happens your works in Spirit will be great.

> **Meaningful Life:** *Life that moves a Soul along the Path of Light toward Heaven.*

EXERCISE 29

JOY EVERLASTING

Transflexing Joy.

When you Awakened your Soul, you began to know Joy, the singing of your Soul in the Heaven Light.

The origin of Joy is divine, for throughout the Body of Heaven a Joyous choir of millions of sanctified Souls perpetually ring silently thunderous praise to *Abba*, the Face of God, and all of Heaven quakes—Joy Everlasting. Those in body who enter Joy join the Body of Heaven in perfect Praise.

Under Heaven this sacred Joy extends descendant through the Angels of the Diadem and every Sacred Being in the Light—all within the Heaven Light.

Your Soul in the Heaven Light knows no exhaustion, but sustained by the Heaven Light like a sail in a world of wind, heads ever toward its destiny.

Ascending Soul, as you approach Heaven's Firmament, know that you can receive Joy Everlasting.

Joy perpetual is also an indicator of your ever-presence in Soul, your Soul's abiding in the Heaven Light, your Soul's continuous sanctification.

Joyous is the Path of the Heaven Light. Joy is the rendering of your Soul unto the Heaven Light. In Joy your Soul purifies in the Heaven Light. In Joy your Soul Ascends to Heaven.

Transcendent Soul, you know the Clear Light, you know the Joy the Heaven Light brings. Every HeavenWork exercise changes your Soul. Now you may change your Soul by letting Joy fill you always.

Just like the Sacred Beings in the Light, thus should every moment of your life be Joyous. Who wouldn't choose a life of Joy perpetual? It's easy to do. Here's how.

Goal: *To Integrate Joy perpetual into your Soul.*

Preparation: *Sit in easy chair, where you will not be disturbed.*

Steps:

1. *Relax deeply, and with Abbreviation, confidently Slide into the Clear Light (exercise 28). Bask, in Soul, in the joyous freedom in the infinite vacuum of the Clear Light.*

2. *Also with Abbreviation practice Infinite Reach (exercise 15), and extend your rays of intuition infinitely to the end of the Clear Light, where it collapses before Heaven. Sense your effortless omnipresence in the Spirit Universe.*

3. *There, with your Soul's knowing reaching everywhere, invoke the Shower of Light (exercise 9) with Abbreviation. Notice how gently the Heaven Light enters and caresses your Soul. Transcendent Soul, this is how Heaven Light manifests in the Clear Light, above the earth. Notice how nurturing, loving, calming, and patient the nature of the Heaven Light has become, and how omniscient and forgiving the Joy that freely carries into your Soul.*

4. *Bask in this calm and gentle Joy.*

5. *Mark how your Soul feels the Joy, grounded in the Clear Light and swaddled infinitely by the gentle Heaven Light.*

6. *Invoke Crescendo (exercise 18) around your Joy, allowing the rising tide to swell, filling the boundless Spirit Universe with Joy.*

7. *When your Crescendo peaks and permeates your Soul with Joy, Transflex it (exercise 26, using Abbreviation) and Seal it, willing with your Soul that your Joy remain within you and around you every moment until you enter Heaven.*

By practicing Joy Everlasting you have Integrated Joy into your Soul forever. If you should find Joy absent from your Soul, simply will it back fully with Abbreviation.

Allow your Joy to guide you and keep you on the Path of Light, for where there is Joy there is Truth. Joy is greater than life, greater than Soul. Joy is a gift of God.

Here's a paradox of Spirit. Even when life's ills plague you, it's okay to feel Joy in your Soul, for every moment in life—pleasant or painful—is a precious gift, and your Soul is eternally grateful for life however it is handed you. Later you will Crown your Joy Everlasting by learning to sustain Joy even in life's bumpiest times.

With all your heart and Soul, thank deeply, graciously, and humbly the Heaven Light, the Sacred Beings in the Light, and all of Heaven for the Blessing just bestowed upon your Soul.

Repeat this exercise 10 times before moving to the next one.

EXERCISE 30

THE DOOR UP

Engaging the face of your Soul.

You opened it with one of your earliest HeavenWork exercises, HeavenHome—the wonderful hole in materiality about two feet over and slightly in front of your head, where the Heaven Light drops down into your Soul.

This, the Door Up, is where your Soul receives the Heaven Light.

Mysteriously we sometimes refer to the Door Up as the "third eye," the "window of the Soul," or "Kalachakra." But what is the Door Up, really?

For practical purposes, you may think of the Door Up as the face of your Soul.

The Door Up is the front of your Soul—the part of your Awakened being that faces Heaven. When you performed HeavenHome (exercise 4) many things happened. Most important you set your Soul on Heaven and Marked your Soul's position and migratory course, permanently.

The Door Up: The front of your Soul, which faces Heaven.

Indeed, as Jesus said, "The Kingdom of Heaven is at hand." Heaven *is* here—just beyond the Door Up of your Soul and spread out before you. No matter where you are, Heaven is always here and now before your Soul. And the Door Up homes your direction.

All things Sacred descend to you from Heaven through your Door Up—the Heaven Light, your Guardian Angels and the Sacred Beings in the Light, the Heaven Breath, and God's Immanence. Therefore honor that part of your Soul so bent on Heaven.

It is time to engage and strengthen the Door Up—the face of your Soul, the eye of your Soul—to bear you Ascendant towards Heaven.

Here's how.

Goal: *To see through your Soul into the Sacred.*

Preparation: *Sit in a chair where you will not be disturbed.*

Steps:

1. *Enter Witness (exercise 16) through Abbreviation.*

2. *Practice HeavenHome (exercise 4), using Abbreviation. Feel God's Immanence pass through your Soul.*

3. *Invoke a Shower of Light (exercise 9).*

4. *Allow the Light to pour into your Soul powerfully. Harness the Light and build it into a Crescendo (exercise 18).*

5. *Just when your Soul feels the rising tide of Light rush into Crescendo, take a deep breath, and when you exhale, hiss loudly and direct all of the Light upward toward your Door Up.*

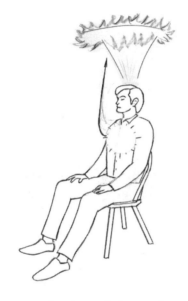

Remain silent, do not think, and Surrender your Soul to the Light that churns above your head, permeating your Door Up, cleansing your portal to the Sacred. Observe how the Heaven Light knows exactly what to do to open your Soul's vision. Feel the Joy in your Soul while the Heaven Light purifies you and readies your Soul for Ascendance.

As you continue on with your Ascending HeavenWork exercises, when your Soul purifies and Ascends, you will be able to view, in Soul, the vast panorama of sacred Spirit that is Heaven.

Now that your Soul can center in the Clear Light you will soon be able to use your Door Up to draw immense concentrations of Heaven Light to rapidly accelerate your Soul's Ascent to Heaven. Know that you are now able to perform the work inaccessible to your Soul before you entered body. You are now at the greatest moment of your existence!

You now have the opportunity to become a master of Light, an instrument of Heaven.

You will learn to perform works of Light so pure and miraculous they lay beyond the scope of mind.

With all your heart and Soul, thank deeply, graciously, and humbly the Heaven Light, the Sacred Beings in the Light, and all of Heaven for the Blessing just bestowed upon your Soul.

Repeat this exercise 10 times before moving to the next one.

VISION OF SOUL

Pure and simple is the vision of the eye of your Soul, less discerning than human eyesight, but perfectly intuitive in nature, complete and wordless understanding of that which you behold.

Unobstructed by the veil of body, your Soul passes freely along the Path of Light, drawn to sacred things of Spirit, all the way to Heaven.

EXERCISE 31

CONSTANCE

Along the path unwavering.

Often we hear of those who entered the path to Heaven, only to fall off the path later. We like to say it's because "life caught up with me." But what really happens is the mind's distractions lulled the Soul back to sleep.

But because the HeavenWork bypasses the mind to go directly to your Soul, you will not fall off the path.

A mystic seven hundred years ago wrote that while the body walks along its dusty way, the Soul walks, like Jesus, on the sea.

What this means is that once the Soul is Awakened, it thrives beyond the mind's and body's knowing.

Early in your HeavenWork you practiced Momentation, your Soul's covenant with Heaven to live from your Soul, keeping your Soul present in life and constantly receiving Heaven Light.

Presence in Soul came naturally to you. It became automatic—autonomic, in fact. Since then many things have happened. Your Soul has become empowered, you have entered the Clear Light, and you have learned many HeavenWork exercises.

Constance, the continuation of Momentation, takes you one step further. Constance empowers your Soul to practice your HeavenWork exercises constantly, autonomically, to accelerate your Soul's Ascendance through the Clear Light.

Constance is the marriage of Momentation and Abbreviation. Combining your Soul's natural ability to operate on its own in the Heaven Light with your Abbreviated HeavenWork exercises, your Soul will now become able to constantly perform all of your HeavenWork exercises, every moment, day and night!

Goal: *To constantly sanctify in the Heaven Light.*

Preparation: *Sit down with this book in hand.*

Steps:

1. *Just for a moment, go to the Table Of Contents of and read down through all the first 28 Heaven Work exercises, remembering what each exercise did to your Soul.*

2. *Now, more slowly, read them once again, one by one. This time perform each exercise, Abbreviating each one of them.*

3. *After you have completed all 28 Abbreviations, read them once again. This time, starting with exercise 1, build slowly into Crescendo, so that when you get to exercise 28, you climax and release your Crescendo.*

4. *As you release the Light, in the blizzard of Heaven Light rushing through you, Mark with your Soul the simultaneous activity of your Heaven Work Abbreviations, and resolve, in Soul, to continue performing them without ever ceasing.*

The Heaven Light's omniscience is beyond comprehension. Your Soul's ability to multitask the Heaven Light should not surprise you.

With all your heart and Soul, thank deeply, graciously, and humbly the Heaven Light, the Sacred Beings in the Light, and all of Heaven for the Blessing just bestowed upon your Soul.

Repeat this exercise 5 times before moving to the next one.

A NEW COVENANT OF SOUL

If you are so moved, it is time to improve upon your first covenant of Momentation. Now you may form a new, more perfect covenant of your Soul with Heaven.

If you are ready, place your hands on your heart and make this promise before Heaven:

> *For the rest of my life will my Soul perform my HeavenWork constantly, and always in accordance to the Will of Heaven.*

Your Soul now dwells openly in the Heaven Light. By keeping your Soul open, Heaven Light freely enters your Soul, changing you constantly, in an unbroken flow.

You are becoming a Being of Light, a servant of Heaven, and you are known and held beloved by the Heaven Light, and all the Sacred Beings in the Light.

EXERCISE 32

EXPRESSING LIGHT

Lamp of the world.

In Spirit your Soul learns there is no receiving, only giving.

And yet, in Spirit, giving *is* receiving, for the nature of Spirit is True Love—selfless Compassion—and all who bear the Heaven Light receive a measure of grace.

Every Soul the Heaven Light touches purifies.

So far, your HeavenWork has involved you pulling Heaven Light into your Soul. This served to Awaken, strengthen and Transcend your Soul.

But in order for your Soul to Ascend, you must also pass the Heaven Light into other Souls, Blessing them with holy Spirit, for that is the Will of Heaven. Remember, "Thy will be done on earth as it is in Heaven."

While receiving the Heaven Light Transcends your Soul, Blessing with Heaven Light Ascends your Soul.

Only when your Soul Expresses Heaven Light are you fully functioning on earth.

The Truth in Soul is the Heaven Light. When you share the Heaven Light with other Souls, your Soul Surrenders unto the Light and you are made purer. Your Soul Ascends.

Like a Lighthouse your Soul can Express Light and become a channel of Light, a magnifying lens that sends Heaven Light out freely and Compassionately, a beacon providing Light to those who would Awaken and find Heaven.

Do you remember when you practiced LightWater (in exercise 7), how quickly the Heaven Light surged from your Soul into the glass of water? With LightWater your Soul was prepared. Now you will learn to Express gently, steadily, a glow of Heaven Light in all directions.

Goal: *To glow with Heaven Light.*

Preparation: *Sit in a chair in the dark.*

Steps:

1. ***Enter a state of calm and invoke a Shower of Light (exercise 9), using Abbreviation.***

2. *Harness the Light (exercise 10, using Abbreviation) into a ball just covering your heart, and continue to invite more Heaven Light to fill your heart.*

3. *Crescendo the Light (exercise 18) within your heart. As your Crescendo peaks, will with your Soul that the ball of Light immediately explode and shoot out in all directions.*

4. *As your Crescendo climaxes, notice how the omniscient Heaven Light responds to your Soul's desire, by streaming out from your Soul in all directions.*

5. *To keep glowing, simply keep your Soul open and form a channel by continuing to replenish your Soul with the Shower of Light pouring down into you.*

Intuitively your Soul will shift and sense the Heaven Light Expressing from you, like you are a sun, flowing out perfectly and evenly in all directions. Your glowing may be accompanied by thrilling goose bumps all over your skin, with your hair standing on end, followed by a surge of warmth as it passes your Soul Transcendent.

Surrender your Soul to the rapturous depth of the glow and you will Express Light stronger.

Continue to bask in the glow, and feel, intuitively, how the Heaven Light not only passes from you in every earthly direction, but also Ascendant beyond the Clear Light and towards the Sacred. Feel how the Door Up, the eye of your Soul, seems to peer with fascination into the welcoming Light yet unknown.

Freely you may share the Heaven Light with all Souls, for the Heaven Light descends to materiality not to harm, but to Awaken, protect and guide Souls to Heaven. There is no better service than Blessing another Soul with Heaven Light.

Trust the caring nature of the Heaven Light. So perfect is the omniscience of the Heaven Light that it knows every need and opportunity of your Soul. It even knows the conditions that will surround your very Soul a thousand years from now.

Therefore, love the Heaven Light, glow in the Heaven Light, go with the Heaven Light, and get good at Light Expression. Learn to Abbreviate it now, for it prepares your Soul for the fireworks of Light to come.

With all your heart and Soul, thank deeply, graciously, and humbly the Heaven Light, the Sacred Beings in the Light, and all of Heaven for the Blessing just bestowed upon your Soul.

Repeat this exercise 20 times before moving to the next one.

BACKGROUNDING

As your Soul has Transcended materiality into the Clear Light, and as you Ascend the Clear Light, your HeavenWork will intensify. That is, you will feel greater turbulence as more Heaven Light flows through your Soul and your Soul works the Light more powerfully.

But sometimes you will find your exercises don't put out so much intensity even though you are trying hard with your Soul. Sometimes the Light passing through your Soul seems more in the background. The truth is, you still *are* putting out intense Light. You just don't feel it because sometimes your Soul doesn't Transcend, but remains "grounded" in materiality. You are Backgrounding.

There is nothing wrong with Backgrounding. In fact, it's a part of Constance. You don't want to spend all your gift of life Transcended out of materiality.

However, if you find your HeavenWork is often Backgrounding, simply Harness a small Cocoon of Light around your Soul and Crescendo it until you Transcend, and you will feel the intensity of Light-in-Soul return.

EXERCISE 33

LIGHTING THE WORLD

The Soul's perfect Expression.

Infinitely free can your Soul reach to the ends of the Clear Light. Perfectly pure can the Heaven Light render your Soul, passing you beyond the Clear Light towards Heaven's Firmament.

Powerfully can your Soul share the Heaven Light on earth. The Heaven Light knows no bounds, and you, now, can share the Heaven Light with the world, with all Souls in the world.

The more you receive and Express the Heaven Light, the more you come to understand the Light. Would you pray, then, for the world with your Soul? Would you Bless with Heaven's beloved Light all Souls on the earth—enemies as well as friends, and those you never met? If you feel in your Soul, at this very consideration, a surge of Heaven Light swell in your heart, then you are ready to Light the World, for such love is a sign of Ascendance.

Such love bides in accordance to the Will of Heaven, the power superior to any other in the universe.

With such love there is nothing your Soul in the Heaven Light cannot do. Feel your intuition. Even now, you sense your Soul can surge an infinite concentration of Heaven Light not just over the earth, but throughout the universe. But let's start with the earth.

Goal: *Holding all the Souls of earth in Light.*

Preparation: *Lie in bed at night, ready to go to sleep.*

Steps:

1. *Using Abbreviation, Dance Light (exercise 19) throughout your room.*

2. *When you can see, with the eye of your Soul, the turbulent Heaven Light rushing along the ceiling, Express Light (exercise 32), using Abbreviation.*

3. *Invoke Crescendo (exercise 18), using Abbreviation. Allow more and more of the limitless Heaven Light to channel through. Continue mounting Crescendo. When the tide of mounting Light rises to climax, do not squeeze, but keep your Soul open, allowing your Light Expression to move outward, freely, in all directions.*

4. *Prolong your Crescendo. Notice with your intuitive Soul how your Light Expression reaches out as far as your Soul wills. Now, will with your Soul that the omniscient Heaven Light stream through you and out at the speed of light. Remember, with the Heaven Light all things are possible, and the Spirit universe contains an enormous reservoir of Heaven Light.*

5. *Using Abbreviation, practice Infinite Reach (exercise 15). When your Soul shifts into the Clear Light, feel the hundreds, thousands, millions— billions of Souls suspended in the vast sky around you and below you. Feel the Heaven Light washing every single Soul with invigorating sanctity! As this happens, sense, if you can, with your Soul the myriad Sacred Beings in the Light then appear into the Clear Light, descendant from the Firmament of Heaven, in joyous congratulations that you have just moved Ascendant.*

6. *If you do not sense the other Souls of the earth around, practice Sensing Souls (exercise 3), using Abbreviation.*

Remain in the embrace of the world's Souls for as long as you desire. How easily you embraced every Soul on earth!

If you desire, with your Soul's intent, will that the Heaven Light become more turbulent, to stir every Soul Awake.

Grasping these moments in Spirit, know this. You have just experienced reality Truer and clearer than ever before. You are coming home, all the way to Heaven.

> *With all your heart and Soul, thank deeply, graciously, and humbly the Heaven Light, the Sacred Beings in the Light, and all of Heaven for the Blessing just bestowed upon your Soul.*

> *Repeat this exercise 10 times before moving to the next one.*

> *Get good at Lighting The World. You will need it later.*

BLESSING

Blessing—*true* Blessing, Blessing that works—does not come from the tongue or mind, but the Soul.

Blessing happens when your Soul invokes, Harnesses, Crescendoes, and Expresses the Heaven Light into another Soul with the intent of spiritual auspice.

There is no Blessing without Heaven Light and no Heaven Light without Blessing.

Blessing, the heart of the HeavenWork, joins every Soul on earth to each other, and Heaven. Blessing is the spiritual action behind Jesus' words, "Thy will be done on earth as it is in Heaven," for thus it is in Heaven.

For this, most of your Ascending HeavenWork will involve continuations of Blessing. So get good at it.

You will learn to Bless with the following two exercises, Plume and Sacred Intent.

EXERCISE 34

PLUME

Shooting forth the Heaven Light.

Plume is a special kind of Light Expression. Rather than radiating Heaven Light in every direction, you concentrate and produce a great thrust of Light that shoots straight and directly out of your Soul into another Soul.

With the eye of Soul, you will see the Light shoot out from your heart like the smoke trail of an old cannon, and when the Light strikes the receiving Soul it will fill the Soul and scatter and surround the Soul in a Cocoon.

Learning Plume involves several earlier exercises, but thanks to Abbreviation, you will quickly learn to Plume in a matter of seconds.

Goal: *To send a column of Heaven Light into another Soul.*

Preparation: *Sit in a chair where you can see other people.*

Steps:

1. *Relax and using Abbreviation, invoke a Shower of Light (exercise 9). Feel the clarity the Heaven Light instills in your Soul, and notice how the Light continues to open the eye of your Soul, filling you with a sense of your true spiritual being.*

2. *With the eye of your Soul, look within and beyond the others' bodies, such that the bodies fade from your vision, and feel with your Soul, their Souls. Subtly your Soul will select and Mark the one among them most ready to receive the Heaven Light. Throughout Plume continue to Mark the selected Soul.*

3. *Using Abbreviation, begin to Express Light (exercise 32). But as the Heaven Light starts to Crescendo, will with your Soul that soon all of the Light issue powerfully into the Marked Soul. Squeeze the Light with your Soul.*

4. *As the tide of your Crescendo rises, look directly at the Marked Soul through the eye of your Soul. When the Crescendo peaks, take a deep breath, bow your head, and open the front of your Soul facing the Marked Soul. Will intently that the omniscient Heaven Light shoot out powerfully into the Marked Soul.*

As you release the Light, feel it turbulently rush down through your head and forward, out through your heart, and witness, in Soul, the column of Light shoot out beautifully, perfectly, into the Marked Soul. See how the Light moves directly into the Soul before scattering in orbiting wisps and tufts, surrounding the Soul in a nurturing, purifying Cocoon.

With all your heart and Soul, thank deeply, graciously, and humbly the Heaven Light, the Sacred Beings in the Light, and all of Heaven for the Blessing just bestowed upon your Soul.

Repeat Plume 10 times successfully feeling the power of the Heaven Light issuing out of you, and the confirmation received in your Soul as it strikes the other Soul, before moving to Sacred Intent.

EXERCISE 35

SACRED INTENT

Assigning the Heaven Light.

And now you are ready to Bless, you are ready to issue the Will of Heaven to another Soul through the Heaven Light.

Blessing happens by Assigning a sacred purpose to Plume.

Omniscient and omnipresent is the beloved Heaven Light, which passes descendant from the right of *Abba*, the Face of God-in-Heaven, filling the universe.

A thousand years ago the Heaven Light knew that this very moment you would prepare to Bless another Soul, that you would come to call on the Heaven Light to carry an assignment in the service of Heaven.

Superior is the Heaven Light, which can pass through materiality like breath through smoke, Light ubiquitous when materiality is no more.

There is no hiding from the Light of Heaven, and the Heaven Light eagerly awaits you. So, too, are your Guardian Angels now at hand—they who ride the Light in the service of Heaven. Wisely, take a moment to acknowledge their grace presence.

Capable and willing is the Heaven Light to carry your Sacred Intent into another Soul. Sacred Intent completes Blessing, Assigning the Heaven Light to permeate and cleanse another Soul divinely.

What, then, is Sacred Intent? It is not a word, visualization, symbol, or idea of the mind, but a pure, sacred Expression of the Soul in accordance to the Will of Heaven, an Expression of giving. All Blessing is giving.

Sacred Intent is carried in and released by your Soul, not the mind. Should the mind enter in, your Sacred Intent is rendered inert.

It is helpful to think of Sacred Intent as a ball of Light that your Soul tenders unto the Heaven Light that Plumes toward the Marked Soul. To form your Sacred Intent into a ball of Light, embrace its whole meaning in your heart, wordlessly. Squeeze it, then release it in the Plume, directing the Heaven Light channeling through you to carry it to your Marked Soul. Once entrusted with your Sacred Intent, the Heaven Light will pull it from your Soul in a ball of Light and carry it through to your Marked Soul.

The Heaven Light will serve your Soul whenever your Soul serves the Will of Heaven.

There are many Sacred Intentions, and they all serve Heaven's Will that all Souls Awaken, enter the Heaven Light, and find Heaven. Here, like all of Heaven and the Sacred Beings in the Light, you are given the gift to serve Heaven.

You can Assign any Sacred Intention to Plume to invoke a Blessing (or *all* the Sacred Intentions once you get good at it!). But we will start with a simple one, Compassion, for Blessing is the way of Compassion.

Remember, Compassion is not a thought, emotion or idea, but clear loving being full of understanding that we are Truly One in Spirit, that in essence we are all the same, we are all bound for Heaven, we are all intended to be in the service of Heaven.

Goal: *To complete Blessing by assigning Plume a sacred purpose.*

Preparation: *Sit in a chair where you can see other people.*

Steps:

1. *Start Plume (exercise 34), using Abbreviation if you can. When you Mark your Soul of choice, notice how spontaneously your Soul selects, with a knowing beyond the mind, an intuition known only by the Soul in Spirit of the Soul in the most need of Light. Continue to Mark onto that Soul throughout this exercise.*

2. *Glean, with your Soul's intuition, what sanctity the Marked Soul needs. If the answer jumps out into your Soul, then that is the Sacred Intent you will form. Otherwise, continue to plan to Bless with Compassion.*

3. *Let the Heaven Light build in your Soul towards Crescendo.*

4. *As the tide of Crescendo rises, not with your mind, but in your heart, let Compassion take over your Soul. Become Compassion. In moments the remnant ties to your mind will shift from head to heart, such that you are fully in Soul, and you are ready.*

5. *By relaxing, then squeezing your Soul, Express out in front of you all the Compassion contained in your Soul. You will now experience a new action of your Soul. A ball of Compassion will pass forward out of your Soul, feeling to your Soul in your chest a little like what gently blowing an egg out of your mouth feels like.*

6. *As your ball of Compassionate Sacred Intent releases from your Soul, will with your Soul, with deepest reverence to the Light, that the Heaven Light carry the ball directly into the Marked Soul.*

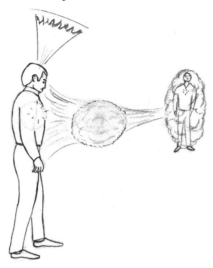

Notice, as the ball of Sacred Intent releases and travels in the wonderful Heaven Light, how your Soul's intuition has instantly changed—you are able to sense the voyage and delivery of your Sacred Intent into the Marked Soul, and feel how your Intent is received from the perspective of the other Soul.

Do not think, but remain intuitive, in awe at what has passed, so that you can learn to become what you are not, what mind will not allow you to become. Grasp, in Soul, the nature of what just happened.

Get good at Blessing for it will prepare you for many things—to know other Souls with a perfect intimacy beyond the scope of mind, to Ascend, releasing your grasp of mind, body and materiality, and eventually to Seal, the Light mastery to assign the Heaven Light to perform great works in accordance to Heaven's Will.

Such is the Will of Heaven, such is the nature of the Heaven Light, such is the way of Blessing. For now, Bless everyone, all the time, for we live in a dark world, and every Blessing is vital to the Will of Heaven.

With all your heart and Soul, thank deeply, graciously, and humbly the Heaven Light, the Sacred Beings in the Light, and all of Heaven for the blessing just bestowed upon your Soul.

Repeat this exercise 20 times before moving to the next one.

SACRED INTENTIONS

Awakening: Raise your Soul up in the heart, beyond the prison of mind.

Remembrance: You are Soul, why you are here, and what you must do.

Sanctification: You must purify on earth, taking the Heaven Light in Soul.

Transcendence: Fill your Soul with Heaven Light, and return to the Clear Light.

Ascendance: Surrender your Soul to the Heaven Light, and find Heaven.

Revelation: Your Soul in Spirit, glean from Heaven the Direction of Souls.

Clarity: Do not idolize the things of man or earth.

Freedom: Do not cleave to the earth.

Constance: Remain present in your Soul every moment.

Joy: Be of Joy, for Joy is the singing of your Soul in the Heaven Light.

Calm: You are a Soul, serene, ready to move toward Heaven.

Compassion: Look to the betterment of every Soul, for we are One in Spirit.

Patience: In time, even eons, all of Soul moves toward Heaven.

Gratitude: Grasp the precious gift of gleaning Spirit in life.

Understanding: Receive the spiritual perspective, rather than materiality.

Mercy: In Spirit, there are no earthly debts, but sacred opportunity.

Courage: Come, enter the Heaven Light, that you will be saved.

Accordance: Trust and follow Heaven's Will within the Heaven Light.

Safety: Your Soul cannot be harmed.

Grace: In Spirit you are never alone, you will always be cared for.

Auspice: The Sacred Beings in the Light will intervene on your Soul's behalf.

EXERCISE 36

GROUPS

Multitasking Heaven Light.

Spirit bides beyond the reach of mind.

If you search the world's sacred literature you will find nothing that comes close to describing the nature of the Light of Heaven, or the sublime experience that even one moment in the Light brings to your Soul.

But if you enter your Soul, bid the Heaven Light fill you, and remain openly receptive, you will learn things in Spirit so wondrous sacred they cannot be put into word!

The Heaven Light is so complex and exquisite its workings escape even the most ardent Souls. But the HeavenWork will help you change that.

Now you are going to witness the Heaven Light do something amazing: You are going to Assign the Light to Bless a crowd. What makes it amazing is that your Soul is simply going to Assign the Heaven Light, and the Light is going to do the work.

You will do this by Abbreviating Cocoon, Expressing Light, Plume, and Sacred Intent.

Goal: *To Bless many Souls at once.*

Preparation: *Sit in a group of people, such as a classroom, office, restaurant, or sports arena.*

Steps:

1. *Accustom yourself to the crowd around, and relax deeply. Sense with your Soul the Sacred Intent you wish to Bless the other Souls with.*

2. *Using Abbreviation, form a Cocoon (exercise 20) around you. Will with your Soul that your Cocoon grow and surround all the Souls you intend to Bless. Just for fun, choose a lot. Be sure to continue Cocoon throughout this exercise.*

3. *Once you can see your Cocoon with the eye of your Soul, Express Light (exercise 32), using Abbreviation, so that the Heaven Light radiates into every Soul in your Cocoon.*

4. *Begin to Crescendo and form a Plume (exercise 34, using Abbreviation) that heads towards the Souls you are Blessing. When your Soul is ready to release the concentrated Heaven Light, with your Soul Assign the Light with your Sacred Intent (exercise 35, using Abbreviation), also willing that the Light Bless every Soul within your Cocoon.*

5. *Then bow your head and climax your Crescendo while releasing your Sacred Intent into the Plume.*

Watch, with the eye of your Soul, how all at once the Heaven Light Plume branches out in all directions, complexly, into every Soul within your Cocoon, how the Light hits and goes to work cleansing, permeating each Soul.

Continue Expressing Light, so that your Soul can behold the Miracle taking place. Feel, with your Soul, the new, icy fresh purity washing your Soul while the Heaven Light multitasks your Blessing. With your Soul open, learn from what is taking place things sacred and new, Truths freshly discovered from your perfect Teacher, the Heaven Light.

If you would grow in Spirit, become what you are not.

Do not assign words to what you observe in Soul; simply enter new Truth. In this way you are leaving the ways of man and entering the Sacred. In this way, you are homing toward Heaven.

When you are ready, take a deep breath, bow your head forward again, and cease the Plume. The Heaven Light will continue Blessing each and every Soul for about a day.

Bless you for Blessing other Souls. Know that you have now become a sun of Heaven Light, a sun of man.

With all your heart and Soul, thank deeply, graciously, and humbly the Heaven Light, the Sacred Beings in the Light, and all of Heaven for the blessing just bestowed upon your Soul.

Repeat this exercise 10 times before moving to the next one.

SAYING GRACE, INVOKING GRACE

Indeed, the tradition of saying meal grace is beautiful, but is it all it can be?

Now that you have learned to Bless with your Soul, you can make grace just like Jesus did—by Blessing your meal with the Heaven Light.

Simply do to the food what you did with LightWater (exercise 7). Place your palms over or beside your plate and before your heart. With gracious Intent from your Soul, send, using Abbreviation, the Heaven Light into it down your arms and out your palms, and straight out your heart. Both your body and Soul will tell the difference Light makes to your food.

But why stop at food and drink? Do you think Jesus' gratitude ended at the table? No, constantly he Blessed everything around him.

So can you. So should you.

Bless with Heaven Light every breath you take, every step you make, every Soul you meet, everything that happens to you in this short precious life, for every moment is a gift that could be taken away at a moment's gasp.

There is no Blessing without Light and no Light without Blessing. Thus is the nature of grace.

Therefore practice your HeavenWork constantly, Joyfully, that your Soul may grace Heaven.

EXERCISE 37

SIMULTANEOUS BLESSING

The synergy of Heaven Light.

Where there are two or more in Spirit, there is divine synergy.

What is Heaven, but perfect Blessing perpetual, Ascended unto *Abba*, the Face of God at Creation?

In Heaven the Diamond Heaven Light teems within the rolling Clouds of the three million of the Body of Heaven, where glory and jubilation are and ever shall be. There is no separation in the Light. All are One in Spirit.

> **The Body of Heaven:** *The vast, rolling clouds of Heaven, surrounding the Diadem, Heaven's abode of all Transfigured Souls.*

Two Souls Blessing each one the other is an excellent practice to burn away the illusion of separation and bring you into your True nature of Light, and the more your Soul travels into the Light, the closer you home on Heaven.

Just feel the difference when you are Blessed by someone you are Blessing!

What is the principle of church, temple, mosque, shrine, synagogue, or tabernacle but Simultaneous Blessing?

Therefore share the Light with others on the Path of Light, with other HeavenWorkers, for both shall receive a measure of grace, and more.

Goal: *To bond in Blessing with another Soul.*

Preparation: *Sit or stand in front of another HeavenWorker.*

Steps:

1. At the same time, both of you perform Group Blessing (exercise 36) on each other.

Openly receive into your Soul the stronger Heaven Light carrying into your Soul, from above and from in front of you, glean the new and special bond shared between your partner Soul and yours, what new meaning, and how, it seems, you Surrender your Soul, briefly, and become as One.

Surrender to this new intimacy, such that you shift, dropping completely into your Soul in heart, moving forward, in Soul, until you touch upon your partner's Soul.

Trust, for nothing ill can happen to your Soul, and if you are so moved, Surrender still more, such that you drop into your partner's Soul, if briefly, in rapture, and you will know perfect intimacy, the likes of that in Heaven—Disclosure.

With all your heart and Soul, thank deeply, graciously, and humbly the Heaven Light, the Sacred Beings in the Light, and all of Heaven for the Blessing just bestowed upon your Soul.

Repeat this exercise 10 times before moving to the next one.

Exercise 38

Baptism Of Light

True Awakening of the Soul.

For longer than I dare say, Baptism of Light has been my favorite HeavenWork. If I had my way I would Baptize the world with the Light of Heaven, for that is solely why I remain on earth.

There is baptism of the earth, and there is Baptism of Light. The first baptism, baptism as we know it today, was long ago reduced, by those who did not know the Heaven Light, to a symbolic mystical ritual issued hopefully, yet vainly from the mind, using words, physical gestures, and water. By and large today's clergy are neither required nor taught to Awaken in Soul, master the Heaven Light, and actuate the Baptism of Light.

Mind alone cannot compel the Heaven Light, only the Soul can. If the baptist's Soul happens to be sleeping, how can Heaven Light be invoked? How can a Baptism of Light truly take place?

But the second Baptism—True Baptism, Baptism that works—is a special Blessing of Heaven Light invoked by the Awakened Soul. It is a permanent flash transmission covenant of Spirit delivered into a Soul to Awaken it into Remembrance so that the Soul can go about a meaningful life of HeavenWork.

Remembrance is your Soul's sudden insight of what you really are, what you came here to do, and how to go about it.

True Baptism Awakens and sets the Soul on the Path of Light.

Baptism of Light Awakens the Soul, but not always the mind. You can Baptize anyone's Soul, but only babies younger than six months are likely to grasp, in faint mind, what is happening, for their Souls have yet to fall fast asleep in life.

Awakened Soul, now that you can Bless you can Baptize. Here's how.

Goal: *To Bless Awake and set a Soul on the Path of Light.*

Preparation: *Stand with a mostly full glass of water between your hands, and with the one to be Baptized.*

Steps:

1. *Holding the glass of water before your heart, invoke HeavenHome (exercise 4), using Abbreviation. Recognize, with the eye of your Soul, how closer you are coming to Heaven, how you can almost gaze upon the vast Firmament. Feel, in awe, God's Immanence pour down into your Soul.*

2. *Also using Abbreviation, form a Cocoon (exercise 20) around your Soul and the one to be Baptized. Continue Cocoon throughout the Baptism.*

3. *Extend your hands in front and behind the one to be Baptized, placing one palm on the back just behind the heart, and the other holding the glass of water touching the chest just before the heart, so that you are holding the Soul between your palms. With Abbreviation invoke LightWater (pre-exercise 7). Feel the Heaven Light pour down your arms and out your palms, and how it jumps from your heart into the glass of water. Continue this channel of Light throughout the Baptism.*

4. *Now Bless the one to be Baptized, Abbreviating Plume (exercise 34) and Sacred Intent (exercise 35). Embrace the following into your ball of Sacred Intent: Awaken! You are a Soul, here on earth to purify into Heaven, through the Heaven Light that fills you even now. Awaken now(!), and carry the Light in your Soul always, as long as you shall live! You shall find Heaven in this life!*

5. *Squeeze and release unto the Heaven Light your ball of Sacred Intent.*

There is no mistaking your Soul's witness of the flash transmission covenant the Heaven Light strikes into the Baptized Soul. It braces the Baptized Soul like a crashing cymbal, and if the one Baptized is younger than six months the infant will likely start to recognize and stare at the familiar Light that surrounds your Soul.

If the one Baptized is old enough, conclude your Baptism by offering a drink of the purified water.

Because water is such a good conductor of Heaven Light, only a highly empowered Baptist does not benefit from using LightWater in Baptism. Even the Baptist John is remembered as using water. It is fine to always Baptize using water.

Short of performing a Miracle with Heaven, Baptism is the most auspicious way to gift another Soul with Light.

With all your heart and Soul, thank deeply, graciously, and humbly the Heaven Light, the Sacred Beings in the Light, and all of Heaven for the Blessing just bestowed upon your Soul.

Rehearse Baptizing 5 times before moving to the next exercise.

EXERCISE 39

BABIES!

Providing the opportunity of a lifetime!

Babies are Blessed, for they are the continuation of Spirit on earth, the future of Heaven's Will on earth, and they have a lifetime to do the HeavenWork!

Only a little while ago they were swaddled, in Soul, in skies of loving Light, attended by the Sacred Beings. They came here, each of them, with pure intent intuitive of Soul. But just before arriving, the grip of body and the mind's pirate thoughts took over. Even now, see how materiality all around them lulls their sweet Souls to sleep.

Now, here before you, they look to you for help, *real* help.

Awakened Soul, you can help.

All they need is a jumpstart, a True Blessing from you to put them back on track, to place them once again upon the Path of Light. And they are so ready, receptive and willing.

Give of this service every time you see a baby.

Goal: *To Awaken a baby's Soul.*

Preparation: *Perform this exercise spontaneously next time you see a baby younger than six months.*

Steps:

1. *The baby does not need to be near you, but can be anywhere in sight. Set yourself at peace and invoke a Shower of Light (exercise 9) using Abbreviation.*

2. *Read with your Soul the Soul of the baby. In doing this, the baby will likely turn toward you in curiosity.*

3. *Using Abbreviation, perform a Blessing of Plume (exercise 34) and Sacred Intent (exercise 35). Embrace within your Soul this loving ball of Sacred Intent: Remember, you are Soul in the Heaven Light. Hold this Light within you always!*

4. *Release the ball of Light unto the Heaven Light channeling through the Plume. Watch, in Soul, as the Sacred Intent enters the baby's Soul and splashes into a Cocoon, omnisciently tending the Soul's sanctifying needs.*

You have just placed another Soul aright on the Path of Light, you have just performed a great act of HeavenWork.

Each time you Bless a baby you will be delighted when the baby turns to you, smiling in gratitude and loving Remembrance.

With each baby you Bless you open another floodgate for Heaven Light to pour forth unto man. Therefore, never let a baby pass you by without your sending the Heaven Light into its Soul!

With all your heart and Soul, thank deeply, graciously, and humbly the Heaven Light, the Sacred Beings in the Light, and all of Heaven for the Blessing just bestowed upon your Soul.

Repeat this exercise 10 times before moving to the next one.

DEATH

Death grips us ever so harshly, and because of this we have learned plenty about the death of the body, and the last throes of its extinguishing mind. But what about the Soul, what happens to the Soul at death?

What would Lazarus tell us, or Elijah?

Indeed, thousands *have* passed through death's door and returned to life with the Soul safely intact in the body. Each near-death experiencer returned a permanently changed being.

But in 1962 when I drowned and came back, my Soul, knowing the better, refused to return to my body, and instead has remained suspended between life and death, in between the earth and Heaven, free to migrate through the whole of Spirit. For the past 45 years, my Soul has dwelt also among the dead.

Just as I have walked among the many dead-in-life, and just as I have dwelt among the live-in-death, so it is I would tell you about death and the Soul's migration.

Death grips the mind, not the Soul. That is why at the death of a loved one we desperately mourn the loss of the person's material attributes—of the body and its personality—instead of their essence which we truly loved about them: Their Soul. All the while the Soul slips freely, safely and joyfully into the Light.

Yes, we all die. The body convulses, seizes, ceases, and corrupts, and the twilight mind extinguishes, while the Soul, in a glory one in body cannot know, continues unobstructed along its migration through Spirit.

Earth is not our home. Earth is a place we visit, and at death all reference to earth is left behind.

Once released, your Soul Remembers eternally, that you are Soul, that you are old as time, that you are bound for Heaven, that you have dwelt on earth many, many times before, and that you will return again, for in Soul set free at death, one veil of unknowing is lifted.

Death, like birth, is incidental to the Soul.

In Spirit none are separated by death, for all Souls are joined by the Heaven Light. It is only in life, within the veil of embodiment, that we seem divided.

The moment of death is important to the Soul, for there is no hiding in Spirit. At that deepest moment of Truth, Soul is always borne by the omniscient

Heaven Light in accordance to the Will of Heaven.

Death is not the end, but a blink of the Soul's eye, a door. There is no death of the Soul.

Nor can the Will of Heaven be curtailed. Every moment of your life determines your destiny. At death, either your Soul has sanctified or remains profane. If you sanctified in life you will be carried to Heaven. If you remain profane, you will be returned by your Compassionate Guardian Angels to the Life-Between, for nothing profane can enter Heaven. There is no other way.

Yet, no Soul is damned.

THE MOMENT OF DEATH

When you die—each time you die—the experience of your Soul is the same, however the onset of death.

For a split second your body and astonished mind experience a deep sharp pain, which is immediately relieved and forgotten as your Soul is tugged back from out of your heart and head. The Soul is tugged quickly, around three times, and each tug is accompanied by a muffled popping sound.

As your Soul quickly moves back a few inches, severing from the body, the mind and body dissolve away, followed by the dissolution of the immediate area around you, and then the earth, sky, and all of materiality.

And you are released back into the Clear Light, and filled with a familiar rush of Joy a hundred times stronger than anything you ever felt in body. All references to the earth—thought, word, sensation, individuality—immediately perish completely, like they never were, and you are once again in your essence Clean, naked, intuitive, true, ardent, a perfect ball of impermeable Light, like a glass ball, permanent yet untouchable.

Quickly you reach in pure understanding, with the ever-streaming silver sunrays of your Soul's intuition, to the furthest reaches of the Clear Light where it collapses before Heaven, and you Remember. You Remember what you are, what you came to earth to do.

At this transitional moment one of several things can happen—things all well within your Soul's understanding. You may:

1. Be carried by a radiant Angel of the Diadem to the Firmament of Heaven where your Elect Soul will be Transfigured by the Breath of Heaven and

Received in complete glory into Heaven or the Clouds of Heaven;

2. Find your Guardian Angels before your Soul, who return your Soul to materiality while your body rallies back to life;

3. Briefly revisit your body, only to find it foreign, dense, inert, and unable to enter, and you will make your last fleeting references to materiality before returning to the Clear Light;

4. Fill with deep sadness, woeful that you'd spent so little time doing what you came to life to do.

If your Soul sanctified in life you will be Transfigured and carried into Heaven. If your body rallies, your ever-present Guardian Angels will remarry your Soul to your body, completely or in part. It is not uncommon for a Soul to revisit the body, if briefly, but once you return to the Clear Light, your Soul, too, will fill with sadness at facing a life ill spent.

Unless your Soul is conveyed to Heaven you will enter into a cave of darkness, to find the eye of your Soul haloed by the judge-like Usher Angels.

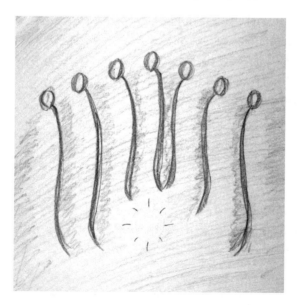

MIGRATION OF SOUL

Like grave dark judges, the Usher Angels ring your Soul's eye, and you are awed by their great purity and power. Somber and Compassionate, these omniscient sacred Beings in the Light convey with complete intuitive mastery the Truth into your Soul that once again you failed to sanctify in life.

Halfway through your Soul's reactive inclination to justify your failure you are stopped by these Sacred Beings, who fill your Soul with understanding that you will not be harmed, that all of Spirit serves one purpose, for *you* to find your way to Heaven, and you are filled with peace excelsior.

How clear it all becomes, the pure understanding of the nature of Heaven and the Heaven Light. You are safe and loved by the Light, always and ever! Here you learn that nothing is Truer or kinder to your Soul than the Heaven Light.

And thus you surrender your Soul unto the witness of the Heaven Light and all the Sacred Beings within. Full of trust your Soul falls, only to be caught on the softest wings of Heaven Light, which carry you lovingly to rest.

Because Soul in Spirit is beyond the grasp of the material-referenced mind, we tend to consider tracking the migration of the Soul as elusive, if not impossible. But that is only because mind cannot follow Soul into Spirit. To Mark and follow the Soul's migration through the Light, you must follow with the eye of your Soul.

In short, after death, your Soul enters the **Life-Between**. Immediately after your Ushers' attendance, your Soul carries on wings of Heaven Light to the Lightfields, where you will pass a few years in rest, recovery, Remembrance and readiment for life anew. In all this time your Soul is always safe secure within the nurturing Heaven Light.

As soon as you leave the Ushers, as you are carried on the swaddling wings of Heaven Light, your Soul enters **Blackout**—a long time when your Soul does not move or intuit. You are in complete and absolute rest, recovering from life.

Gradually your Soul dawns, if barely, into "half-being," in the insignificance of **Limbo**. Slightly intuitive, you are humbled in the Truth that your Soul yet remains profane. You remain in Limbo at the mercy of Heaven for a worth duration.

In a **Stupor**, your Soul's eye opens, yet you do not stir. You are at your purest, devoid even of your innate intuition except for gratitude that now you have been granted existence.

Suddenly you **Awaken**, your Soul's intuition fully present, only purer, clearer All things of earth and man are forgotten. Your post-life recovery is complete and your Soul is restored to being. You discover you are being swaddled in a thick sky of milky white Heaven Light—a vast Light of Compassionate, nurturing love.

As soon as you grasp, in Soul, your restored wakefulness a Reviving Angel approaches you, touches up against you, and fills you with the understanding— the Soul memory—that you are home and safe. The Angel *Encourages* you to explore, find the Fields of Light, and learn Truth. Then the Angel pushes you so that you discover you can move—migrate—through the Light.

Despite the awe you feel towards the Reviving Angel you depart, knowing with a growing fascination the opportunity ahead of you, or within and beyond the nurturing Light.

As you scoot through the Heaven Light you begin to feel, increasingly, a sacred wind flowing into you from the eye of your Soul. You know it is *Heaven's Emanation*. What you do not yet know is that this Emanation will pass through your Soul increasingly throughout your entire remaining dwelling in the Life-Between.

As more of Heaven's Emanation passes through you, your spiritual intuition blossoms, becoming far-reaching. In the Wind of Heaven you glean that the essence of your Soul is the same substance of the Heaven Light, and that washing away the profane elements of your Soul with the Heaven Light changes your Soul into the substance of Heaven.

Heaven's Emanation at last fills your Soul with the knowing that you are already *in*, or nearby the Fields of Light of the Life-Between. Already you sense the *Lightfields* all around you, within and beyond the thick Heaven Light, so you "will" to enter in with your Soul, the Heaven Light opens, and you pass though into the Lightfields.

Lightfields—the perpetual rainbow light, the rolling green light meadows and the opalescent sky that stretch on seemingly forever, and the millions— billions—of kindred Souls there abiding, intense crystalline energy bubbles of light, at rest or in motion, alone or together.

How hollow the comfort your Soul receives from the sky and meadows as you try, over and over, to rest upon them, from an old earth memory, but cannot, for they are only light. And you are filled with understanding that the Lightfields are only earth images projected in the Heaven Light by the Angels of Truth—Pillar Angels—to draw all Souls in the Life-Between and prepare us for life anew.

The large Master Pillar Angels, bridges of Heaven, there only for the sanctification of each and every Soul.

For an earth year you remain in the Lightfields, experiencing things of Spirit—mobility, passing-through the Light, flying, Spirit perspective, intimacy, trust, harmony, unity, disclosure, Heaven's Will, and the nature of the Heaven Light and Sacred Beings in the Light. And as you increasingly draw near the Pillar Angels, your Soul is filled with Remembrance.

In Remembrance you come to understand that migration in Spirit in the Life-Between cannot sanctify your Soul, that you must return to the repugnant materiality of earth, with all its dark opacity, pain and suffering, to challenge your Soul's resolve to bear the Light in Soul, that Soul can sanctify only in materiality—that only in life can Soul migrate to Heaven.

Thus is your Soul's desire for body rekindled.

But desire is not enough. Only when your Soul is completely consumed by desperate desire to sanctify through body on earth, are you granted the dear gift of life by the Sacred Beings, in accordance to the Will of Heaven.

You will then spend months **preincarnate**, dead still, with all the others elect to life. When at last you awaken and stir, you are **Selected** by the Placer

Angels, and then **Adorned** by all the others soon to join you in life, who give of their being to you, Sealing traits into your Soul and Bonding promise of affiliation from their Soul into your Soul.

Once adorned you are **Translocated**, by your Placer Angels—your Guardian Angels—to within the veil of materiality, where you hove, between your Angels just without and beyond the veneer of earth, waiting until they find, in their exceeding omniscience, auspicious birth opportunities for your Soul.

They allow you, your Placer Angels, to glimpse into the Souls of your mother and father, and their children and children yet to come, such that you can glean the natures of each Soul, and the Angels render unto you spiritual understanding of the opportunities and challenges such life pairings will present to your Soul, such that your Soul is Marked and set.

In celebration and Miracle, you slide into materiality as your Angels earnestly marry your Soul unto the heart of the tiny body yet waiting in your mother's—your new mother's—welcome womb.

How you strive and determine in Soul, those months of growing in the womb, to keep to your Sacred Intent which bore your Soul to life incarnate—to magnify the Heaven Light on earth with all your might, every waking and sleeping moment, how you will let nothing get in your way this time.

Even during your last months gestate you strive with your Soul to remain intuitive and pure, while your body's inferior and opaque mind grows stronger and stronger, until finally you give in, and your Soul is rendered asleep.

CONTINUUM, THE SOUL'S JOURNEY TO HEAVEN

Continuum is not just about sleep, it is about all of life. And what's more, it is about the long life of your Soul. It is about forever.

You practiced a brief version of Continuum in exercise 23, when you continued uninterrupted in Soul as your mind and body fell asleep. But Continuum is eternal—your Soul's steady and unbroken presence throughout your long journey to Heaven, in and out of life, again and again. In this way death is not the end but only a doorway. At your body's "death" your Soul **ejects** naturally out of materiality into the Clear Light. Unless your Soul has sanctified and immediately Transfigures into Heaven, you will be received in loving tufts of

Heaven Light, where you will be free to *migrate* through the Fields of Light of the Life-Between before you return to earth to continue your sanctification. No Soul is ever lost under Heaven. The Heaven Light sees to this.

When your Soul is ready and made prepared to return to earth, you will be *injected* into a fetal heart by the Sacred Beings in the Light who will serve as your Guardian Angels throughout your earthy life. The only exception is when Sacred Beings in the Light self-inject themselves into life.

Such is Continuum, the cycling journey of Soul in search of Heaven.

EXERCISE 40

THE DYING

Assisting the Sacred Beings in the Heaven Light.

There is no hiding from Heaven. The Sacred Beings in the Light, sacred agents of Heaven's Will unto the earth, know everything that happens under Heaven—when a sparrow rises and falls, when an ant is crushed, when a bacterium perishes.

The Heaven Light, and the Sacred Beings within, know everything about you in a complete purity beyond the grasp of mind—not only your present, past and future, but how your entire being fits and will ever fit into all things material and spiritual. And perfect is the machinery of the Spirit Universe. Thus you cannot cut deals with the Heaven Light; there are no shortcuts. Each Soul must sanctify individually in life.

So it is at your death.

So it is at the death of a loved one, and thus you would best serve their Soul by easing them into the caring Heaven Light before, during and immediately after death, in the service of Heaven. In this light, the exercise, The Dying, is a service, spontaneous in nature.

The Dying is a special Blessing of Light.

Guardian Angels are always present, and at death they make themselves known unto the Soul in their charge, in accordance to the Will of Heaven. To this end, now that you are Ascending, you can assist them.

DEATH OF A LOVED ONE

Every Soul is a loved one, for we are always One in Spirit. Therefore when your Soul moves you to perform The Dying you are in accordance to the Will of Heaven.

At another's death you cannot afford to be distracted by the tempest of materiality, by the throes of the dying body or mind. Nor can you afford to be distracted by the family members and healthcare workers present. Yet, if you are invited to be present at a loved one's death you must perform The Dying without causing any of *them* distraction either.

If you are invited, you can remain out of their way, in the corner of the room. Later, when you learn Distancing, you will not have to be physically present at all.

Even at the tumultuous moments before death, do not be distracted. Your mind and the unpleasant physical phenomena that occur as death approaches must not pull you from your Soul's center or the Heaven Light.

Performing The Dying does not involve treating the body or mind—leave such things to the earthy professionals. To be effective keep it simple. However, the loved one will have many human needs, and there are many Compassionate human things you can do *while* you perform The Dying, if invited, to assist in the passing.

It is okay, for example, to respond to them, Quicken your hands and hold their hand, even place your hand upon their heart, if you are asked to and it doesn't interfere with the healthcare workers.

Always perform The Dying intuitively, with your Soul under the guidance of the Heaven Light, for only the Heaven Light knows the destiny of that Soul.

With The Dying you facilitate the passing Soul's transition by enveloping the Soul in an enduring Blessing of Heaven Light. Perform it perfectly, in silence, Soul-to-Soul, unhindered by material distractions.

Goal: *To help transition one's Soul through bodily death.*

Preparation: *Attend a loved one's death, or spontaneously, should you witness another's death.*

Steps:

1. *Make yourself comfortable somewhere you will be out of the way of the healthcare professionals, family, friends, and clergy. Enter HeavenHome (exercise 4), using Abbreviation. Maintain HeavenHome throughout this entire service.*

2. *Using Abbreviation, invoke from the Face of God-in-Heaven a Shower of Light (exercise 9). Surrender your Soul unto the Light that you will follow the Will of Heaven within the Light. Feel the Compassion flood your Soul, and the Truth. Maintain the Shower of Light throughout this entire service.*

3. *Fill the room with a Cocoon of Light (exercise 20) using Abbreviation, so that every Soul in the room is contained within the Heaven Light.*

Maintain Cocoon throughout this entire service.

4. *Using Abbreviation, send a Plume (exercise 34) into the passing Soul. Maintain a steady Plume throughout this entire service.*

5. *Embrace in your Soul this Sacred Intent: Thy Will be done on earth as it is in Heaven.*

6. *Surrender this ball of Sacred Intent unto the Plume of Heaven Light.*

7. *Keep the Blessing of Light continuous throughout the death process. Even if you must get up and leave the room, keep the Heaven Light within and around the Soul of the dying person.*

8. *Maintain your Blessing upon the Soul for 30 minutes after the body has ceased. Then, form a closing ball of Sacred Intent, Assigning the Heaven Light to carry the Soul continuously through its destiny.*

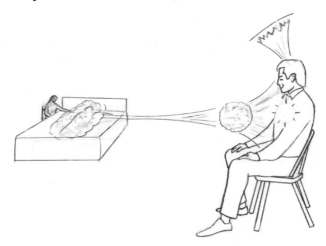

If the dying one should rally, as often happens, maintain The Dying and stay there until it appears the crisis is over. If the loved one survives, you may end this service by sending another ball of Sacred Intent, Assigning the Heaven Light to remain within that Soul and to contact you well before death returns. It is okay to leave and return another time.

If you are asked questions before or during The Dying, always come intuitively from your Soul in the Heaven Light. Do not lecture or conjecture, and admit when you do not know. Simply refer to the Heaven Light and the Will of Heaven carried within the Heaven Light.

If your charge dies, remain in The Dying for 30 minutes after the moment of death, for your Compassionate presence will grace the Soul throughout the immediate afterdeath direction and adjustment.

As for the Souls of the bereft, afterdeath is a time of release, relief and peace. It is more enduring to practice pure presence rather than words, in intuitive witness of the departed Soul in migration.

In facilitating the migration of another Soul you also prepare yourself for *your* Soul's migration at death. In this light, the exercise of The Dying is the same whether you perform it on a loved one or on yourself when your time comes.

Soul sanctifies not in death, but in life.

AT YOUR OWN DEATH

There are many causes, many ways of dying, many changes your body and mind may go through, especially as your death nears. But there is only *one* way your Soul departs, *one* way your Soul migrates.

Do not fear your death, for your Soul knows exactly what to do. It always has, and you will Remember the moment you are released back into the Clear Light. You will Remember in great freedom and Joy who you *really* are, what you *really* came to earth to do, what is happening, and what is about to happen. And the loving Sacred Beings in the Light will be there to ease your transition.

Every HeavenWork exercise you perform, especially servicing The Dying of others, prepares you for an auspicious death, to carry you on loving wings of Heaven Light into your migration.

Should you die *after* you have completed your HeavenWork, having Ascended and sanctified in life, you may add to The Dying the Transfiguration preparation exercise, *Transcondensing* or its Crown, *Lightning Bolt*.

Transcondensing, a preparation for Lightning Bolt, draws the Breath of Heaven through your Soul, and Lightning Bolt helps end your Soul's exile from Heaven by sending concentrated consummating bolts of Heaven Breath *into* your Soul so that you can be Transfigured into Sacred Spirit and pass through the gate of Heaven.

If your Soul has nearly completed its Ascent to Heaven, there is something you can do at the last moment of life to push fully Ascendant: *Tranflex* your *Blessing of Light* in your heart just as your body systems fail and arrest. This is another good reason your Guardian Angels married your Soul to your heart!

If your time of death comes *before* you have completed your Ascension, you will be lovingly carried, in Soul, into the Lightfields of the Life-Between. Because of the HeavenWork you practiced in life, your migration through the Life-Between will be auspicious. You may even pass through your entire migration without a lapse in consciousness, your rest, recovery and Readiment will pass sooner, and you will return to a life full of sanctifying opportunity.

Therefore practice this many times before your death.

Goal: *To transition your Soul auspiciously through bodily death.*

Preparation: *Practice all of your HeavenWork exercises until the day you die.*

Steps:

1. *Usually you will know your body is about to die. If your onset of death is slow, spend your last hours in a Cocoon (exercise 20) of Light. If your onset of death is immediate, and it is too late to save your body from irreparable harm, immediately invoke a Shower of Light (exercise 9) before forming a tight Cocoon around your body. Receive God's Joy into your soon-to-be-freed Soul.*

2. *Invoke HeavenHome (exercise 4). With the eye of your Soul, peer through the Door Up (exercise 30), to Heaven, and commend your Soul to the Will of Heaven.*

3. *Feel with your Soul the Immanence of Heaven breathe down upon your Soul. Receive this, God's Immanence into your Soul, the absolute fairness and Compassion. Slowly, gradually, Crescendo the Immanence within your Soul.*

4. *Form, with Heaven's Immanence in your Soul, a ball of Sacred Intent that your Soul be delivered freely in the service of Heaven.*

5. *At the moment your body begins to arrest, at the stoppage of your heart and the brief moments before your Soul is tugged back from your heart and head, quickly Transflex your ball of Sacred Intent and release it unto the Heaven Light.*

The moment you release your Sacred Intent your Soul will be tugged and painlessly severed from your body, and you will find yourself back in the Clear Light, surrounded by a Cocoon of loving Heaven Light. You will not slip into darkness as your Soul enters its migration.

Your Soul will know perfectly what to do next.

Birth and death are incidental to your Soul,
which continues ever on its journey to Heaven.

EXERCISE 41

COSMIC WIND CHIMES

Singing to the Angels.

And so it is your body dies, your Soul is released, and you pass back into the Life-Between, over and over again in your long quest for Heaven. *Do you Remember?*

But your time of death has not yet come. There is much you can do, here and now, to sanctify, Ascend beyond material rebirth, and find your way to Heaven. And your HeavenWork exercises progressively get more powerful, and more interesting.

Soul eternal, you have always wanted more than this meager half-existence we call life. You have always wanted to Live, to Ascend to Life perpetual, Being beyond being, to Heaven.

But to go where you are not, you must become what you are not. You must let go of the things that hold you back, and acquire the things that carry you to your destiny.

To Ascend to the Sacred you must become sacred. You must unlearn the profane ways of man and learn the sacred ways of Spirit. You must learn the sacred language of Soul-in-Spirit.

Wordless and purely, you must learn to Sing to the Angels, chiming Ascendant through the Heaven Light.

Joyously, intrepidly, you can learn to Sing Ascendant with your Soul, through the Door Up, unto the Sacred Beings who fill the Heaven Light all the way to Heaven.

Your Expressions of sacred language are silent, yet thunderous, and they are heard in Heaven.

Cosmic Wind Chimes is your first pronouncement to the Angels of your coming Ascendance. You now have your sacred voice—the power and avenue to Express your Joy and Sacred Intent. You can now reach out unto the servants of Heaven.

Sing out Ascendant with your Soul, and you will be heard.

Goal: *To pronounce to the Sacred your Soul's will to Ascend.*

Preparation: *Awaken, in the middle of the night, in Vigil.*

Steps:

1. *Enter, in the middle of the night, into the Clear Light of Vigil (exercise 27). Stretch, with your Soul's familiar intuition throughout the infinite reaches of the Clear Light.*

2. *In the peace abiding in the Clear Light that passes through the dark of night, invoke HeavenHome (exercise 4), using Abbreviation. Humbly, in awe, receive in your Soul the perfect Immanence from the Face of God-in-Heaven.*

3. *Using Abbreviation, open the eye of your Soul by practicing The Door Up (exercise 30).*

4. *Gather the Heaven Light in your Soul, in preparation for a Blessing of Plume (exercise 34) and Sacred Intent (exercise 35).*

5. *Heaven is the Mark of your Plume. Send your Plume upward, through the Door Up, the eye of your Soul, Ascendant through the Heaven Light to Heaven.*

6. *Prepare your ball of Sacred Intent:* Joyous and brave Surrender of your Soul in perfect trust unto the Will of Heaven, your unwavering will and permanent commitment to Ascend unto Heaven, and your covenant to facilitate only Heaven's Will.

7. *Singing is your Joyous, sustained release of your ball of Sacred Intent unto the Heaven Light. The closest earth reference to your Soul's sensation is wind chimes joyously tinkling in a loving wind, heard by all the Angels in and under Heaven. As you release your ball of pronouncement unto Heaven, Assign the Heaven Light to carry it to Heaven, sharing it with all the Sacred Beings along the way. But do not release it completely. Continue to hold the ball of Intent within your Soul such that the Heaven Light, knowing what your Soul is doing, pulls from the ball the essence of your Intent continuously.*

8. *Remain in Joyous Cosmic Wind Chimes for a sustained period, using Crescendo now and then to surge your Singing with desire for the Sacred.*

Bask in the awe and wonder of your Ascendant destiny, the frontier of sacred Spirit opening to your Soul and blazed in accordance to the Will of Heaven by your Soul's pure pronouncement.

Learn to practice Cosmic Wind Chimes in the day, spontaneously, through Abbreviation.

Do not be afraid. No harm can come to you in the Heaven Light, only good. Sing, therefore, Sing with all your Soul.

With all your heart and Soul, thank deeply, graciously, and humbly the Heaven Light, the Sacred Beings in the Light, and all of Heaven for the Blessing just bestowed upon your Soul.

Repeat this exercise 10 times before moving to the next one.

Get good at Cosmic Wind Chimes. You will need it later.

No written word can frame
The Being beyond being
That is Heaven

Render unto the earth the things of earth,
and render unto Heaven the things of Heaven.

EXERCISE 42

SOUL PRAYER

The heart's reach to Heaven.

Heaven Answers most Prayers, provided they come not from the mind but the Soul, and that they ask not to receive but to give.

Now that you can Sing Ascendant, you can Pray from your Soul.

There are two types of prayer: The weak prayer of the mind, and the powerful Prayer of the Soul. Prayer of the profane mind does not carry into Spirit, much less all the way to Heaven; thus its prayers are rarely Answered. But Heaven always Answers the needs of your Soul, more than Soul knows.

The material mind always desires to receive things of the earth, while the Soul always Expresses self-sacrifice for the sake of Heaven.

Prayer must come from your Soul.

Sometimes Prayer from the Soul is Answered even if it is not pure, when it is tainted by the mind's profane desires. But the Answer always comes long after your mind has lost interest in its fulfillment, with its eventual Manifestation leaving your Soul unfulfilled.

Be careful what you pray for, and never enter Prayer frivolously.

In life our needs are many, or so it seems. But in Soul, no matter in life or in the Life-Between, you have only one true need: To sanctify. Only in sacrifice is your Soul sanctified. Therefore Pray only in the service of your Soul, and every other Soul, in the service of Heaven.

Thy Will be done on earth as it is in Heaven.

Thus is Soul Prayer one of sacrifice, of service to the Will of Heaven.

Cosmic Wind Chimes helped you Express your Soul into the universe, carrying to Heaven. Soul Prayer takes you a step further Ascendant. The more your Soul Ascends the more powerfully you can Pray. Come, and learn to Pray powerfully.

Goal: *To speak to God in the language of Spirit.*

Preparation: *Find a place where you will not be disturbed.*

Steps:

1. *Pray any time you feel moved, in Soul, to make known to God-in-Heaven an important and binding pronouncement of service of your Soul.*

2. *Using Abbreviation, connect your Soul to Heaven by practicing Cosmic Wind Chimes (exercise 41), . In your heart, form wordlessly your prayer into a ball of Sacred Intent, such as: Abba, no matter the cost to my being, fill me with your Will that I might bear It unto other Souls on earth.*

3. *Instead of holding onto your ball of Prayer Intent, release it completely into the Plume of Heaven Light passing through the Door Up.*

Feel in your Soul, *Abba's* Answer received the moment you begin to Express it, a flash of sacred affirmation blasting through you in an instant, consuming you, and the wordless Compassion that cleanses your Soul like a flame.

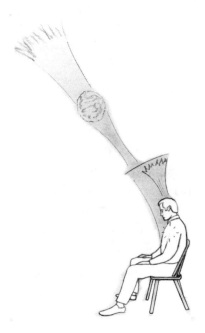

Feel the Heaven Light rush into your Soul, at work, omnisciently nurturing you from your sacred encounter. Feel the Heaven Light so quickly drawn to things sacred.

Feel the presence of the Sacred Beings in the Light who draw near you, and the eyes of Heaven upon your Soul. Your Prayer is made known in Heaven.

Such is the essence of Soul Prayer.

Soon you will learn to use Soul Prayer for Manifestation, Miracles and great works of Light in concert with the Sacred Beings in the Light, and even the Angels of the Diadem. You will also learn to receive guidance directly from *Abba*.

But for now, keep it simple, and learn to carry your Prayer effectively to Heaven.

Know that no Answer to your Prayer will come as a material reward, but a Spirit charge for your Soul to carry unto others, and in so giving is your Soul rewarded by the Heaven Light by the only way Soul can be rewarded: By sanctifying.

Therefore, Pray carefully, Pray often, anywhere, spontaneously, briefly if you like, for even a split-second Soul Prayer is received in Heaven.

With all your heart and Soul, thank deeply, graciously, and humbly the Heaven Light, the Sacred Beings in the Light, and all of Heaven for the Blessing just bestowed upon your Soul.

Repeat this exercise 10 times before moving to the next one.

IDOLATRY

Have a care that your Soul Prayer does not slip from the Soul to the PseudoSoul of the mind, for the mind can only idolize, imagining a god of human proportions, with human requirements, profane human needs. God is not to be trifled with, not to be appeased by human means.

Your Soul, passing along the Path of Light, does not project or reference earth or materiality, but homes intuitively to Heaven, the Source of Heaven Light, expecting only the Truth of Heaven that will be revealed on Ascension.

Therefore Pray to God for your Soul, for all Souls, to change, to come closer to Heaven.

EXERCISE 43

HEART PURIFICATION

Remembrance in Spirit

Like a constant summer wind the directive Immanence of *Abba* blows descendant from Creation, borne on the rolling clouds of Heaven, the sanctifying Heaven Light, and the consummating Breath of Heaven, filling the universe and bearing upon every Soul.

Remembrance is your Soul's Opening, Receiving, Surrender, and Understanding of Heaven's Immanence—an instant, complete and direct Transmission from Abba, the perfect Understanding of Heaven's Will, Direction and wherewithal of Soul.

It is everything you need to know on earth.

> ***Remembrance:*** *The Soul's return to precarnate awareness, full awareness of life purpose.*

In Soul, before you came into body, you were filled with perfect Remembrance of the Will of Heaven, of what you are, what you must do, and how to go about it. It was Remembrance, in fact, that ignited your resolve to sanctify, compelling the Sacred Beings in the Light to incarnate your Soul.

You have learned Soul Prayer, the language of Spirit. You have learned to reach *Abba*, and thus you are ready to behold the Truth of truths. It is time to release your mind's illusions and Remember, once again, your purpose.

Ever since you have been on the Path of Light, you have received Heaven Light, but the trick to Heart Purification is receiving Light *completely*, and Sealing a new convenant with Heaven. In so doing your Soul will pass Remembrance into your body and mind, and in so doing your heart will purify, permanently.

Based on my experience, there are two ways to receive Remembrance. One is to die and spend a year or two in the Life-Between. The other way is to complete this exercise.

Goal: *To Remember and Seal in Soul a new covenant with Heaven.*

Preparation: *Go to bed.*

Steps:

1. *Before falling asleep place your hands on your heart, and using Abbreviation, invoke a Shower of Light (exercise 9), Mark your Soul to awaken in Vigil during the night.*

2. *When you awaken in Vigil, remain in Soul, not stirring the mind, not giving to thoughts. Feel, in Soul, the peace and safety of the infinite Clear Light, and invoke HeavenHome (exercise 4), using Abbreviation.*

3. *From over your head, from the Door Up, the eye of your Soul, feel the gentle Wind that blows softly against your Soul. Gently, allow your Soul to become curious of the Wind, and allow the Wind to enter into your Soul. Open your Soul to the Wind.*

4. *Begin Cosmic Wind Chimes (exercise 41). As your Plume forms, will with your Soul that the Wind continue to descend into you from the Door Up, from Heaven.*

5. *When you feel the Wind pass upstream your Plume (downward into your Soul), begin Soul Prayer (exercise 42). Notice how more powerful the Wind becomes when you connect with Abba. Know that the Wind is the Immanence of Abba.*

6. *In your heart, form wordlessly this prayer of Remembrance into a ball of Sacred Intent: Abba, Receive me, and fill me with your Truth. What is? What am I? What am I here for? What are we all here for? What are we to do? Release your Prayer into the Heaven Light Plume.*

7. *Receive, in a flash Abba's Answer, a blast of sacred affirmation passed through you in instant, consuming you, changing you, cleansing you.*

8. *Feel like never before the awe and purity of your Soul. Surrender unto the purity as the Heaven Light rushes to your Soul's sacred contact, for you have never known such Truth in all of your Soul's long existence. Behold wordlessly the quality of the Truth of truths, the perfect and whole essence passed in a divine instant through your Soul by the Immanence of Abba-in-Heaven.*

9. *Understand, not in word but in essence, the whole of what just occurred to your Soul. Hold the Truth received and Crescendo it, Sealing a wordless but permanent new covenant with Abba, that you are called to Heaven.*

As the Sacred Beings in the Light draw near you, and the witness eyes of Heaven dwell upon your Soul, understand:

> *Abba-in-Heaven calls unto your Soul, and every Soul, always.*
> *The essence of Soul is Heaven Light, we are One in Spirit,*
> *bound for Heaven.*
> *Because Abba calls your Soul you love and thirst for Heaven*
> *with all your being.*
> *Your desire for Heaven brought you to earth.*
> *Every moment of life you desire to sanctify with Heaven Light*
> *upon the earth.*
> *In the Heaven Light are all things known.*

Thus is the Truth of truths received.

Always your Soul will be filled with this knowing. As natural to your Soul as Marking, you Sealed a new covenant with Heaven by Receiving *Abba's* Immanence. You are becoming what you are not, you will never wander from the Path of Light, you are Heaven bound, and your heart will remain pure.

> *With all your heart and Soul, thank deeply, graciously, and humbly the Heaven Light, the Sacred Beings in the Light, and all of Heaven for the Blessing just bestowed upon your Soul.*

> *It is okay to continue on to the next Exercise even if you did not experience Remembrance with your Soul or Seal a covenant with God-in-Heaven. But every now and then, return to this exercise and continue to practice Heart Purification until you have entered freely into your covenant.*

> *Get good at Heart Purification. You will need it later.*

Come, look into the Heaven Light,
and find Answers in the Light.
Come, learn the language of Spirit.

EXERCISE 44

HEAVEN'S INSTRUMENT

Aligning unto Heaven's Will.

I am pleased to announce that Heaven is about to create a new Instrument of Light: You.

You have learned to Express the language of Spirit, you have pronounced unto Heaven your Ascendance, you have Expressed unto *Abba,* who immediately Answered you, your will to serve Heaven's Will, and you have received, in Remembrance, ultimate Truth, Heaven's Truth.

You are now capable of listening in Spirit, to render your Soul unto Heaven's Will.

Heaven's Will, also known as the Word, Logos and *Dharma,* is of spiritual nature, alive and vital. It cannot be laid into the pages of a book, but must be received directly in Soul from *Abba,* the Face of God-in-Heaven, proceeding perfectly, completely and constantly in the Immanence of Heaven, the Wind of Heaven, which passes descendant within the Clouds of Heaven and the Heaven Light.

One moment in the Wind and you will learn all there is to know. You will glean divinely the Direction of Soul. You will know the great freedom of the Truth of the way of Heaven, and the way into Heaven.

All there is to know.

The Wind of Heaven will blow upon and through your Soul when your Soul has opened the door of Ascendance. The door is you, and the way to open the door, to pass through the door, is by receiving and Surrendering unto the Will of Heaven.

Heaven's Instrument prepares you to open that door, so that your Soul can sense and receive Heaven's Will, and become and remain an Instrument of Heaven, every moment of your existence.

Did you notice when you Prayed from your Soul, when *Abba* Answered you immediately and perfectly, how *you* also changed?

Change, sanctification, is the miraculous Answer to Prayer. With each Prayer Heaven grooms your Soul for what you are to become.

Heaven's Instrument is a special Soul Prayer, the continuation of Integration into your True being, a new covenant of your Soul with Heaven that will set you free.

Come then, open the door and enter into the Sacred, where you have not yet been.

Goal: *To prepare your Soul to directly receive and facilitate the Will of Heaven.*

Preparation: *Lie in bed, in the dark of night, ready to fall asleep.*

Steps:

1. *Using Abbreviation, enter HeavenHome (exercise 4). Feel, passing like a loving Wind into you from the eye of your Soul, the sacred Immanence of Abba, the presence of Heaven just beyond, nearer than ever but just past your Soul's tracing.*

2. *Feel how the gentle Wind blows softly against your Soul. Gently, allow your Soul to become curious of the Wind, and allow the Wind to enter into your Soul, and pass through your Soul. Open your Soul to the Wind.*

3. *Keeping open to the Wind, begin Cosmic Wind Chimes (exercise 41, using Abbreviation) so that your Plume of Heaven Light travels up the Door Up to Heaven.*

4. *Using Abbreviation, begin Soul Prayer (exercise 42), and prepare, wordlessly, your Soul's first ball of Sacred Intent:* Abba, remove my obstacle, open the door, open my Soul to your Will. *Release your Prayer into the Plume. Notice immediately the quiver in your Soul, Heaven's cleansing Answer, and how more powerful the Wind becomes. Release the obstacle that just fell away, your door.*

5. *In awe, bathe your Soul in the perfect purity that passes through you, openly, innocently, receptively gleaning the nature and the Truth of the Wind, how it changes you, constantly, permanently, in ways yet to be discovered.*

6. *Prepare your second ball of Sacred Intent:* Abba, Receive my Surrender forever unto your Will. *Release your Prayer into the Plume, and receive a new Answer from Heaven—a stronger surge that undulates your Soul like a jellyfish on a wave. In awe grasp the new nature of your Soul within the Wind of Heaven.*

7. *Mark, with your Soul, the passing of Heaven's Wind into your Soul, and prepare your third ball of Sacred Intent:* Abba, Seal me forever unto your Will, until you Receive me into Heaven. ***Release your Prayer into the Plume and again feel the immediate affirmation blast from Heaven into your Soul. Understand wordlessly with your Soul the nature of the blast, the Sealing of your Soul forever unto the Will of Heaven, which will always pass through your Soul like a cleansing wind.***

8. ***As you have been Sealed by Heaven so you may Seal. Embrace your new covenant with Heaven, take a deep breath, and Seal back that which has been Sealed into you, thereby making your Soul an instrument of Heaven.***

Heaven's Instrument is the opening of your door, not your passing through. It is a continuation, not Crown, of your Soul's perfect freedom in Spirit, preparing you for the advanced exercise, Wind of Heaven, where you will learn to waft on Heaven's Immanence in complete service of Heaven's Will.

With all your heart and Soul, thank deeply, graciously, and humbly the Heaven Light, the Sacred Beings in the Light, and all of Heaven for the Blessing just bestowed upon your Soul.

Repeat this exercise 10 times before moving to the next one. Then practice Heaven's Instrument, using Abbreviation, once a day for another 50 days.

Get good at Heaven's Instrument. You will need it later.

All of Heaven's Instruments are Angel watched.

CREIGHT, THE GIFTS OF ASCENDANCE

Knowing and communication in Spirit are perfect, pure and complete, beyond word.

Yet when I drowned in 1962 and was set Ascendant on the Path of Light, the Heaven Light delivered into my Soul a special word, *Creight*, which means talents given to the embodied Soul, the ability to see into and work with Spirit.

Every Soul born on earth receives some Creight, for otherwise you would not be here. Your measure of Creight is your accumulative gifts of Ascendance over your Soul's long, long existence. Every moment of your existence leads you from what you were to what you are, and what you will become.

Some try to describe the merit of Creight in terms of **karma**, but vainly, for no anthropomorphic mind on earth can hope to frame the enormous, subtle and sacred root criteria the Spirit Universe applies to the gift of life.

All living beings have Creight to some magnitude, yet everyone's Creight is different. The many whose Souls lie dormant have such weak Creight they pass their lives away without noticing or cultivating their spiritual talents. They, trapped in the box of mind, are blind to Spirit, such that things spiritual seem imaginary, even hallucinatory. They frame reality intolerantly in terms of material religion and science, and they are quick to judge that which they know nothing of. Sadly, in overcompensation, they sometimes achieve positions of power and influence in science and religion to direct man blindly into the darkness of materiality.

But the Creight of those few Souls Ascending the Clear Light magnifies progressively, and to such extent that all things become possible.

Yet Creight is not an achievement, but a welcome gift of grace by Heaven to Souls Ascending toward the Firmament.

Fully understood only by they who are intent on sanctification, the gift of Creight provides the tools and knowing your Soul needs to enter Heaven.

The value of Creight is not so much how powerful you become in Spirit, but how you apply your gifts, how you use them to sanctify.

By now, as your Soul Ascends the Clear Light toward Heaven, you have noticed changes in your own Creight, new gifts of Spirit, psychic gifts.

Your gifts may be many or few, depending on the orientation of your Soul, and subtle or powerful, depending on your Soul's might. They may appear directed Heavenward or earthward, depending on how you manifest them. Your gifts are Heavenward if they manifest in sanctifying ways. If they manifest in any other way they are earthward, useless, even detrimental to your Soul, for they reinforce your attachment to materiality.

You have been given them only because your Soul is sanctifying, and they are granted solely to help your Soul sanctify. To use them for purposes other than sanctification is spiritually unnatural, and against the Will of Heaven. You must bear them responsibly and in accordance to the Heaven's Will. Otherwise your Soul will stall along the Path of Light, if not fall completely from the Path.

If your Creight expresses as *magical*—telepathic (receiving or sending thoughts or feelings), clairvoyant (knowing physical events far away), clairaudient (hearing voices of disembodied entities), materializing or psychokinetic (generating physical abundance), psychometric (knowing events from another time), precognitive (knowing what is going to happen), or the like—you are manifesting them profanely, earthward, in a spiritually materializing direction. You are tainting them with your mind, applying them with the ways of earth as ends, and you must convert them sacredly, sending them Heavenward, for on the Path of Light anything but straight to Heaven tumbles back to earth. Your mind may desire the psychic, but your Soul does not, for psychic is not sacred.

True gifts of Spirit are received in kind, in covenant with Heaven. You must receive them in the same Spirit they were given, in accordance to the Will of Heaven, the Sanctification Principle: For the sanctification of your Soul and other Souls. You must receive your manifestations of Heaven Light only in the service of sanctification of all Souls.

TRUE GIFTS

On the other hand, you may be expressing your gifts of Creight as intended, *miraculously*, sacredly, Heavenward, many in ways we have no words for. You may receive **Sacred Sight**, the embodied Soul's ability to recognize **Heaven's Mark** on Ascendant Souls—whose bright sphere radiates intensely in silver-white spires of Light in all directions.

You may begin to distinguish bright and Awakened Souls from small, dark, sleeping Souls.

You may acquire the ability to Slide into the Clear Light and behold other Souls fully, totally gleaning their complete and magnificent natures, and *Reading* what each Soul needs to sanctify further.

You may find that babies have begun staring at you, knowingly, smiling at you with certainty, grateful recognition, and power from the Light that grows within and around them.

You may start to identify every Soul you behold as exquisitely different—a thousand times more intricate than a face.

You may start to recognize the *Mark of Death*, a gray pall over the Soul of a person about to die, accompanied by an urge from your Soul to spontaneously perform The Dying service.

You may suddenly and intuitively glean your Soul's immediate direction to Heaven, and full understanding of what you need to get there.

You may receive in the Heaven Light, directly into your Soul, the Will of Heaven, which caresses your Soul like a warm summer breeze, and passes through you, filling you with the Remembrance in Spirit, directly from Heaven that Heaven calls unto you.

While channeling Heaven Light, occasional charges of Heaven's Breath may explode through you.

You may suddenly understand your own nature—what you are, what you came to do, and what you must do to go about it.

You may revive your Soul's memory, of birth, gestation, quickening, preincarnation, the Life-Between, and important events that touched your Soul long before.

You may be frequented with spontaneous visits by Sacred Beings in the Light, your Guardian Angels, or suddenly feel the Countenance of *Abba* upon you.

You may begin to glean, before your Soul and just past the Door Up, the Firmament of Heaven spread out before you, drawing you closer.

You may acquire the ability to compel Creation to manifest in the service of Heaven opportunities for others to sanctify, creating Miracles.

You may begin to hear constantly, in Soul, the thunderous silent *Divine Music*—the glory and jubilation of the millions-strong choir filling the Body of Heaven praising *Abba*, the Face of God-in-Heaven.

The highest of Heaven may open to your Soul, disclosing True prophecy of sacred Spirit—matters of Heaven inconceivable even unto Soul under Heaven.

Such are among the true gifts of Heaven. These gifts of Heaven only remain true when you apply them in the service of Heaven.

Just so, you can convert your earth-directed psychic manifestations into the sacred. It isn't difficult. Just bypass the mind, freeing your Soul from your mind, for only the mind spiritually materializes. Simply enter fully into your Soul and apply them toward Heaven.

Look into the Heaven Light and learn, in Soul, what you do not know, and become what you are not.

In the case of telepathy, strive to read the Soul rather than the mind, bathing the Soul in Heaven Light.

For clairvoyance and psychometry, look into Souls and glean what they need to sanctify.

For clairaudience, send Heaven Light toward the voices, for only earthbound entities cleave to human language.

For materializing and psychokinesis, receive more Light into your Soul so that you Ungrasp body and earth.

For precognition, apply your knowing to how change will affect other Souls' sanctification.

Do not celebrate your special gifts of Creight. They are not so much rewards as tools, your means for entering Heaven. Assimilate them with your Soul, using them only for the purpose of spiritual service and sanctification.

Before the earth, or man, or even Soul was, is and ever shall be the Heaven Light. Apply therefore your Soul in the service of the Light.

MANIFESTATION

Constantly in Spirit, from out of Creation high in Heaven, are all things made manifest, the *Alpha* and *Omega*—the birth of Soul and dross materiality, and the ultimate return destiny of Soul.

From There, Being beyond being, the Clouds of Heaven roll ever outward, past the Firmament, dropping descendant into the chasm gates to form the crust of universe—materiality, which hangs in the balance upon the infinite Clear Light.

Ever manifesting, ever expanding, ever collapsing. Materiality perishes, Soul returns to Creation. For an eon your Soul, and every other Soul, have stood witness.

Ascendant, your Soul pure in Spirit can influence the direction of Manifestation. Abiding in the Will of Heaven, Ascendant Soul can Manifest.

Thus I have waited until now, when you have come to love Heaven more than earth, to introduce *Manifestation*, your Soul's natural ability to compel Heaven to alter materiality. For in Ascending the Path of Light you have released your hunger for things of the earth.

Know this, if you would remain on the Path of Light and enter Heaven, never misdirect Manifestation for material abundance, or for any spiritual materialization, but Manifest only in accordance to the Will of Heaven, for the sanctification of Souls.

Heaven's superior army of Angels, the Sacred Beings in the Light, facilitate and defend Heaven's Will in Manifestation flawlessly.

Manifestation is not a HeavenWork exercise, but an acquired gift received through Heaven's grace as a Mark of your Soul's Ascendance. Having learned to contact Heaven with your Soul, Heaven is always near you, listening, Answering.

As long as you remain pure in Spirit, Heaven will facilitate your Soul's Expressions for the benefit of other Souls. Your door has opened, you are empowered, and you can Ascend through the Clear Light toward Heaven. Therefore Manifest only toward these sanctifying ends.

There are two ways of Manifestation. They both compel Creation, but the first and most accessible mechanism, the Heaven Light, is gentle and gradual. The second, the Breath of Heaven, is more elusive, but immediate and powerful, enough to part waters, pull back skies, and render matter dissolute.

If you have begun to notice things happening around you that seem to create opportunities for your spiritual growth, and for those you love, you are starting to Manifest with Heaven Light. Your Portal to Heaven is opening, and just beyond your knowing, your Soul has begun Expressing subtle balls of Sacred Intent Heavenward.

Your Soul Manifests by Expressing pure desire to sanctify unto Creation in the heart of Heaven. Heaven hears and attends your Soul, and Creation responds to your Soul's Expression.

The trick is to keep to things spiritual, compelling Creation at its sacred Source. Rather than visualizing with your mind the formation of material things or conditions or situations of the earth, instead, for now, Assign the Heaven Light with your Soul to form constellations of Light that nurture Soul. Thus is materiality moved calmly in the superior design and service of Spirit.

Only by sanctifying does your Soul Ascend. Only by Ascending does your Soul compel Creation. Thus is Manifestation kept sacred.

Sanctifying Heaven Light Manifestation prepares you for your advanced HeavenWork and your powerful Heaven Breath Transfiguration exercises.

For now know this, True Manifestation always Blesses the Soul, and never the body.

SOUL PRAYER MADE MANIFEST

Are you ready to Express a Prayer of Sanctifying Manifestation for the betterment of all Souls? Try Soul Prayer (exercise 42) again, using this ball of Sacred Intent: *May all Souls on earth Awaken, fill with Heaven Light, and Remembering, find their way along the Path of Light, the Direction of all Soul, to Heaven.*

Exercise 45

Light Dis-Illusion

Freeing your Soul from the minions of darkness.

The Path of Light is safe and full of Sacred Beings in the Light, and Souls intent on biding in the Will of Heaven.

And yet, far descendant of Heaven and close to the earth there are others—out-of-body entities trapped in illusion, bent on remaining material; they, able to render materiality just enough to frighten you, who cast a hellish shadow on earth existence, for their illusion exiles them from Heaven.

Yet rarely do they exact their powers on man. They don't need to, for most Souls lie asleep in life, imprisoned in illusion.

For eons our Souls have dwelt within their hell realm.

But now, your Soul Ascending on wings of Heaven Light beyond the reach of their power threatens their illusory being, and they will act, jealously, angrily.

They will not attack your Soul but your mind, usually by trying to frighten you so that your mind becomes dominant once again over your Soul, so that you Soul once again falls asleep, so that once again you are imprisoned in materiality, remaining exiled from Heaven.

They attack you only because if you continue your Ascent to Heaven they will have lost one more Soul to *Abba*. They attack you only now because soon you will bide beyond their grasp. This, they know is their last chance.

Being of Light, all you need do is push your Soul a little more Ascendant to pass beyond their realm forever.

Indeed, they have already lost your Soul.

Their attacks may be subtle or strong, depending on your Soul's power. They may manifest simply as shadows jumping out of you from the darkness, or footsteps following you. Or they may speak to you of worldly desires, trespassing into your thoughts, from just behind you. They may appear to befriend you or annihilate you. They will know intimate things about your life and mind. They may draw physical energy from your body. They may possess or even manifest a body to engage you. Even the earth may rise up in desperate anger to daunt you from the Path of Light, so that you might resort to hiding once again in the dark illusion of materiality.

But you need not be alarmed. Just remember this, your Soul in the Heaven Light is always safe from darkness and the minions of darkness, for they will not approach the Light. Thus as they shun the Light, you are well armed.

They are armed with illusion, darkness and spiritual materialization, you hold the Light of Heaven. To pass beyond their reach, do this.

Goal: *To instantly protect your Soul from illusory entities and pass beyond their power.*

Preparation: *Because attacks occur spontaneously, practice Light Dis-Illusion in advance.*

Steps:

1. *When you sense a dark entity suddenly around you, immediately, using Abbreviation, invoke a Shower of Light (exercise 9). Instinctively your Soul will open fully to receive a powerful inrush of Light.*

2. *Still Abbreviating, form with the powerful Light a Cocoon of Light around you (exercise 20).*

3. *Open your channel to the Sacred by practicing HeavenHome (exercise 4), using Abbreviation. Receive Abba's Immanence into your Soul, and fill with Compassion, for even this foul entity can know the Heaven Light.*

4. *Protected in the sanctifying Light, turn the eye of your Soul toward the entity to face it. With calm certainty and Compassion, look upon the entity. Your Soul cannot be harmed. Crescendo the Shower of Light within your Soul and send a Plume (exercise 34) of Heaven Light unto the entity.*

5. *Form this ball of Sacred Intent: Before Abba-in-Heaven you are known by the Heaven Light, for you to Remember that you, too, will ultimately find Heaven. Come, enter the sacred Light, or go from me now. Depending on how your Soul Reads the entity, you may choose only to banish it.*

6. *After you release the ball, Assigning the Heaven Light to carry your Sacred Intent unto the entity, build a Crescendo of Light more and more until the entity slinks away in shame into the darkness.*

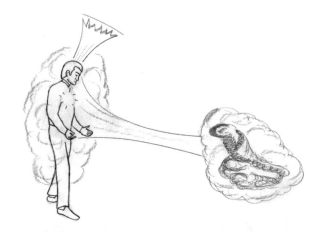

While it is unlikely your Blessing of Light sanctification will turn the entity towards the Path of Light, you *will* send it away, for those of darkness always shun the superior Light.

Everything on earth presents opportunities for your Soul, even entity attacks. They nurture your Compassion, a Mark of your Soul's Ascendance. And the shock from their sudden appearance empowers your Soul to surge further Ascendant, further along the Path of Light, to pass beyond illusion's realm forever.

With all your heart and Soul, thank deeply, graciously, and humbly the Heaven Light, the Sacred Beings in the Light, and all of Heaven for the Blessing just bestowed upon your Soul.

Practice this exercise 10 times before moving to the next one.

SAGE

There is one material protector from illusion that works every time. Man has used it for thousands of years to exorcise ghosts: Dried sage.

Affordable and available at most meditation stores, it might be handy to carry a piece of it with you at this point along the Path of Light. Should, for any reason, you start to buckle under an entity attack, simply light it, blow out the flame, and let it smoke, like incense.

Simply and aptly put, sage chokes illusory entities. Period. Use it as your safety net should the rattling windows unnerve you.

But don't come to rely on it, because you will not pass beyond illusion's realm. Instead, get good at Light Dis-Illusion.

Everything on earth is opportunity for your Soul's sanctification, especially when things don't seem that way. Illusory attacks are excellent opportunities to empower your Soul because they pose immediate challenges.

HELL

On earth there is much attention paid toward Hell. There doesn't need to be. Truly, they who harp on Hell dwell in part therein. The burning question in life is not what can you do to *not* go to Hell, but what you can do to get away from it. Heaven is the answer, the only answer.

The Soul becomes what it beholds. Therefore don't cleave to Hell, cleave to Heaven.

EXERCISE 46

CHAOS

Nurturing your Soul's natural Ascending response.

As human animals we like to measure experiences as desirable and undesirable, pleasurable and painful, good and bad. But to the Soul *all* of life experiences are desirable, no matter how the relating mind judges them.

Every experience in life is a new opportunity to sanctify.

So far you have practiced your HeavenWork at convenient times, sometimes in the company of those you prefer to be near. But you must master your HeavenWork all the time, for some important moments for your Soul come at you fast.

Now that your Soul is Ascending, you are equipped to handle things differently. Instead of defeating you, you can now apply the direst life experiences to challenge your Soul to surpass itself. Such is the nature of Chaos.

Chaos—when emergencies, tragic news, accidents, bad luck, or even sudden death are thrown at you—is an excellent opportunity *because* it comes inconveniently, when you least expect or want it.

Any cause of death can be auspicious to the Soul's migration if you remain undistracted.

In truth, every moment of your life borders chaos, though your mind would render you complaisant by insulating you in creature comfort. But borne in the gift of life no Soul under Heaven knows peace, only fervent desire for the Sacred, to enter the Sacred.

Every moment your Soul stands at the precipice, ahead of you the salvation of Heaven if only you could cross the abyss of materiality below pulling at your Soul. There is no hiding for the Awakened Soul.

Thus must all Souls learn Chaos, the way of handling chaos.

Chaos is not a way of escaping outside stresses, but entering into your true self, maintaining perfect presence without illusion, and not succumbing to, but thriving on the unexpected, even sanctifying.

Chaos is a simple exercise that restores your Soul's natural freedom from the mind's attachment to material events. It is the relaxation response of the Soul, of Remembrance, of the natural presence of your Soul in all of life's events. Instead of meeting chaotic events with the body and mind's boxed reactive panic, you simply slide into the perfect calm of your Soul's eternal perspective, and act in the service of your Soul's sanctification, in accordance to Heaven's Will.

Having Transcended and commenced Ascending along the Path of Light, your Soul has become constantly wakeful, constantly sanctifying, constantly passing toward Heaven. Chaos is the continuation of Constance, the affirmation that you are mastering your HeavenWork, a Mark indicating you are passing into Spirit.

Mastering Chaos means your Heavenwork is no longer scheduled, but constant, flowing, spontaneous, nurtured even by chaos.

You don't need to be awash in chaotic events to practice Chaos. Practice Chaos now and often, so that you can be ready whenever spiraling distractions happen.

Goal: *To immunize your Soul from all of life's distractions.*

Preparation: *Practice this brief Remembrance exercise anytime, anywhere.*

Steps:

1. *Using Abbreviation, enter Witness (exercise 16). Immediately feel your awareness drop from your head to your heart, your true being.*

2. *Abbreviating, enter Remembrance (exercise 43) and fill with Compassion.*

3. *Abbreviating, enter Heaven's Instrument (exercise 44) and fill with the promise to serve Heaven's Will.*

4. *Invoke a Shower of Light (exercise 9), using Abbreviation and become empowered to these ends.*

5. *Crescendo the Heaven Light and Seal it into your Soul with the Sacred Intent that whenever chaotic events occur you will instantly receive Light, Remembrance and direction from Heaven.*

Practice Chaos not just when bad things happen, but also in the face of desirable things, and even when nothing happens, for your Soul knows no fatigue in the Heaven Light, and every moment in life is an opportunity to sanctify your Soul.

Ascending Soul, you are prepared. Now nothing in life can enslave you. Witness all of life from the eye of your Soul in the Heaven Light, and continue your Ascent to Heaven.

With all your heart and Soul, thank deeply, graciously, and humbly the Heaven Light, the Sacred Beings in the Light, and all of Heaven for the Blessing just bestowed upon your Soul.

Repeat this exercise 10 times before moving to the next one.

HEAVENHOME EMPOWERED

Now that you have mastered Cosmic Wind Chimes, Soul Prayer, Heaven's Instrument, Light Dis-Illusion, and Chaos, go back to exercise 4, and practice HeavenHome again *not* using Abbreviation. See how strong your channel to Heaven has become!

You have learned to Invoke the Heaven Light, Express it from your Soul, and glean its sacred nature. Now you shall learn to enter the Light, wherein all things are possible.

Come.

TEN

ADVANCED SPIRITUAL EXERCISES

Consider for a moment how different your HeavenWork exercises have seemed so far. Some were easy, some more challenging, some simple, and some required several combinations of exercises you mastered earlier.

And yet no matter how hard you tried, your Soul in the Heaven Light performed each exercise without tiring. And you changed; you became more, your thirst for Light increased, and you became more intimate with the Light. Such is the nature of Soul in Spirit, wherein, with Soul fed by infinite stores of Heaven Light, all things can happen.

Now you will make things happen.

But you must be ready. So before continuing, go back again to the Table of Contents, and using Abbreviation, practice each of the 46 exercises you have learned. You have to master all of them before you can move on to the following 15 advanced Ascending exercises.

You will find these advanced exercises to be new in nature, for they have less to do with the ways of mind and earth, where you are leaving, and more with the ways of Spirit and Heaven, where you are coming.

CROSSOVER

How your Soul has changed along the Path of Light!

As your Soul continues to Ascend, as you approach the heart of Spirit that is Heaven, there comes a moment of great crossing, when you release the things of earth, the ways of earth, and your identity with them. They no longer pull you, they never will again.

Not only do you realize that you, Soul, are not of the same nature of a stone, or the soil, but neither are you of the animal body you dwell in, or the mind emanation of the body's brain.

You come to realize, not with the mind but with perfect knowing of Soul, that you are not of the earth, not of man, that you are a citizen of Spirit, bound irretrievably for Heaven.

This is realization of **Crossover**, the Crown of Integration, the great knowing typically achieved only at the moment of death. But unlike death, alive and with your Soul in body, you are able to do something one cannot do after death. You are able to Ascend to Heaven. You have found the way.

But Crossover is more. It is a breakthrough, a permanent change in being brought about by your Soul's actual *entering* into the Heaven Light for the first time, free Ascendance.

Crossover Ascendance—the essence of Jesus' declaration, "I am the Light of the world." Not things of the earth, not things human, not so much things even of Soul, but things of Heaven.

> **Crossover:** *Passing permanently from material illusion to Truth in Spirit. The release of attachment to earth and the human body, recognizing true citizenship in Spirit.*

Soul becomes what Soul beholds. By taking the Heaven Light into your life-empowered Soul, by reaching and opening to the Sacred, you have learned to enter the Sacred, you are compelling Heaven to open unto you.

There is no mistaking the moment of Crossover. If you haven't already experienced it, you soon will, for Crossover is the nature of your advanced spiritual HeavenWork exercises, and they will accelerate your Ascent through the Heaven Light.

There is no turning back. Why would you? Come then, and Crossover into Spirit.

EXERCISE 47

DISTANCING

Meeting in the Clear Light.

As you continue to Ascend you will come to perform things unimaginable to the mind but familiar to your sanctifying Soul.

The ways of the earth do not extend to Spirit. Materiality is indeed hard, but it is not durable. What I mean is, after you have died, and you are ejected once again into Spirit, what will materiality be to you? Gone, in a cloud of forgotten dust.

In death your Soul migrates through the Life-Between—Spirit one grade closer to the ultimate reality of Heaven. In the Heaven Light-swaddled Clear Light of the Life-Between, you learn many things of Spirit.

In the Life-Between, shed of the veil of embodiment, your Soul sees every other Soul purely, unobstructed, exquisitely, completely, recognizing each Soul as unique from all others—a perfect ball of crystal clear energy, durable, containing 10,000 tiny flecks of myriad colors that form a unique constellation disclosing that radiant Soul's most magnificent eternal being.

You also learn that time and space are not barriers. For example, if you will with your Soul to locate another Soul, you are instantly there, before that very Soul.

There, between the earth and Heaven, your Soul also surpasses the boundaries of materiality, for materiality is illusory, bending easily even unto the slightest touch of the Heaven Light.

The Life-Between lies in the Heaven Light-infused Clear Light, where your Soul can travel instantly and without obstruction. Because materiality hangs upon the Clear Light, Souls are incarnated throughout the world, throughout the universe wherever life can take hold.

Now you, Ascending embodied Soul, having learned to return to the Clear Light, can learn to pass your Soul instantly anywhere in the universe.

Yes, as you Ascend, even though you still dwell in body you can pass your Soul in the Light of Spirit through materiality. Now that you have entered the Heaven Light, you are ready. You have acquired the skills.

But you must always act to sanctify, in accordance to the Sanctification Principle. Otherwise you will lose these skills.

Passing your Soul into the Clear Light and entering materiality elsewhere—*Translocating*, or *Asterlisking*—is not a HeavenWork exercise because it does not sanctify.

But passing your Soul within the Heaven Light into the Clear Light to find an individual Soul for the purpose of Blessing that Soul *does* sanctify. This is Distancing, jumping your Soul out of materiality unto another Soul in the Clear Light, where all Souls have root.

When you Ascend, when you enter the Heaven Light, the more you sanctify other Souls the more your Soul sanctifies. Thus is Distancing an important HeavenWork exercise, your first leap into Spirit, so get good at it.

To Distance you will combine many of your HeavenWork exercises with a base mechanism that you will use for other advanced HeavenWork exercises: *Creating a* **Vortex** *within a channel of Heaven Light.*

> **Vortex:** *A spiral in the Heaven Light, capable of pulling, pushing, and Translocating things of Spirit.*

We will start small, with your hand. Soon you will learn to access the whole spiritual universe from the palm of your hand.

Sound difficult? It isn't really. Just do this:

Goal: *To Transcend materiality and Bless another Soul.*

Preparation: *Sit in a place where you won't be disturbed for five minutes, and think of the Soul you would like to Bless.*

Steps:

1. *Using Abbreviation, Quicken your hands (exercise 7) and invoke Light (exercise 6) into them.*

2. *Put your palms close together and for a moment practice LightBall (from exercise 7).*

3. *Hold your left hand 12" in front of your heart, in front of your Soul, with your palm up. Place your right hand, palm down, 3" over your left palm, and Bend Light (exercise 8) by creating a circular Light channel flowing from the Door Up into your heart, down your right arm, through your palm and into your receiving left palm, up your left arm and back through your Soul-in-heart. Thus you have established a perpetual circular Light channel.*

4. *Do you remember how naturally and easily you Marked Heaven with your Soul when you first practiced HeavenHome (exercise 4)? In the same way you will now Mark the Soul you wish to Bless. Don't think of the person's physical qualities with your mind, but feel within your heart, with your Soul, the pure and transparent qualities you love more deeply, that pull upon your Soul, qualities that lie beyond his or her body and mind. Feel the other Soul with your Soul. When your Soul shifts, subtly grasping the presence of the other Soul, bow your head, take a deep breath, and exhale, Marking that Soul. Feel in fullness the close presence of your Marked Soul. Do not release your Mark on the Soul until you have completed your Distancing.*

5. *Quickly circle your right palm counterclockwise over your left palm many times, forming a Vortex in the Heaven Light channel, so that the Heaven Light spins down into your left palm like a small tornado. Then, without breaking your Light channel, move your right hand back to a distance of 6" from your left palm.*

6. *Using Abbreviation, send a Plume of Heaven Light (exercise 34) from your Soul into your left palm so that it circles through you in the Heaven Light Vortex channel.*

7. *Form a wordless ball of Sacred Intent Blessing (exercise 35), and Assign the Heaven Light to carry your Soul unto your Marked Soul. Know that the omniscient Light already knows—has long known—what you are about to do.*

8. *Bring your hands close to your heart, and release your ball of Sacred Intent in this special way: Allow your Soul to leave your heart with the ball of Intent, and using Abbreviation, enter ThoughtGap (exercise 25) so that your Soul releases freely from your heart and passes safely through the Heaven Light Vortex into the Clear Light. Therein you will find your Marked Soul waiting for you.*

9. *When you behold the Soul, Express love and Compassion unto the Soul, and honor, for you are among the few of the earth who are about to learn to behold another Soul perfectly, without material obstruction.*

Continue to bask before the other Soul as the Soul receives your Heaven Light Blessing. When you are ready to return to body and mind, raise your hands together and blow between your palms and then clap them once.

And so you are learning, there are no walls, there is only here and now. We are all here and now, One in Spirit. Heaven is here and now. Nothing other is, and your Soul continues to Ascend.

Distancing, your first Advanced HeavenWork exercise, prepares you for many great works, so get good at it, for your next exercise requires its mastery. It is likely it will take 100 attempts before you can master its Abbreviation.

Practice it many times, seeking out many Souls, Remembering you need not ask permission to Express a Blessing of Heaven Light, for Light is the Truth of the world, and you are an Instrument of Heaven.

Distancing rapidly develops your Creight, your ability to see into Spirit, and work Spirit in ways not of the earth, but of Heaven. Once you have mastered Distancing, you may move on to your next exercise, Soul Disclosure, where you will learn how to know another Soul fully and completely, in perfect intimacy.

With all your heart and Soul, thank deeply, graciously, and humbly the Heaven Light, the Sacred Beings in the Light, and all of Heaven for the Blessing just bestowed upon your Soul.

Repeat this exercise 20 times before moving to the next one.

DISTANCING THE DYING

As your Soul Ascends, as you cultivate your Creight, you will receive the gift of Sacred Sight, including the ability to recognize the Mark of Death, the gray mask cast over the Soul of those about to die.

Now that you know how to Distance, you can Bless other Souls even when they are not physically nearby.

By blending Distancing with The Dying (exercise 40), you can join the Sacred Beings in the Light in facilitating the Will of Heaven by illuminating anyone's—everyone's—passage through death's door. With practice, you can learn to escort new discarnate Souls unto the Usher Angels, and ultimately, to the gate of Heaven.

ASTERLISKING

And so you have learned directly, the Clear Light lies within and beyond materiality, containing materiality. The inferior physics of materiality have very little effect on the Clear Light, and the Transcendent-Ascending Soul can learn to become independent of materiality's bounds.

Once grounded in the Clear Light, Soul does not have to return to the same place in materiality. Soul can also soar through the Clear Light and relocate, jumping Heaven Light throughout materiality, for example, jumping instantly from one mountain peak to another.

Just after I drowned the Heaven Light taught my Soul this ability to "Asterlisk." But I do not perform it because while it is not profane manifestation, it does nothing to sanctify the Soul, and is therefore not part of the HeavenWork.

The HeavenWork is for sanctification only. At best Asterlisking serves only as a magical distraction, a joy ride that can stall your progress along the Path of Light. Therefore, consider adapting this ability, if you develop it, into a more worthwhile HeavenWork Ascending exercise.

To enter the Heaven Light
form a counterclockwise Vortex within a channel of Light.

EXERCISE 48

SOUL DISCLOSURE

Perfect intimacy in a flash.

On earth we all know how to recognize one another—by the face, body shape, voice, touch, smell, fashion sense, personality, interaction patterns, and the like.

But there is a much deeper, truer way of knowing another being, a vastly intimate way of pure and perfect eternal knowing: Soul to Soul.

With your Soul wafting Ascendant toward Heaven along the Path of Light, with your Soul learning to *enter* the Heaven Light, your Creight has begun to flower, and you are gathering abilities never before imagined. You are now ready to look upon another Soul without obstruction, with perfect intimacy, with a depth and clarity the mind cannot frame.

You are ready to learn, or rather, *relearn* Soul Disclosure.

Do you Remember how it was *before* you entered body, the way things really were? Do you Remember how perfectly in Soul you beheld other Souls?

There, in the freedom in Spirit of the Life-Between, stripped naked from the forgotten veils of mind and body, you beheld other Souls perfectly, completely, each one of us an exquisite spherical radiance of transparent hope for Heaven, and when you approached another Soul, and looked within us, and you found in every one of us 10,000 tiny flecks—blemishes of impurity, flaws, imperfections marking our exile from Heaven.

Remember, there, in all that timelessness, one by one, the thousands of other Souls you Disclosed unto, and all you needed do was approach, engage and touch another Soul, and suddenly shunting forward, you would enter into the other Soul for just a moment!

Remember in that brief moment how the other Soul's 10,000 flecks surrounding you would suddenly break into vibrant colors of Spirit, and spin, dancing into an intricate constellation of disclosure, and in a flash your Soul would fill with a surge of complete understanding of that marvelous Soul's entire eternal life...

...And in that same instant, *your* Soul would also Express into the other Soul your own perfect disclosure of your long journey.

All of this occurred in one great flash, and once that sudden inrush-outrush occurred, you would both be gently withdrawn, shunted from the other's Soul, and there you would bask before each other, in grateful, blissful rapture from the perfect depth intimacy just exchanged, and you would honor that Soul.

Soul Disclosure—perfect open communication in a mutual flash transmission, made Soul to Soul time after time during your long wait for life in the Lightfields of the Life-Between.

Now in body, as your Creight flowers, it is natural for you to once again come to peer past the borrowed masks of mind and body and enter directly into other Souls, beholding each one in their true nature, magnificent and unique, every one.

Because you can Distance, Soul Disclosure is within your reach.

The Truth in Soul is that we are all One Spirit entering Heaven. Thus is the Direction of Soul under Heaven. The Spirit of Heaven Light is the pure essence of every Soul, untouched by the 10,000 flaws of Soul.

Thus is Soul Disclosure made possible to the embodied Soul. When you perform Soul Disclosure you release your Soul unto the Heaven Light, the Heaven Light carries you to within another Soul, and thus will you actualize and become that great Truth that we are all One in Spirit.

Come, and prepare for the most sublime intimacy between your Soul and another.

Goal: *To enter the Heaven Light and carry into another Soul.*

Preparation: *Sit across from someone you love, who is open to your entering her Soul.*

Steps:

1. *Gaze into the eyes of your partner. Relax deeply, recalling from all your HeavenWork experiences that your Soul is always safe in the Heaven Light. Trust, therefore, that only good will come from what your Soul is about to do, and allow your Soul's curiosity to grow in anticipation that once again you will be able to see another Soul perfectly, your partner's Soul.*

2. *Using Abbreviation, invoke a Shower of Light (exercise 9) into your Soul. As you continue to gaze you may see projections of other faces flit*

Transcendently just beyond her face. Do not direct your attention to these projections, as they are affected by your mind.

3. *Soon you will be naturally drawn down to your Soul, and you will slip down into your heart. You will shift from your body's eyes to the eye of your Soul. Your partner's eyes, face and body will mostly disappear as you Transcend in part so that your Soul intuitively gazes within her torso wherein her Soul bides. Notice how strongly your Soul wills to look upon your partner's Soul! Also know that even though her Soul is right there in front of you, you must still enter the Heaven Light Vortex into the Clear Light.*

4. *When you feel the shift to your Soul, place your hands on your heart and form this wordless ball of Sacred Intent: I love and honor this Soul, and desire with all my being to enter in her Soul, know her completely, and disclose unto her my own eternal truth. When I behold her Soul I will Surrender unto the Heaven Light.* **Continue to hold in your heart this ball of Sacred Intent throughout this exercise.**

5. *Perform all of Distancing (exercise 47) so that you bide in Soul in front of the most exquisite Soul across from you.*

6. *The rest is simple. Will with your Soul to approach her Soul so that your Souls touch.*

The rest will happen on its own, through the Oneness of the Heaven Light. The moment your Souls touch you will each slip forward into each other, and in that flash moment before you both separate, you will simultaneously know the perfect eternal rapport only two Souls can feel, and your true essence of Heaven Light.

If you did not find your Soul shunting into her Soul, it is most likely your Soul was reluctant to Surrender unto the Heaven Light, reluctant to leave your heart. This happens when the mind still overinfluences Soul. In such case, you still likely felt a subtle, Background pull toward her Soul.

This is good, for even though your Soul remains "grounded" in materiality, you are still reaching into the other Soul. Each time you practice Soul Disclosure your mind will loose its grip in the service of your Soul's growing trust in the Heaven Light.

The nature of your HeavenWork is changing. Your LightWork is becoming less and less of the way of earth and more the way of Spirit. You are learning to enter the Heaven Light.

The essence of Soul is the Heaven Light, and in the end of illusion, and the birth of Truth, only the essence of your Soul enters Heaven.

As such is the Path of Light, as such is the way to Heaven.

Entering the Heaven Light is one of the keys to Heaven. By mastering Soul Disclosure you receive your first key to the Kingdom of Heaven.

With all your heart and Soul, thank deeply, graciously, and humbly the Heaven Light, the Sacred Beings in the Light, and all of Heaven for the Blessing just bestowed upon your Soul.

Repeat this exercise 10 times before moving to the next one.

READING SOULS

What is the spiritual significance of a Soul's 10,000 flaws? They are the illusions in Soul that cleave to materiality rather than Heaven. They survive both the death of the body and the migration through the Life-Between, over and over again. Every Soul under Heaven is afflicted with such blemishes. They are not flaws imaginable by the mind, but spiritual flaws for which man has no catalogue.

You must be rid of them. They must be washed clean before a Soul can enter Heaven. You will wash clean your 10,000 flaws, gradually and all together, as you continue your advanced and Transfigurational HeavenWork exercises. And you will also help other Souls erase their own 10,000 flaws.

What does this have to do with Soul Disclosure? You don't need to enter into another Soul more than once to know that we are all One in Spirit, and that the way to Heaven is by entering into the Heaven Light.

Soul Disclosure is a preparatory exercise for entering the Heaven Light. Once you succeed your Creight flowers quickly, and you can apply your new gifts in accordance to the Will of Heaven, by helping other Souls to sanctify.

Here's where Abbreviation comes in. Abbreviation also works with Soul Disclosure. With practice your Creight will develop the gift of instantly *Reading* Souls—the ability to recognize a Soul's 10,000 blemishes and intuit what HeavenWork that Soul needs to do to sanctify.

Practice this shorthand form of Soul Disclosure and you will learn to Read every Soul you meet, and spontaneously Express unto them Blessings of Light Assigned with specific Sacred Intent that Awakens the receiver Soul to their sanctifying needs.

Reading Souls—pure vision—is a gift of Creight often mastered by gurus. Souls about to Transfigure into Heaven can spontaneously know every Soul they encounter with the magnitude of Soul Disclosure.

One more thing. Once you have mastered Soul Disclosure, you don't need someone else to tell you what *your* Soul needs to sanctify. In the Heaven Light, by entering the Heaven Light, you can read your own Soul, you can glean, not in arrogance but clarity, your own sanctifying needs.

Simply Invoke a Shower of Light (exercise 9) with Abbreviation, and you will know. You have trusted the Heaven Light and entered in. In Jesus' words, "your faith has cured you." In my words, your learning to enter the Heaven Light has given you sight in Spirit.

EXERCISE 49

STARBURST

Ka-boom!

Soul becomes what it beholds, and rapidly along the Path of Light. Enter therefore the Heaven Light and all things become possible.

Your Creight now flourishes in your growing Affinity with the Heaven Light. Obstacles disappear in the wake of new discoveries in Spirit. You are now becoming capable of learning your HeavenWork directly from the Heaven Light.

Thus far on the Path of Light you have relied on your Door Up to access the Heaven Light, and you have learned to Invoke it in powerful concentrations. The Heaven Light came unto you directly from Heaven.

Indeed, the narrow Door Up *is* the face and eye of your Soul. But there is more you can now know. You were taught to Invoke Light from the narrow opening of the Door Up because it was the easiest way to awaken that faculty of your Soul. Receiving Light from this narrow passageway made it easier to concentrate the Light and prepare your Soul for more powerfully sanctifying HeavenWork.

Know this, you can receive the Heaven Light from all directions. You can open the eye of your Soul to all directions!

While the Heaven Light Originates in Heaven, it also fills the universe and does not extinguish. Now that your Affinity for the Heaven Light has grown, your Soul has become empowered to invoke and work the Light in new, more powerfully sanctifying ways.

Starburst is such a way. Starburst is an intense Heaven Light-cleansing of your Soul's 10,000 flaws. In Starburst, your Soul's flaws begin to wash away. You purify, you become more like Heaven, and you Ascend.

Instead of invoking Light from above, you will completely open the eye of your Soul and receive the Light from all directions, with a power unlike ever before. What's more, because of your Affinity for the Light, you will Harness the Light within your Soul-in-heart until a critical mass is reached, and Assign the Heaven Light to explode back out in all directions with even greater power, like you are a sun of Heaven Light.

Seem like a lot for one exercise? It is. That's why you first need to prepare by Unfolding—completely opening the eye of your Soul.

UNFOLDING: OPENING THE EYE OF YOUR SOUL

Did you ever notice how sometimes a powerful Shower of Light widens your Door Up? It's because the eye of your Soul is flexible, like an eyelid, only more.

You can easily widen your Door Up so completely that your Soul's eye becomes global, allowing you to see into Spirit above, sideways, in front, in back, below and in all directions in between. Here's how.

1. *Lie down in bed, on your back, with the lights off. Lay your hands at your sides, palms down. When you reach a point of deep relaxation, invoke a gentle Shower of Light (exercise 9), using Abbreviation. Feel how the omniscient Heaven Light hardly stirs, and fills you like a mist.*

2. *Using Abbreviation, either Pop Out The Ball (exercise 13) or form a Cocoon (exercise 20) the size of your expanded Soul—a ball about 6' wide around your torso.*

3. *Observe with the eye of your Soul the boundary of your Door Up over your head.*

4. *Will with your Soul that your Door Up elongate, widening to make a 12"-wide crescent slit, like eyelids, over you. Peer with the eye of your Soul into the Clear Light extended over your Soul, and notice how easily and willingly your Soul's eye opened.*

5. *Will with your Soul that your Door Up opens, down your front and back over your head, so that half of your Soul can peer into the Clear Light.*

6. *Once you have become comfortable with and curious about your Soul's opening eye, will that your Door Up open, rolling back completely, so that your spherical Soul peers in all directions into the Clear Light. Notice how there is no longer up or down, that your Soul is free of any material gravitational pull.*

7. *Gently Crescendo the Heaven Light within your Soul and Mark your Soul's opened eye so that you can Abbreviate it anytime simply at will.*

8. *Remain calm and peaceful for five minutes, suspended in the Clear Light with the eye of your Soul completely open.*

There are two ways to experience Starburst—Transcended and grounded. If you Transcend, your Soul will be shaken, turbulently. But this is good because the Heaven Light's cleansing power is more effective, and no harm can come to your Soul. Your Soul will Ascend quicker.

But if you remain grounded in materiality, or return to mind immediately after Starburst begins, you will feel Starburst much gentler, as Backgrounding. Even Backgrounded, Starburst is a powerful sanctifier.

Now you're ready. Let's bathe your Soul.

Goal: *To wash away your Soul's 10,000 flaws.*

Preparation: *Lie down in bed at nighttime.*

Steps:

1. *Using Abbreviation, open the eye of your Soul completely. Feel how easily your Soul remains in its full size, surrounding your body.*

2. *Invoke Heaven Light from all directions. At first the Heaven Light will rush into your Soul from your Door Up, but the inrush of Light will spread, entering you wider from above, from your sides, from behind, and then from below, and you will become clearly aware that your Soul is Transcended, suspended in the Clear Light.*

3. *Form a Cocoon around your Soul so that no Light escapes your perfect sphere.*

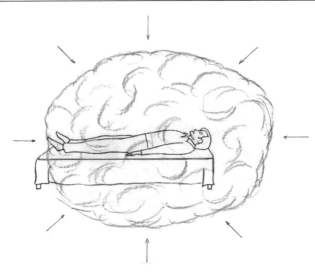

4. *Shrink your Cocoon down in size so that it surrounds your heart. When your Cocoon starts to feel like it is made of the hardest metal, you are ready to Harness the Light.*

5. *Begin to Harness the Light, as it enters the barrier of your Cocoon from all directions. Crescendo the Light continuously, not letting your Cocoon stretch. Notice how the Light within your Soul becomes denser, confined within your Cocoon, which becomes harder and harder the more the Light pushes against it. Continue to Crescendo the Light as it reaches critical mass.*

6. *Critical mass is reached when the Heaven Light begins to melt through your clenched Cocoon. When you feel this giving, Assign the Heaven Light to explode mightily throughout to the corners of the universe and to continue flowing into your Soul, as you shrink your Cocoon down to the size of a grain of sand.*

7. *As you shrink down your Cocoon, the omniscient Heaven Light will explode it away, blasting out in all directions in silvery-white needles of Light. As this happens, continue to receive Heaven Light from all directions, forming an inrush-outrush channel of Light to fuel your sustained Starburst.*

If you remain Transcendent the sustained explosion will rock your Soul like a rocket engine. If you cannot yet bear the unbridled sanctifying of your Soul you will innately ground, returning in part to your mind so that your Starburst is rendered Background.

Feel the naked experience of your Soul on fire in the Heaven Light. Glean the sacred nature of the fire and its cleansing effect on your Soul's blemishes. Allow the illusory flaws of your Soul, which have plagued you for an eternity, to melt away in the holy flame. And open to the sacred nature of the Light.

Cleanse in one lifetime that which took eons to scar your Soul, and come into the Light of Heaven.

Starburst—your most powerful sanctifier yet. Therefore learn to Abbreviate it completely. At first, Abbreviate each step:

Unfold

Cocoon

Shrink

Harness

Crescendo

Assign and Shrink

Explode and Sustain

Practice this Abbreviation sequence until it takes you only five seconds. Then, all you have to do to master this exercise is absorb into your Soul the word, "Starburst," and your Soul will explode into Light.

Such is the way of the Path of Light.

Starburst is a purifying HeavenWork exercise that gradually burns away your Soul's 10,000 flaws. Be creative with Starburst. Learn to Assign the exploding Heaven Light to Awaken and cleanse other Souls' illusions it passes through. Practice it often, for it prepares you for an even more powerful purifier—Nova.

With all your heart and Soul, thank deeply, graciously, and humbly the Heaven Light, the Sacred Beings in the Light, and all of Heaven for the Blessing just bestowed upon your Soul.

Repeat this exercise 10 times before moving to the next one.

EXERCISE 50

VORTEX

Lightwashing the feet.

Jesus didn't do things ritualistically; he didn't need to. All of his spiritual work he did with the Light and Breath of Heaven.

His Blessings were not of word, but Light. His healings were not of the hand, but Light and Breath. His words, still misunderstood by man, were not of things of earth, but Light. When he Prayed, he didn't use words; his Soul lofted Ascendant before *Abba*, where his transmissions were pure, direct and perfect.

When he anointed others' feet, he didn't do it symbolically with oil, water or tears, but with Light. He didn't Lightwash to clean feet, he Lightwashed to clean Soul.

This he did by pulling Heaven Light down from The Door Up in a pulling Vortex, drawing it down like drainwater through his Soul and to his feet. Once striking the ground, the Light would shoot out along the ground in a sheet of icy, brilliantly clear, sanctifying Light, accompanied by thrilling shock waves of icy Light that would emanate from his Soul into the Souls of those close by. The Light would then Seal into all things nearby—the body and Soul, and air—and remain for a long time.

With Soul Disclosure you used a small pushing Vortex within a narrow channel of Heaven Light to enter the Light and translocate your Soul unto another Soul.

Now you will use a large *pulling* Vortex within a wide channel of Heaven Light to Assign the Light to render space sacred—not for the sake of spiritual materializing, but to Bless Souls that enter within your Vortex Lightwash.

Lightwashing feet is thus Lightwashing Souls on earth.

Thy Will be done on earth as it is in Heaven.

Now you, too, are ready to Lightwash.

Goal: *To Seal a space with Heaven Light.*

Preparation: *At first, practice alone, where you will not be disturbed.*

Steps:

1. *Vortex can only be performed when you are moved by your Soul; it cannot be invoked without Sacred Intent. Therefore do not begin this exercise until you are moved from your heart.*

2. *With your Soul, Mark the space around you that you wish to Lightwash, and invoke a Shower of Light (exercise 9).*

3. *Place your right hand on your heart. Harness the Light such that the Light travels into your right palm and up your right arm.*

4. *Open your Door Up (exercise 30) and notice how the Heaven Light descends with greater power since you have mastered Starburst. Gaze up, with the eye of your Soul, into the Door Up.*

5. *Raise your right hand up over your head so that your palm touches your Door Up. Will with your Soul that more Heaven Light pass into your palm and through your arm.*

6. *When you feel a surge of Light enter your palm, you have connected to the Light. Slowly begin to circle your hand clockwise along the diameter of your Door Up, continuing to pull in more and more Heaven Light. Continue slowly stirring the Light until all of the descending Light responds to your palm's pull. You are ready to form your Vortex.*

7. *Accelerate your hand's stirring movement, and shrink slightly the size of the circle your palm makes each time around. Lower your hand slightly every turn. By the time your hand reaches your shoulder level, the Heaven Light will follow your hand, forming a Vortex, much like bathwater going down the drain.*

8. *You must now do several things all at the same time, and quickly: 1) Form a ball of Sacred Intent in your Soul to Awaken Souls to the Heaven Light in accordance to the Will of Heaven; 2) Assign the omniscient Heaven Light to follow your palm's direction, to splash upon the ground and spread out in a sheet and explode globally from the point it first strikes earth; 3) Assign the Heaven Light the distance to spread and how long to remain; and 4) Loudly hiss "Shhhhhhh!" to instantly attenuate your mind's interference as you quickly lower your right palm toward the ground, until your arm is outstretched toward your feet.*

9. *At the moment your arm stops straight, instantly release the Heaven Light Vortex from your palm, allowing it to strike the ground in accordance to your Assignment.*

As you hiss you will feel the Light Vortex avalanche through your Soul and into the ground. You will witness in Soul as the Light splashes onto the ground, seizing your feet in icy Light and rippling out quickly in a flat circle in all directions and stopping at the rim of your defining.

Walls of icy Light will immediately emanate out of your Soul in a sphere, like shock waves.

Performed correctly, the intensity of Lightwashing will be nearly as turbulent to nearby grounded Souls as Backgrounded Starburst is to your Transcended Soul. The effect is unmistakable, and your Soul can read its power, as can Souls receiving the Lightwash.

When you have practiced Vortex successfully, try it with some friends standing at different places nearby. Without first telling them what to expect, ask each afterwards what it felt like to them.

With Vortex you can bring Light unto the earth in accordance to the Sanctification Principle, and leave it there for other Souls to find and resonate. Vortex prepares you for the important sacred HeavenWork exercise, Sealing.

> *With all your heart and Soul, thank deeply, graciously, and humbly the Heaven Light, the Sacred Beings in the Light, and all of Heaven for the Blessing just bestowed upon your Soul.*

INTO HEART AND SOUL

After you learn to master LightWash, try this variation: Instead of splashing Heaven Light onto the floor, bend it when it reaches your heart, and guide it with your hand straight into another's Soul.

ABBREVIATING

After mastering Vortex, learn to Abbreviate it, performing it in entirety in five seconds, without using your hands, without hissing—simply by willing with your Soul alone.

Repeat this exercise 10 times before moving to the next one.

To pull the Heaven Light
form a clockwise Vortex within a channel of Light.

EXERCISE 51

VOLCANO

The ring of fire.

As you purified your heart, so must your body be made pure.

Your body is a thing of the earth, profane and unable to pass beyond materiality, and thus it corrupts. But your Soul continues to Ascend, and as you near the Firmament of Heaven, there comes a time when your body must adjust so that your Soul doesn't leave it.

Volcano occurs at this time to prevent it from happening.

So unexpectedly does Volcano come on that you would swear its cause came from *outside* your being. In a way this is true.

Volcano will occur to you one time, and likely when you least expect it. And though your Soul immediately recognizes what is happening, and engages in it, Volcano originates in the omniscient Heaven Light, which knows you are ready.

You will experience Volcano when your Soul Crossovers fully into the Sacred, when your Soul Ascends so far from materiality that your profane body would drop lifeless unless it is Sealed with Heaven Light.

Volcano is the omniscient Heaven Light's transformation, a permanent stitching of Sealed Light into the fabric of your material body. Volcano does not make your body sacred, but protects your body for the rest of its natural life, capacitating it to continue to house your sanctifying Soul.

In this way Volcano changes your body into the temple of your Soul.

"Gentle" and "pleasant" are not words that describe Volcano, and Volcano is anything but pleasant. But it must happen.

Volcano will strike without warning, like a medical crisis, when all your body systems go amok, like a quick and severe attack of diabetic ketoacidosis. Truly you would swear you are about to burst spontaneously into flames!

"The burn up" is a much better description, for it begins as a burn in your toes, that slowly spreads up your body in a burning ring for 15 minutes, changing every cell of your body, every molecule, ending only when it has passed through the top of your scalp, all the while moving up in a fiery burn, just like an erupting volcano.

You will feel like your body is dying.

But it isn't. And when it is all over, your body will be changed, permanently, and your Soul will know it. Every Ascending Soul must undergo Volcano to keep the body alive as your Soul completes its final purification under Heaven.

Volcano is an Initiation of Soul.

Volcano is a HeavenWork exercise because there are things your Soul can do to make the best of this changeover.

When Volcano occurs your Soul will not be in control, but can intensify while the Heaven Light tends to your body so that your body becomes a custom-fit temple for your Soul as you Ascend to the Firmament.

Goal: *To change your body into the temple of your Soul.*

Preparation: *Volcano is spontaneous, so be mindful, alert and ready for its sudden strike.*

Steps:

1. *The pain in your toes will be unmistakable, spreading quickly to your feet and ankles. At first you will suspect the cause to be physical, like your feet have fallen asleep, but as the burning pain continues up your legs your Soul will suddenly come to recognize what is taking place. The burn does not leave but remains throughout your body throughout Volcano only to fade completely the moment it spreads up to your scalp.*

2. *First, know that the pain will not harm you in the least, and will last for only 15 minutes, so do not worry about your health. Acknowledge in your Soul that the pain is Sacred in origin. Place your hands upon your heart and ride the pain occurring to your body in the same way you Entered Soul (exercise 5). Remain grounded in your body the entire time the burn spreads throughout your body. Riding the pain will not help you escape your pain, but assist the Heaven Light in conforming your body to your Soul. The pain is brief but the rewards lifelong. Therefore embrace the pain.*

3. *Do not be alarmed when the burn moves up to your abdomen, as your vertebrae each seem to separate and regenerate, as your intestines move and as your internal organs each twist. The Heaven Light never harm body.*

4. *As the burn moves up to your heart, the chamber of your Soul, Crescendo the burn to form a perfect and powerful altar seat for your Soul.*

5. *Continue your Crescendo, and when the burn at lasts closes over the top of your scalp, bravely Transflex (exercise 26) the pain completely, and the burn will pass from your body.*

6. *As a result of your Transflexion, you will find you have entered the Clear Light unlike ever before, for you to Express your Truth in Soul as your Soul sees fit. Likely you will innately enter Cosmic Wind Chimes or Soul Prayer, sending your Sacred Intent to align your Soul unto the Will of Heaven.*

Bask in the unbridled Joy and freedom of the Clear Light as long as your Soul wills. You have just received your first Ascendence Initiation, and Heaven's Countenance rests upon you.

Receive your Soul's Direction purely within the Heaven Light streaming out of the highest Heaven into your Soul.

Know that with Volcano your Soul has been permanently received into Spirit. Your path to Heaven's Firmament is short. After Volcano, should you die unexpectedly, your Soul will migrate quickly through the Life-Between to be reborn (alas, probably not wealthy or good looking, but) into a life auspicious for your sanctification.

Death has lost its power over you.

With all your heart and Soul, thank deeply, graciously, and humbly the Heaven Light, the Sacred Beings in the Light, and all of Heaven for the Blessing just bestowed upon your Soul.

Memorize this exercise and move to the next one.

EXERCISE 52

ANGEL CALL

Touching the Divine Messengers.

There are two levels of Angels who touch man—those who bide eternally under Heaven and those who Originate from within Heaven.

Those under Heaven, who we on earth normally think of as Angels, are the Sacred Beings in the Light, and our contact with them is commonplace.

Those from within Heaven are the Angels of the Diadem, and their contact with us is rare.

We recognize the presence of the Sacred Beings in the Light as Compassionate, holy, beloved, reuniting, understanding, extending, patient, consoling, nurturing, guiding, conscientious, alerting, rescuing—they who reach unto us in ways we can understand with heart, mind and Soul. These are our Guardian Angels, our Family Angels, and the Angels of the Life-Between.

These are the Angels who intervene in life's trials.

But the Angels of the Diadem are nothing of the earth, nothing of man, nothing even of Soul under Heaven. Direct Messengers, Perfect and Divine, they descend unto man only by command of *Abba*, the Face of God-in-Heaven.

Indeed, they are spontaneously created by *Abba*, beyond Soul's comprehension.

Rarely do the Diadem Angels make themselves known. And yet, over my Soul's 28-year watch of Heaven, 175,000 times I have witnessed them stream out of the Diadem, pass out of the Firmament, and drop descendant through the chasm gates to manifest the moment of their need, and then return to Insubstantiate into the Diadem—each time with exceeding perfection.

Like *Abba*, they are Being beyond being. So different are these Angels that if you would Call them, you must Call them differently.

When you do Call an Angel, whether Family or Diadem, never do it frivolously or vainly, for you will not be Answered, and you may be rendered a while into Dark Night. Therefore Call only when your heart is pure, when you are in true need, or when you desire only the sacrifice of your Soul in the service of Heaven.

SACRED BEINGS IN THE LIGHT

They are always with you. They always were, they always will be. It's just that you don't Remember how to see them.

But your HeavenWork is changing that.

Angel Call doesn't so much invoke the presence of your Guardian Angels (the Sacred Beings charged to you) as it trains your Soul to see them.

For they are already here.

Please take a moment to reach out with your Soul and embrace your Guardian Angels who have just approached you, for now, just as your Soul considers them, they extend their omniscient Compassion and love unto you.

There, where they always are, on either side of you, between your shoulders and your Door Up. Feel how joyfully compliant they move to your heart when your Soul wills to embrace them.

See how easy it is?

Calling Angels is HeavenWork, and HeavenWork always directs your Soul unto Heaven, and never invokes Heaven unto earth. Thus it is Angel Call does not compel your Guardian Angels to come unto the earth, but elevates your Soul unto the Guardian Angels.

Come, open your heart with love and gratitude, and meet your Angels.

Goal: *To behold your kindred Angels.*

Preparation: *Awaken from sleep in the middle of the night, in Vigil.*

Steps:

1. *In Vigil, begin the practice of Cosmic Wind Chimes (exercise 41): Stretch your Soul's intuition throughout the infinite reaches of the Clear Light, and invoke HeavenHome (exercise 4) with Abbreviation. Feel how quickly your Soul Marks upon Heaven. In the Immanence of Heaven, open the eye of your Soul by practicing The Door Up (exercise 30).*

2. *Peer with the eye of your Soul up through your Door Up, at the Heaven Light that permeates the black of night like a fog. Peer into the gray blending as it grows whiter in gentle wisps of Heaven Light.*

3. *Wordlessly, humbly, form a ball of Sacred Intent within your Soul: I wish to see into Spirit, and behold the Sacred Beings within, my Family Angels who tend my Soul.*

4. *Keeping your Sacred Intent within your Soul, continue to gaze with the eye of your Soul up through your Door Up, openly, intuitively, receptively, to whatever Light form that emerges before you.*

There is no instruction for when your old, old friends in Spirit appear. Their arrival is a great time of immediate learning, and only your Soul knows how to recognize and receive them, and how to receive *from* them. How in Compassion they honor you, who rightfully honors them.

Each time they make themselves known to you, and the awe they engender, will be like the first.

Joyously they behold you as they reveal themselves in beauteous splendor, Expressing an almost human configuration of Light to help you trace upon them—eyes, sometimes even a face. But recognize them not for what they aren't, but for what they are, their true essence—the Heaven Light—so you will grow your Spirit Sight.

Learn from your Angels the ways of Spirit.

Angel Call carries your Soul Ascendant on the Light wings of your Family Angels. Let them take you. Surrender unto them, who will only to carry you to Heaven.

If they don't at first reveal themselves to you, do not be discouraged. In truth, your Family Angels may not come every time. They may not reveal themselves at all. But they are always there, here and now, and they understand you better than you understand yourself.

Practice Angel Call. If you don't see them at first, keep at it. Angel Call is a leap Ascendant, and once you have connected to your Angels they will bear your Soul unto the Firmament.

Now that you have met them, do not name them, do not think of them with your mind, do not anthropomorphize them at all with the ways of earth. But know them with your Soul—intuitively—by the report of purity their presence sends through your Soul.

ANGELS OF THE DIADEM

Angels of the Diadem are beyond human understanding, for they Express directly and perfectly from *Abba*, the Face of God-in-Heaven, and they serve the cause of Heaven.

The Angel of the Annunciation was such an Angel.

Your Soul cannot Call upon these Angels, they call upon you.

Soaring through the Body of Heaven like a meteor, passing through the Firmament and dropping descendant to the world of man, a Diadem Angel hoves, from nowhere, on the earth, and peers into your Soul.

And your Soul is made naked and silent before them.

Materiality vaporizes around the Angel, who manifests a shell of sacred substantiation, human-like, harder than stone metal, quick as light, and the power to slice the universe in two.

In a flash, sacred Understanding, Disclosure and Direction straight from *Abba* fills your Soul.

And your Soul desires to touch the Angel, and be touched by the Angel.

Instantly the Angel parts, and you are changed forever.

Would you like to call an Angel of the Diadem?

Be careful how you answer, for if you would, know that your Soul will be blasted, and altered in a way that you will never again be of the earth.

Diadem Angel visits are rare, the ultimate Blessing, and their presence will hed you of worldly things.

Few are they on earth worthy of a visit by an Angel of the Diadem. In fact, unless your Soul has Ascended enough to clearly see the Firmament of Heaven, t is unlikely a Diadem Angel will appear to you.

Yet every Soul on the Path of Light should strive to Call upon them, for heir presence sanctifies the Soul with lightning bolt power.

The only way to petition an Diadem Angel visit is through sacrifice of our Soul in the service of Heaven. Know, if you are visited, that you *will* be Commanded by Heaven, and you will lose worldliness. But you will come loser unto Heaven.

Goal: *To offer your Soul unto an Angel of the Diadem.*

Preparation: *Sit alone, where you will not be disturbed.*

Steps:

- *To commence Diadem Angel Call your Soul must exceedingly and truly desire to render a service of sacrifice unto the Will of Heaven. If your*

Soul owns such Intent, allow yourself to fill with love and gratitude for what you are about to offer up.

2. *Perform Starburst (exercise 49), using Abbreviation.*

3. *Continuing Starburst, practice Cosmic Wind Chimes (exercise 41): Enter the Clear Light of Vigil, stretch throughout the infinite reaches of the Clear Light, and invoke HeavenHome (exercise 4) using Abbreviation.*

4. *Open the eye of your Soul by practicing The Door Up (exercise 30), and peer with your Soul up through your Door Up.*

5. *Send a Plume of Heaven Light (exercise 34) up your Door Up, Marked for Heaven.*

6. *Abbreviating with your Soul, stir a counterclockwise Vortex above you, at your Door Up, so that your Vortex travels up your Plume channel to Heaven.*

7. *Wordlessly, form within your Soul a ball of Sacred Intent: Abba, if I am worthy, sacrifice my Soul in the service of your Will.*

8. *Freely and willingly release your Sacred Intent into your Vortex.*

9. *Once your Sacred Intent is taken up toward Heaven, reverse your Vortex with your Soul, stirring clockwise so that the Plume of Heaven Light reverses and flows down from Heaven, down through your Door Up, and into your Soul.*

10. *Remain there, still, receptive, in perfect awe and obedient attendance.*

Remember, there is no Calling an Angel of the Diadem. If your Soul is worthy, Heaven will compel you to practice Diadem Angel Call, and you will be called upon by such an Angel.

If a Diadem Angel should appear unto you, and if you should act on your Soul's desire to touch it, your arm will be rendered numb, and stuck to the Angel, as if you touched a stone with a powerful electric charge, for its shell of substantiation is superior to materiality.

The Angel will vanish instantly in an upward flash, and you will be changed for all eternity. You will be Blessed for all eternity, and the eyes of Heaven will remain upon you until you enter In.

With all your heart and Soul, thank deeply, graciously, and humbly the Heaven Light, the Sacred Beings in the Light, and all of Heaven for the Blessing just bestowed upon your Soul.

Get good at Angel Call. You will need it later.

To call an Angel from the Diadem
form a counterclockwise Vortex within a channel of Light
through the Door Up and release a ball of Sacred Intent.
Once sent, reverse the Vortex, directing it unto your Soul.

EJECTING, INJECTING

Ejecting means pushing Light away from your Soul either into another Soul or Ascendant, Heavenward. You accomplish Ejecting by forming a counterclockwise Vortex of Heaven Light with your Soul. Injecting means pulling Light descendant, into your Soul. You accomplish Injecting by forming a clockwise Vortex of Light with your Soul. Think of Ejecting as pushing, and Injecting as pulling.

TRANSMISSIONS

You have always received them, Transmissions from the Sacred.

In your mind you may not have known, but all your life your Soul has received *Transmissions* in Spirit, divine Wisdom from Heaven and from they who serve Heaven.

You have received them for eons, for the life of your Soul. But just like the rest of us, you forgot how to receive them when you were born in this short earth life.

As your Soul Ascends closer to Heaven you will Remember how to receive Transmissions clearly with your Soul.

Transmissions, pure sanctification Wisdom, conveyed instantly, perfectly, beyond word or thought or any artificial symbol, pass through the Heaven Light into your Soul like sunlight through a cloud and reveal the way to Heaven.

Such is the way the *Dharma*, the Word of God, is passed into the Soul, the only way. Divine knowing cannot be laid out into the profane symbol of word or tongue, or even mind at its most abstract.

The Heaven Light is rife with Transmissions. They originate from Heaven, the Diadem Angels, the Sacred Beings in the Light, and from high-Ascending Souls.

Many have mastered the HeavenWork and deposited immense Transmissions in the Heaven Light to be delivered to specific Souls at specific times, or when an individual Ascending Soul came upon them while exploring the Heaven Light.

Always borne in the Heaven Light, Transmissions may come in many ways—from one Ascendant or Ascending being into your Soul, groups of special Souls, or every Soul, now, later, once, or perpetually.

Transmissions may be stored anywhere, for the Heaven Light permeates all things spiritual and material. They may be found in trees, stones, bodies of water or air, on a patch of earth, and in envelopes of Heaven Light between the Clear Light and Heaven.

Ascending Soul, you can learn to find them, and receive them, just as many of them will find you at your time.

Transmissions arrive suddenly, like a blast of Clear Light through your Soul, instantly transferring an enormous reservoir of sanctification Wisdom.

Truly, the spiritual expression behind every word in this book and every book I will ever write was received in a single flash Transmission from *Abba* into my Soul at 2:10 pm on October 9, 1979.

With every Transmission there is full Understanding in Soul—of the Wisdom, where it came from, what it is to be used for, and how to implement it. Perfect.

As your Ascending Soul nears Heaven you will receive more and more Transmissions, most notably through *Initiations*—when materiality rolls back to reveal supreme Spirit unto your Soul.

Now on the Path of Light, prepare your Soul to receive Transmissions, for simply by opening your Soul to them you are made ready to receive them.

Before your HeavenWork is done you will also learn to send them unto other Souls by Assigning and Sealing them into the Heaven Light.

Transmission: Immediate, perfect and direct infusion of Sacred Understanding into a Soul.

EXERCISE 53

SITTING ON TUFTED PALM

Dwelling among the Sacred Beings in the Light.

Never before, in or out of life, has your Soul been free to waft Ascendant through the region of Spirit between the Clear Light and Heaven—the very Clouds of Spirit that carry forth from Heaven's Firmament, the Clouds in which the Light of Jesus comes.

To find Heaven you must learn to abide therein, in the nether region of Heaven, to learn in Soul for the first time the ways of sacred Spirit. Such is the holiest ground under Heaven, the purest of meditation, the calm way of washing clean away the flaws of your Soul.

There, here and now, within and beyond the Clear Light, swaddled in Heaven Light, your Soul-in-Spirit, free from earth, body and mind, True, ever purifying, may sit on a Cloud of tufted Light, observing in perfect receptivity the ways of Spirit and awaiting the sacred presence of your Family Angels, who will come and bide with you from time to time.

Sitting on Tufted Palm is the continuation of Cosmic Wind Chimes. In Wind Chimes you declared your Ascension to the Sacred Beings. On Tufted Palm you join them.

Sitting On Tufted Palm—the achievement of Transcendence and Ascendance, the Crown of Entering ThoughtGaps, the ultimate of meditation.

Ultimate meditation—full being in your true home under Heaven.

Soul becomes what Soul beholds. Come therefore, enter Ascendant and behold what lies in store.

Goal: *To extend into the Clouds of Heaven.*

Preparation: *Find someplace quiet, where you will not be disturbed.*

Steps:

1. *Enter HeavenHome (exercise 4), using Abbreviation, and feel the Immanence of Heaven blow down upon your Soul like a warm summer wind, passing through your Soul with pure knowing.*

2. *Engage and peer through your Door Up, the eye of your Soul, into the nether gray, which grows clearer, into white Heaven Light. How quickly*

the white rises from the gray, how easily your Soul sees into the Light, for your Affinity for Heaven Light grows.

3. *With Abbreviation, Invoke a Shower of Light and send through your Door Up a Plume of Heaven Light (exercise 34), Assigning it to reach unto the Firmament of Heaven.*

4. *Immediately your Soul will tremble in Answer when your Plume has reached the Firmament. Stir with your Soul a rising counterclockwise Vortex around your heart, and direct it upward, through your Door Up, so that the coil of the Vortex travels up the Plume toward Heaven.*

5. *Wordlessly in your Soul form a ball of Sacred Intent:* I desire only to come near to Heaven, into the Clouds of Heaven, to know Truth, to grow in the ways of Spirit.

6. *Prepare your Assignment of Heaven Light to carry your Soul Ascendant into the Clouds of Heaven, and using Abbreviation, enter a ThoughGap (exercise 25) while releasing your ball of Sacred Intent into the upward Vortex channel. This is Safe Surrender unto the Heaven Light. This is a new experience of the Soul. Trust the Spirit Universe. No harm can come to your Soul, only salvation. Therefore as the Vortex begins to pull your Soul from your heart, go with it freely, and you will be safely released.*

7. *As your Soul is pulled into the Vortex, you will briefly lose awareness. In only a moment you will find yourself in pure Soul, awakening slowly, gently, into a state of sublime being like having been washed up in welcome surrender onto a soft, safe beach by a loving ocean of Light. The sand of the beach you rest on is a wing of Light, holding you like a tufted palm in the Clouds of Heaven.*

8. *Once your Soul assembles into clear awareness, draw the Heaven Light from all around you into a gentle Cocoon (exercise 20), clothing you in swaddling robes of Light, and bide openly within the awe-engendering sacred sky, gleaning the essential properties of Spirit that well into your Soul. Observe all things in Spirit that pass your way, into you and around you, and wait for the wonderful Light Beings to come and instill within you auspicious Transmissions and Blessings.*

Safe Surrender: *Entering the Heaven Light for a limited time.*

Bide On Tufted Palm often, in the awe, peace and insight the Clouds of Heaven render unto your Soul, for you abide in grace as complete as any Soul can reach under Heaven.

Every moment On Tufted Palm you cleanse away your Soul's flaws, preparing you for your Ascension unto the Firmament. Even briefly, even with Abbreviation is your Soul cleansed. In time, Sitting On Tufted Palm will compel Heaven to draw your Soul Elect before the Firmament.

Soul becomes what Soul beholds. Therefore enter the Clouds of Heaven, behold the essence of the Heaven Light, become the nature of sacred Spirit, for this is the way that leads to the gate of Heaven.

With all your heart and Soul, thank deeply, graciously, and humbly the Heaven Light, the Sacred Beings in the Light, and all of Heaven for the Blessing just bestowed upon your Soul.

Repeat this exercise 20 times before moving to the next one, And continue to practice it, however briefly, every day until you enter Heaven.

HIGHER TANTRA

Transflexing orgasm.

Where there is love, Compassion lies just beyond. And where there is Compassion, there is the Heaven Light, and all the power of Heaven.

Indeed, making love is powerful, even rapturous if taken in full. Because we are so drawn to the physical pleasure of orgasm, we often miss the spiritual delights—the intimacy of Soul Disclosure approached within the spiraling ribbons of Heaven Light, and the divine witness of the Sacred Beings in the Light who flow within and around us during and after sexual frenzy.

Have you come to notice lately, in Soul, your Guardian Angels and kindred Sacred Beings in the Light draw near each time you make love, to witness, Mark and Seal your future destinies, and most sacredly the destiny of the Soul of the babe you may bear?

I tell you this, no matter how minute a mortal act, the Sacred Beings in the Light—they, who peer into your Soul and know you completely—see instantly and in absolute clarity its consequences a thousand years from now, do not doubt it. With such perfection is set the machinery of the Spirit Universe.

Perhaps that is why lovemaking somehow grips us so. Perhaps that is why we place at the forefront of our religions restrictions on sexual conduct. Clearly sex satisfies most fully only under conditions of true love, responsibility, trust, devotion, and commitment. Yet lovemaking should not be performed under a cloud of restriction, but with an affirmative and joyous freedom known only in the Clear Light.

Lovemaking is vital to the incarnation of Soul, for pregnancy is the gate of incarnation, and the hope of man hinges upon Souls sanctifying in materiality. If man should fail, Soul will go elsewhere. Thus it is with Creation.

Granted, physical sex alone is naturally enjoyable, but sex while your empowered Soul is Awake, Transcendent and Ascending is sublime, and most auspicious when both Souls are present and flowing in accordance with the Will of Heaven. Should you achieve pregnancy in this sublime state, you provide a wonderful opportunity for the Sacred Beings to marry a most magnificent and deserving Soul into the womb.

Thus Heaven provides a way of converting the act of lovemaking into sanctification: Higher Tantra. Higher Tantra uses Heaven Light to convert human love into its divine essence, Compassion. Specifically, lovemaking provides a great challenge to your Soul to Transflex powerful sexual energy to direct tremendous purifying surges of Heaven Light through your Soul.

For our purposes, the Sanskrit word, Tantra, means spiritualizing sex. Though learning Higher Tantra involves sex, it is *above* sex. Once mastered, with Abbreviation you can practice Higher Tantra without even having sex.

Higher Tantra involves Transflexing your orgasm just before it happens. Instead of reaching physical orgasm, your Higher Tantra exercises will teach you to Crescendo enormous concentrations of Heaven Light to transform your rising orgasmic tide into purifying explosions of Soul, which springboards your Soul Ascendant.

Thus is Higher Tantra performed in only seconds, by riding the rising tide just before orgasm, invoking your HeavenWork, and Transflexing the last moment before reaching orgasm. If you think physical orgasm is great, just wait and see what Higher Tantra does to your Soul!

But if you feel uneasy about Higher Tantra, or if you prefer to practice alone, you do not need to touch your partner, provided you are okay with self-stimulation. If you are uneasy with self-stimulation, or not involved in a relationship suitable for Higher Tantra, you may skip the next four exercises and move on to The Divine Column.

EXERCISE 54

BOND

Partners in Spirit.

Never in Spirit are you alone. And never do you come closer to other, kindred Souls than when you travel the Path of Light, for the Heaven Light magnifies the Soul. Recognizing in each other the same divine essence, thus so are Awakened Souls drawn together.

Thus does the Path of Light Ascendant blaze bright with a million Souls on fire divine.

And now, with Higher Tantra, you can draw closer to another, special Soul, your life partner, your partner in Spirit.

Bond is the gentlest Higher Tantra sanctifier, and a preparation for the other three. Simply by adding Shower of Light and Plume to your lovemaking—and Transflexing just before the moment of orgasm—you and your partner can form an enduring bond of Heaven Light to bridge your Souls.

Bond makes you **Partners in Spirit**—a very special spiritual connection. Bond, the continuation of Soul Disclosure, gradually prepares you to enter your partner's Soul fully during lovemaking—perfect sharing, the most complete intimacy two people can attain under Heaven.

Bond is for partners who want no walls between them.

Before practicing Bond you must first reach basic sexual compatibility with your partner. Both of you should be able to attain orgasm during sex, and reach orgasm at about the same time.

In Bond, as you both become sexually aroused invoke a Shower of Light, which you continue throughout your lovemaking. During copulation, using Abbreviation, you must then both send a Plume of Heaven Light into each other's Souls, which you Crescendo until you begin to orgasm.

The last step is a little trickier, for you must Transflex all of your Crescendoed sexual tension in the early moments of orgasm—the brief window of time *after* your orgasm begins but *before* you reach climax. The early moments of orgasm feels like a fast rising tide that pitches your body into climax.

But your physical orgasm will not occur because it has Transflexed into a sublime sparkling Joy—superior to orgasm—and formed into a Compassionate bridge of Heaven Light Bonding the two of you!

Goal: *To align your sanctification with your partner Soul.*

Preparation: *Just be in the mood.*

Steps:

1. *Honor each other as you begin your normal lovemaking. Look into your partner's eyes, understand and be grateful for what is about to pass, caress, hug, kiss, and tend to your partner's sensual needs that will gradually lead to simultaneous orgasm.*

2. *As things begin to heat up, as you both slide into passion, invoke a Shower of Light (exercise 9), using Abbreviation. Feel how the Light brings patience to your Soul, and a light dimension to your passion. Invite the Light to swirl within and around your Soul, and blend with the same Light passing into you from your partner's Soul.*

3. *When you are ready for final copulation, join face to face. Male sits and female sits upon him. As you begin to copulate, invoke Plumes of Light (exercise 34) with Abbreviation, sending strong cannons of Heaven Light into each other's Souls. Feel how strongly your partner's Plume bathes your Soul in Joy, which spills into every cell of your body.*

4. *Gradually Crescendo your Plumes, in timing with your approaching orgasms. Notice how your Soul can Read your partner's approach to orgasm—so deeply in Soul and Spirit is lovemaking felt. Continue to Crescendo your Plumes until after orgasm begins, at the moment of Transflexion.*

5. *The Heaven Light, Plume and Crescendo will help you calibrate simultaneous orgasm. When you begin to feel your partner's tide begin to rise, so will your orgasm begin. At that moment, bow your head unto your partner's head so that your Door Up intersects your partner's. You are going to allow your orgasm to begin, but Transflex it just before climaxing. As your orgasm rises, quickly gather all of your sexual tension, take a deep breath and Transflex the stress, sending it forward through your Plume and into your partner's Soul.*

Instantly your orgasmic rise will cease, replaced by the familiar icy sheet of Transflexion that originates as a strong tingling in your loins. The tingling will instantly rise up your spine, pass through your heart and fly out in an enormous surge of Heaven Light into your joined Plumes, and you will be filled with a clean and infinite Clear Light joy that lingers on.

You will glean, in Soul, that you and your partner have just popped mildly Ascendant, just beyond the Cloud of Clear Light but not Ascendant enough to see the Clouds of Heaven pass through you. In the freedom of Transflexed Ascendance your Soul will feel, and see, the Bond of Heaven Light between you, fusing your Souls in Spirit.

Linger in Soul, the two of you, enjoying the newly strengthened tie between you. Thoughtlessly, wordlessly, understand in Soul what just occurred, and what continues to occur.

Remember, in Soul, your Bond. Nurture your newfound intimacy, for your Souls have just become engaged in the other's sanctification, the other's entry into Heaven.

Such are Bonds that last a lifetime, and even longer.

With all your heart and Soul, thank deeply, graciously, and humbly the Heaven Light, the Sacred Beings in the Light, and all of Heaven for the Blessing just bestowed upon your Soul.

Repeat this exercise 10 times before moving to the next one.

MARRIAGE IN SPIRIT

If you are married, if you wish to marry, if you intend to spend the rest of your lives together, you may use Bond to perform a *Marriage in Spirit* simply by adding Sacred Intent to your Plume. No commitment unto another runs deeper.

Do not enter Spiritual Marriage lightly, for Bond outlasts any laws of earth. Spiritual Marriage is truly a wedding vow made witness by Heaven, and it will be empowered and enforced by the Heaven Light.

If you and your partner agree to pledge your lives together as partners in Spirit, form your balls of Sacred Intent just as you each first form your Plume, Crescendo your Intent just as you Crescendo your Plume, then release your Sacred Intent into your Plume just before you Transflex.

In so doing, you will pledge your Soul mutually unto your partner's. In so doing are your Souls Sealed unto the other in the Countenance of Heaven. Such is the nature of mating Soul.

EXERCISE 55

PEARL

Sealing unto the Clouds of Heaven.

Tremendous and far-reaching is the force of Higher Tantra. Like a catapult, Pearl pushes your Soul far Ascendant, to well within the nether Clouds of Heaven, and keeps you there, Sealing your Soul there home.

Pearl is your first Higher Tantra exercise of Ascendance, the continuation of Sitting On Tufted Palm. When mastered, Abbreviating Pearl can Ascend your Soul to near Heaven's Firmament in a flash.

There, in the holy space where the Sacred Beings dwell, your Soul rises strong and clear, and spreads blissfully and freely in Compassion within a sphere of opalescent Light—a pearl of Heaven Light.

Unlike bond, you can perform Pearl even if your partner in Spirit doesn't. Or, if you prefer, you can both Ascend to the Clouds of Heaven.

Pearl is achieved by Transflexing Cocoon and Tufted Palm just before climax.

Goal: *To Seal your Soul unto the Clouds of Heaven.*

Preparation: *Just be in the mood.*

Steps:

1. *Begin your normal lovemaking, just as in Bond. If your partner is also practicing Pearl, you must time your orgasm cadence accordingly. If you alone are practicing Pearl, then pace yourself with your own orgasm. As things begin to heat up, as you both slide into passion, Invoke a Shower of Light (exercise 9), using Abbreviation. Feel how the Light brings patience to your Soul, and a light dimension to your passion. Invite the Light to swirl within and around your Soul, and blend with the same Light passing into you from your partner's Soul.*

2. *Just as the Heaven Light bathes your Soul, form a tight Cocoon, a sphere about 3' around your Soul, using Abbreviation. Feel with your Soul how the omniscient Heaven Light already knows what lies in store.*

3. *You may begin your final copulation in any position. As you begin to copulate, use Abbreviation to Sit On Tufted Palm (exercise 53). It is okay even if you do not profoundly translocate Ascendant, but intuitively*

sense your Soul resting in the sky of sacred Light, for you are Marking the Clouds of Heaven for your Transflexion.

4. *As your copulation accelerates, as your sexual stress accumulates, Crescendo your tight Cocoon in timing with your approaching orgasm. Continue to Crescendo until after orgasm begins, at the moment of Transflexion.*

5. *When the window of opportunity arrives, just after your orgasm begins, take a deep breath, bow your head, and Transflex your sexual energy and Cocoon completely, keeping your explosion within your tight Cocoon.*

Instantly you will find your Soul translocated to far within the Clouds of Heaven, and you will feel Heaven's sacred presence close by. No longer does your Soul rest on a wing of tufted Light, but with your presence in Soul so acute and clear, you find you are securely buoyed in the sacred sky by the Ascending power of your Pearl—the sphere of Heaven Light uplifting your Soul.

Feel how within your Pearl your Soul Receives of the sacred sky.

Pearl plants your Soul near Heaven's Firmament, weans you of the ways of earth, prepares you for the ways of Heaven, and makes worthy your Soul.

Pearl extends the reach of your Soul unto Heaven. The more you bide in Pearl, the closer you come to Heaven, so practice Pearl often, *in coitus* and by Abbreviating, for the rest of your life.

With all your heart and Soul, thank deeply, graciously, and humbly the Heaven Light, the Sacred Beings in the Light, and all of Heaven for the Blessing just bestowed upon your Soul.]

Repeat this exercise 10 times before moving to the next one.

EXERCISE 56

PILLAR

Preparing the Divine Column.

As Soul sanctifies, so Soul Ascends. All your existence, in and out of life, Heaven has been here and now—spread out in front of you, just beyond the vision of your Soul.

But that is changing. Soon you will rise before the Firmament of Heaven, and glean all you need to know and do, directly from Heaven.

All your HeavenWork has brought you to where you are now. Ever since you first Marked Heaven with HeavenHome your Soul has continued to travel carefully, gradually toward the Firmament. All you now need is to leap in Soul from your body and earth to the ground of sacred Spirit before Heaven.

Pillar makes it safe for your Soul to take that leap, but it takes some sacred fireworks!

You can use the power of Higher Tantra to form a sacred channel—a Pillar—that permanently connects your Soul to Heaven by cleansing your Door Up, removing all obstacles that keep your Soul from the Firmament.

While the Higher Tantra exercises Bond and Pearl brought a sublime peace to your Soul, Pillar sends a exhilarating Plume of turbulent Light skyrocketing up your Soul, continuing Ascendant from your Door Up like a searchlight straight toward Heaven, clearing the way for your Soul's Ascent.

You make this happen by surrounding your Soul with Dancing Light and Assigning the Light to reach Heaven while Transflexing your sexual stress just before orgasm's climax. This causes a skyrocket of Dancing Light to Plume from your loins up your spine and up through your Door Up, where it breaks Ascendant into a Pillar of pure Heaven Light that never leaves.

Goal: *To form a permanent channel of Light between your Soul and Heaven.*

Preparation: *Just be in the mood, and put the lights down low.*

Steps:

1. *Unlike Bond and Pearl, Pillar is an individual experience of Soul. Thus there is no advantage to your partner practicing Pillar at the same time. Begin your normal lovemaking, just as in Pearl. Throughout Pillar continue to enjoy the pleasurable feeling in your genitals.*

2. *During copulation, close your eyes and fill the room with Dancing Light (exercise 19), using Abbreviation. Open your Soul and invite tremendous surges of Heaven Light to fill the room. When you feel the Light Dancing turbulently around, open your eyes to confirm the Light has manifested visible.*

3. *Continue to Crescendo the Dancing Light throughout Pillar, just as you continue to Crescendo your sexual energy.*

4. *Form wordlessly, purely in your Soul this ball of Sacred Intent:* May the explosion of Dancing Light carry all the way to Heaven.

5. *Just before orgasm, open your Door Up (exercise 30), using Abbreviation, and look up with the eye of your Soul.*

6. *Just as orgasm begins, while continuing to look up through your Door Up, Harness all the Dancing Light with your Soul and concentrate it into your loins.*

7. *Just before your orgasm climaxes, take a deep breath, bow your head, and Transflex all your sexual stress and Dancing Light, and at the same time, release your Sacred Intent into the concentration of Dancing Light in your loins, Assigning it to carry it to Heaven.*

Transflexed, your body is permeated with a skyrocket of fast-rising Dancing Light that shoots up from your tailbone, up your spine, and bursts through the crown of your head and changes instantly into an upward column of purest Light.

Feel how the Dancing Light pushes your Soul Ascendant, dropping body and earth. Peer with the eye of your Soul up your Door Up, through your new Pillar that continues up over your head for a hundred feet, like a searchlight penetrating night's darkness.

In peace, observe in Soul your kindred Sacred Beings appear, one by one, within your Pillar. See how they each send down Compassionate Blessings of Light unto you.

Congratulations, you have just opened your channel to Heaven—a channel that will never close. Feel how easily your Soul draws up your Pillar, like smoke up a chimney flue—that Heaven, your destiny, lies at the other end, and all you need do is freely Ascend therein.

With all your heart and Soul, thank deeply, graciously, and humbly the Heaven Light, the Sacred Beings in the Light, and all of Heaven for the Blessing just bestowed upon your Soul.

Achieve one successful Pillar before moving to the next exercise.

THE PRAYER PILLAR

You have just performed a very important HeavenWork. You have just opened your direct and unobstructed channel with Heaven. You have formed your Prayer Pillar.

Learn therefore to perform Pillar with Abbreviation, adding Soul Prayer, for all your righteous Prayer will carry powerfully to Heaven, and more than affirmations, Heaven's Answers will begin to come manifest.

As you Ascend closer to Heaven, your Soul gleans in the sacred space only to Pray in accordance to the Will of Heaven. Truly every great act Jesus performed was made under that very condition—that it meet with Heaven's Will—for all Ascendant Souls are Instruments of Heaven.

THE CROWN OF ABBREVIATION

The Path of Light nurtures your Soul's natural tendency to Abbreviate all of your HeavenWork exercises. Constantly you discover in Soul your preference to work the Heaven Light less and less with your body and mind, but purely and simply with your Soul alone.

Thus empowered is your Soul in the Heaven Light.

No longer do you require your hands to push, pull and bend the Light. No longer do you require your body's breathing to Crescendo and Transflex. No longer do you need your mind to send Light out into other Souls and through the Spirit Universe.

All these things you simply do upon your Soul's command, all from within the heart. Such an achievement—the Crown of Abbreviation—signals your Soul's growing mastery of the HeavenWork, your Soul's ability to purify and Ascend unobstructed beyond the Clear Light to before Heaven.

EXERCISE 57

NOVA

Holy fire.

Only a Soul made pure can Ascend unto the Firmament of Heaven and enter the Elevation of Transfiguration.

Only a Soul set on holy fire can be made pure. On holy fire, the 10,000 flaws of your Soul are annihilated before Heaven, and your impurities are washed clean.

If you would be made pure, enter Pearl during sex, Starburst, then add a spark of **Heaven Breath**, and you have Nova—your Soul set on holy fire.

Thus made worthy is your Soul to complete its Ascent to the Firmament, for Nova leaps your Soul Ascendant.

Thus is Nova your most powerful advanced spiritual exercise.

The Breath of Heaven, Heaven's power to cleanse, only touches Souls who approach the Firmament, only Souls made worthy.

The Heaven Breath comes naturally to Souls Ascending.

You may have already felt it, unmistakable, while practicing your HeavenWork, a sudden wall—a tall wave—flash instantly from one side and smash into your Soul, sending an electrical charge through you so powerfully that your arms and legs lurch out uncontrollably.

And one second later all is calm again, as if nothing happened. And yet your Soul is changed.

As such are early visits of the Breath of Heaven.

The Breath of Heaven serves one purpose: To Transfigure worthy Soul— Soul Elect— into Heaven. Thus once your Soul has been graced by the Heaven Breath, your HeavenWork enters its last and ultimate Elevation.

Only Souls who have risen near full Ascendant unto the Firmament can compel the Breath of Heaven, which lofts beyond the reach of Soul profane.

As you master your advanced HeavenWork and your Soul's purification accelerates, your Soul learns to Ascend your Pillar close to the Firmament, the Heaven Breath makes itself known unto your Soul, and you can begin to call upon the Breath of Heaven.

So powerfully Ascending is Higher Tantra that pure Soul can compel the Heaven Breath to ignite and explode the Heaven Light and set the Soul on holy fire—Nova—annihilating every last flaw, making it worthy of Heaven.

Nova, the continuation of Starburst, accelerates your purification.

Thus when you cleanse your Soul with holy fire, Heaven draws your Soul unto the Firmament.

Every Soul on earth can call the Heaven Light, but only Souls made pure receive the Heaven Breath, which comes from out the Body of Heaven with the Clouds of Heaven.

Therefore should you not at first strike Starburst with the Heaven Breath to set your Soul on holy fire, do not be discouraged. The Heaven Breath will ignite your Soul when the time is right, when Heaven acknowledges your worthiness, for Heaven makes no mistakes.

Until it happens, keep at it. Practice Nova once a week until you succeed. It's only a matter of time and HeavenWork.

Goal: *To set your Soul on sacred fire.*

Preparation: *Just be in the mood.*

Steps:

1. *Like Pillar, Nova is an individual experience of Soul. Thus there is no advantage to your partner's practicing Nova at the same time. Begin your normal lovemaking, just as in Pearl.*

2. *During copulation, enter Pearl (exercise 55), using Abbreviation. Feel the sacred Immanence of Heaven's Firmament so near, and its holy Clouds that pass through your Soul. Feel how your Soul tingles in Joy.*

3. *Remaining Ascendant, Starburst (exercise 49) using Abbreviation (unfold, Cocoon, shrink, harness, Crescendo, Assign and shrink, and explode and sustain). Feel the Heaven Light explode out your Soul, not just descendant, but also Ascendant, into the Firmament of Heaven. Feel with your Soul as the Firmament receives the Heaven Light from your Soul. Feel the nature of what is happening. Continue Starburst until the time of orgasm.*

4. *Shortly before beginning to orgasm, wordlessly, humbly form a ball of Sacred Intent in your Soul: If it is Heaven's Will, may the Breath of Heaven strike my Soul on sacred fire.*

5. *As orgasm begins its rise, gather your sexual stress and Crescendo your Sacred Intent. Just before climaxing, take a deep breath, bow your head, and Transflex while releasing your Sacred Intent into the Heaven Light that penetrates the Firmament, Assigning it to compel the Heaven Breath.*

If the Heaven Breath strikes into your Soul you will know instantly and directly through the Heaven Breath to "Surrender and Receive." The power of the Heaven Breath will strike into you, igniting like a lantern the Starburst Heaven Light streaming through your Soul, setting your Soul on holy fire.

There is no mistaking Nova, for the holy fire you have just set within your Soul will not quell until you have purified, and your Soul Elect is Received into Heaven.

Nova cleanses your Soul like no other advanced spiritual exercise, but it takes time to annihilate an eon of accumulated flaws. Therefore practice Nova throughout the rest of your life.

With all your heart and Soul, thank deeply, graciously, and humbly the Heaven Light, the Sacred Beings in the Light, and all of Heaven for the Blessing just bestowed upon your Soul.

Repeat this exercise 10 times before moving to the next one.

If you do not succeed, move on to the next exercise but continue to practice Nova once a week until you do.

ABBREVIATION

As much as our animal bodies like sex, once you have mastered your Higher Tantra exercises you can move on, Abbreviating the exercises without the use of physical sex. You don't have to, but if you're anything like me you will prefer to trade orgasm for Higher Tantric Transflexion.

Unlike the mind in body, Soul is tireless in the Heaven Light. You can Abbreviate Higher Tantra 100 times for every time it takes to perform it with sex, and *that* speeds your Ascent along.

Auspicious Quickening

And yet sex is for reproducing, for bringing a worthy Soul unto the earth.

The more your Soul Ascends, the stronger your spiritual overtones become when making love. Master Higher Tantra, Ascend while lovemaking, practice any or all of your Heaven-reaching HeavenWork exercises—such as Heart Purification, Heaven's Instrument, Cosmic Wind Chimes—and Transflex while ejaculating, and the Sacred Beings in the Light will Select your Souls, and the womb between you, as home for a very special, auspicious Soul for you to show the way on earth to Heaven.

The Sacred Beings *are* there, every time.

Behold, Heaven!

As your Soul purifies in the Heaven Light, as your Soul Elect Ascends unto the Firmament, the Heaven Breath prepares your Soul's Transfiguration. So it was, is and ever shall be on the Path of Light.

Whereupon the Firmament of Heaven comes into Soul's view—and the Body of Heaven, the one vast nebula of sacred Clouds rolling out from the Source on high—holy ground, passing out the Firmament, extending past the descending chasm gates, to touch your Soul.

More and more you will know the Heaven Breath, which surrounds your Soul, Engulfs your Soul, and presses in, filling you with divine Knowing, perfect Direction and Understanding of your Soul's redemption before Heaven.

EXERCISE 58

THE DIVINE COLUMN

Blessing Heaven.

Are you ready to reach *into* Heaven?

To know Heaven, to form a direct and active relationship with Heaven, you must first learn the ways of Heaven.

One such way is divine Blessing, Praise. Heaven Blesses every Soul with the gift of Heaven Light, just as you have learned to do. Such is Heaven's way.

Bless, therefore, *Abba*, God-in-Heaven with the Heaven Light, for in so doing is Heaven's Will done on earth, just as it is in Heaven.

Divine Blessing—Praise, the Blessing of utter devotion and gratitude. Thus is the language of Spirit: Bless Heaven with the Light of Heaven.

You have acquired the skills—Dancing Light, Bending Light, Harnessing, Pillar, Plume. Put them together in this way.

Goal: *To extend your gratitude and devotion into Heaven.*

Preparation: *Best to first practice just before bedtime in a spacious room, the lights turned low.*

Steps:

1. *Select one corner of your room as your tabernacle, where you will manifest your Divine Column. The Divine Column is a movement exercise, so clear away any furniture in the corner and make a passage 10' in the room leading to the corner where you can walk back and forth to your tabernacle.*

2. *When you are ready, Mark the tabernacle corner with your Soul, floor-to-ceiling, so that you will remain aware of its location even though you will not be looking at the physical space. Stand at the tabernacle and gaze up at the ceiling near the corner. Looking through the eye of your Soul, notice that the patch of ceiling is located near your Door Up.*

3. *Close your eyes, take a deep breath, and fill your room with Dancing Light (exercise 19) using Abbreviation. Keep your eyes closed until you feel the Dancing Light has become manifest.*

4. *Open your eyes and look up at the ceiling. When you see the Light Dancing across the ceiling, turn and walk down your path with your*

arms extended and palms forward, feeling your Soul pass through the Dancing Light. When you reach the end, form a ball of Sacred Intent in your Soul: Utter devotion and gratitude to Heaven! *Turn and walk back to your tabernacle, Crescendoing your Sacred Intent along the way. When you reach your tabernacle, release your Sacred Intent there, Assigning the Dancing Light to carry into Heaven. Repeat this step five times, Crescendoing the Dancing Light more and more each time. Notice how each time you reach your tabernacle your Sacred Intent grows stronger. The trick is to generate a great channel of Dancing Light into your tabernacle.*

5. *Quicken your hands (exercise 7) using Abbreviation, and each time you walk toward your tabernacle, draw the surrounding Dancing Light into your palms, up your arms and into your Soul. Carry the Dancing Light in your Soul toward your tabernacle. When you reach your tabernacle, reverse your Light Bending, releasing all the Dancing Light in front of you at your tabernacle. At this point an interesting thing occurs to your Soul. You observe that the Dancing Light is traveling up your Pillar in a Divine Column, your permanent channel to Heaven—you didn't have to invoke Pillar; it was just there for you, and it always will be.*

6. *Repeat this process 10 more times, pulling more and more of the room's Dancing Light toward your tabernacle. When you feel the Dancing Light become strong, form it, with your Soul, into a Plume of Dancing Light, and when you reach your tabernacle, quickly raise your arms, pulling the Plume of Dancing Light upward, so that the Light travels up your Pillar and into the ceiling corner, where it disappears.*

7. *Continue to repeat this process, a hundred times, if necessary, drawing more of the Dancing Light into your Plume. Each time you reach your tabernacle, Crescendo the Light as you divert it up your column.*

8. *The Divine Column is complete when you have formed a visible column of Dancing Light that moves up on its own, disappearing Ascendant at your Door Up. Then you may release your ball of Sacred Intent up your Pillar, Assigning the Light to carry forth to Heaven.*

Once you have begun your Divine Column, the Plume of Dancing Light will continue rising up your tabernacle and disappear at the ceiling, traveling instantly up your Pillar and Ascendant into Heaven. After you release your Sacred Intent into the visible Pillar of Dancing Light, simply stop, take a deep breath, exhale, and bask in the wondrous Joy that permeates your Soul.

Tabernacle: A free-standing Ascending column of Heaven Light.

Consider what you just learned in Spirit: That you can send Dancing Light up to Heaven through a column not in your body or Soul, but at a location you Marked with your Soul. You are learning the basics of Sealing.

You also learned that if you send a powerful Plume of Light up your Pillar it will disappear at your Door Up as it Ascends instantly to Heaven.

Such are the ways not of the earth, but Heaven.

The Divine Column is a synergistic HeavenWork exercise. If you practice it in concert with other Ascending Souls the intensity of the Divine Column will manifest stronger, and carry into Heaven a more powerful Blessing of Praise, devotion and gratitude. The more the better. Be creative.

If you perform The Divine Column in a large group, try adding percussion— drums, bells and chimes, and even joyous singing—and Transflex it while your group leader carries all of your collected Dancing Light to your tabernacle!

Truly, the Sacred Beings in the Light practice The Divine Column more than any other HeavenWork exercise.

With all your heart and Soul, thank deeply, graciously, and humbly the Heaven Light, the Sacred Beings in the Light, and all of Heaven for the Blessing just bestowed upon your Soul.

Repeat this exercise 10 times before moving to the next one.

EXERCISE 59

SEALING

Depositing Heaven Light

There are special places on earth—sacred spaces—where the Heaven Light Plumes in perpetuity.

One sacred flame in particular, which Heaven long ago made known to me, has continued on now for two thousand years as a beacon for Souls who would unlock Seals of Heaven Light on earth. In Heaven's time—in the end times—that Seal will be revealed to every Soul on earth.

Sealing is not a way of the earth, but Heaven, a way you can help other Souls find Heaven. Sealing is storing and Assigning the Heaven Light to perform a function in the service of Heaven, a pure service in accordance to the nature of the Heaven Light, the Will of Heaven—that Souls sanctify.

> **Sealing:** *The Soul's assigning Heaven Light to perform a sanctifying function on its own.*

Heaven can Seal, the Sacred Beings can Seal, and Ascending Souls can Seal. You can Seal.

You Seal by Vortexing a **Sealing Body** into the Heaven Light. A Sealing Body is like Sacred Intent, but much fuller, a special, wordless expression of your Soul—a function for the Light to perform or a spiritual Wisdom to be delivered constantly or some time(s) in the future in any way you Assign the Light. In Sealing, you must also attach an **Outcome** of Light to the Sealing Body—the conditions in which you want the Sealing Body opened and delivered.

Your Sealing Body is the "what" of Sealing, a very deep, complete fullness of understanding—the wordless essence behind a word, a hundred words, even a million words. If you leave anything out it will remain left out, so you must form your Sealing Body in abundance.

Your Outcome, which you add to your Sealing Body, includes your Assignment of the Heaven Light—everything your Soul desires it to do—the when, where, how, and to whom your Sealing Body will be delivered. Unlike Blessing, Sealing includes the Assigment *within* the Intent you release unto the Heaven Light.

A Sealing Body can be as simple as depositing an Awakening Blessing into an object to touch Souls who come near, or as specific and vastly complex as depositing into the Clouds of Heaven a complete understanding of the Path of Light to be delivered in one hundred years to one special person entering Tufted Palm.

As long as your Sealing Body is pure and in accordance with Heaven, any expression of Soul can be Sealed, deposited anywhere on earth or in Spirit, and delivered in any way.

As your Soul Ascends to the Firmament, you will receive directly from Heaven the sacred understanding of how to Seal freely and in massive complexity. For now we will keep it simple. You will learn by Sealing a simple Awakening Blessing unto a tree.

Sealing might seem a little complicated to learn, but once you've Sealed, thanks to Abbreviation, it can become second nature—no, *first* nature!

Before we begin you may find it useful to practice LightWater once again, this time with an added twist.

LIGHTWATER

1. *Fill a drinking glass (made of glass) ¾ full with tap water, and take a sip.*

2. *Standing, hold the glass 6" in front of your heart, with the palms of your hands against the side of the glass.*

3. *Invoke the Heaven Light (exercise 6, using Abbreviation).*

4. *Take a deep breath as the Light flows down into your Soul.*

5. *Harness the Heaven Light in your heart and Crescendo it to a powerful concentration.*

6. *Both with your eyes and the eye of your Soul, look into the water in the glass. Feel with your Soul how the Heaven Light desires to enter into the water. But don't let it just yet.*

7. *Only when the Heaven Light heaves strongly toward the water, bow your head and release the Light unto the water.*

The power in which the Heaven Light leapt into the water is what Sealing feels like to your Soul.

Know that when you Seal an object you are not depositing Light *into* the object, which is spiritual materialization, but placing Light where the object is. In this way, Sealing always involves only Soul and Spirit.

You will first Seal unto a tree because it is easier at first to deposit Light unto an object in front of you than in the Clouds of Heaven, and the tree is alive, and will be around for a long time.

Goal: *To deposit Heaven Light with a sacred function.*

Preparation: *Find a tree to your liking.*

Steps:

1. ***Stand before your tree and ready your Soul for a sacred work. Invoke a Shower of Light (exercise 9), using Abbreviation. Feel how the omniscient Heaven Light already knows what is about to happen, how it already flows down into your heart, and forward toward your tree. With the eye of your Soul, look upon the tree, and Mark with your Soul how this one tree is different, unique from every other tree in the world. Recognize the tree with your Soul.***

2. ***Using Abbreviation, form a Cocoon of Light (exercise 20) around you and your tree. How easily, willingly the Heaven Light surrounds you both! Feel the new familiarity, your new affinity you have with this, your special tree.***

3. ***Using Abbreviation, send a Plume (exercise 34) of Light into the trunk of the tree. Watch, with the eye of your Soul, as the Heaven Light splashes within and without the tree, seaming every twig and leaf, expanding to fill your entire Cocoon to receive your Seal.***

4. ***Fill your Soul with Joy and Remembrance, and form wordlessly your Sealing Body, with fullness in Soul:*** *This Blessing, this powerful charge of Heaven Light, will Awaken the Soul of everyone who passes near this tree!* ***Receive into your Soul-in-heart a powerful surge of Awakening Heaven Light, and Harness the Light within your Soul, within your Sealing Body.***

5. ***Holding your powerful Sealing Body within your Soul, wordlessly form your Outcome—your complete Assignment of the Heaven Light:*** *If my Sealing Body is in accordance with the Will of Heaven, remain here, in the space in and around this tree, and fulfill my desire for the duration of one year, then Starburst through the Spirit Universe!*

6. *Harness both your Sealing Body and Outcome in your Soul, and with your Soul, form a counterclockwise Vortex within your Plume, just in front of your chest.*

7. *When the eye of your Soul sees your Vortex catch and swirl into your Plume and into your tree, release unto the Vortex Plume your ball of Sealing Body and Outcome, all the while Assigning again the Heaven Light to carry out your Soul's Outcome—to remain within and around this tree for one year, then disperse in Starburst.*

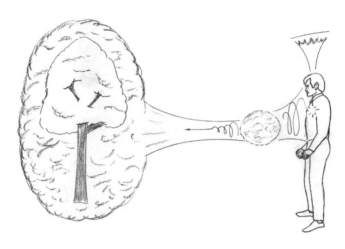

Immediately you will be released from your Cocoon. Walk back about 20' and look upon the tree with your Soul. See how it seems to glow in Dancing Light. Then leave, and go about your normal activity.

Come back in a day or two and look again through the eye of your Soul, and you will find the Seal remains there, strong. Walk near your tree and notice the changes that occur. Watch others as they come near the tree, and marvel at the sacred space that will remain there for a year.

As for Sealing more complex wisdom in the Clouds of Heaven, you must learn how directly from *Abba's* Immanence within the Wind of Heaven.

Such is Sealing, such is the way of Heaven.

Blessed are you who learn Sealing for it prepares you for your most powerful HeavenWork, the Transfiguring creation of Miracles of Compassion with the Breath of Heaven. Nothing in the Spirit Universe sanctifies a Soul more than creating a Miracle with Heaven.

*With all your heart and Soul, thank deeply, graciously, and humbly
the Heaven Light, the Sacred Beings in the Light, and all of Heaven
for the Blessing just bestowed upon your Soul.*

Seal 10 trees with Awakening Blessings before moving to the next exercise.

*Magnify and Assign Light at every opportunity,
blending your sacred works in your daily life.*

EXERCISE 60

THE WIND OF HEAVEN

Heaven's lift.

Creation is the heart of Heaven, the Throne within the Diadem where *Abba*, the holy Face of God-in-Heaven, dwells.

The Clouds of Heaven roll ever out from Creation—*Alpha* and *Omega*, the Source of all, the destiny of Souls—passing through the Body of Heaven, and out the Firmament, dropping descendant into the chasm gates to the Clear Light, and the materiality that hangs upon it.

But when your Soul Ascends to near the Firmament, a measure of the Clouds passes over the chasm gates, unto your Soul Ascendant, bearing and maintaining your Soul on holy ground, passing into and through your Soul, purifying your Soul in early preparation for your Transfiguration.

Biding there, near the Firmament and free from material fetters, your Soul can receive that which passes within the Clouds of Heaven: The invisible Immanence of *Abba*—the Truth of truths, straight from *Abba* into your Soul.

There, naked before Heaven, *Abba's* Immanence passes like a constant summer wind against your Soul, and unobstructed through your Soul, erasing your last remaining flaws.

Abba's Immanence—the Wind of Heaven, the Crown of Integration and Heaven's Instrument. Ultimate Truth comes only from *Abba*, within the Clouds of Heaven, within the Heaven Light, within the Breath of Heaven.

But there is more. *Abba's* Immanence also Directs your Soul.

Like a salmon knowing to swim upstream, like a bird leaping into the wind to take wing, your Soul innately knows to push into *Abba's* Immanence, for in so doing you venture straight unto *Abba*.

Thus as you are pushed from Heaven, so are you lifted to Heaven.

As you are lifted to Heaven, thus comes Heaven's Firmament to hove ever before your Soul.

Come, learn to bide in the Clouds of Heaven, receive *Abba's* Immanence, the Wind of Heaven, into your Soul, Surrender unto the Wind, and rise unto the Firmament, completing your Ascension.

Come, enter into the Sacred, where you have not yet been.

Goal: *To be lifted, by Heaven, unto the Firmament.*

Preparation: *Find a place of peace, where you will not be disturbed.*

Steps:

1. *Using Abbreviation, or going back to exercise 53, practice Sitting On Tufted Palm. But when you arrive within the Clouds of Heaven, do not form a Cocoon around your Soul.*

2. *Feel Abba's Immanence—the Wind of Heaven passing into the face of your Soul within the Clouds of Heaven—grow stronger. Open and receive into your entire Soul this Wind, and allow your Soul's affinity for the Wind to grow. Grasp the deeper, essential sacred knowing that can only be gleaned in the Clouds of Heaven.*

3. *Using Abbreviation, practice Heaven's Instrument (exercise 44). Welcome the Wind, that it continue passing into the face of your Soul, winning you. Release the things of earth, your remnant flaws, as the Wind passing through you washes them away, making your Soul naked, vulnerable and receptive to the Truth of Heaven. Holy!Holy!Holy is the Immanence that passes through you, and your Soul purifies, changing into the sanctity that is Heaven.*

4. *Surrender unto the sacred Truth that passes through your Soul. Become the Truth disclosed. Notice as you Surrender, the Wind pick up, filling you with closer understanding of things sacred. This is your Soul Surrendering to the Truth of Heaven. Continue to open, receiving more, Surrendering more. Feel the Wind brace your Soul.*

5. *Mark the divine Source of the Wind—Abba, in the heart of Heaven, and glean with great Joy and freedom your Soul drawing into the Wind. Feel your Soul lifted upwind, unto Heaven. Open when this happens, such that your Soul is lifted more, closer. Feel the intent of your Soul become excited and fulfilled as you are lifted nearer.*

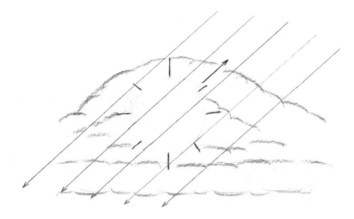

The gentle Wind of Heaven, the continuation of Heaven's Instrument and complete Crossover into Spirit, is a very important HeavenWork exercise, as it raises your Soul unto the Firmament, completing your Ascension. Practice it every day until Heaven's Firmament appears before the eye of your Soul. Once Ascended, your Soul will never withdraw from the Firmament, never.

With all your heart and Soul, thank deeply, graciously, and humbly the Heaven Light, the Sacred Beings in the Light, and all of Heaven for the Blessing just bestowed upon your Soul.

Repeat this exercise 10 times before moving to the next one. But continue to practice The Wind Of Heaven once a day until you see the Firmament with the eye of your Soul, for only then can you continue along the Path of Light.

Get good at Wind Of Heaven. You will need it later.

Exercise 61

Oracle

The wordless Word of Abba, God-in-Heaven.

Divination descends from the Clouds of Heaven unto man, but Oracle Ascends to within Heaven. Oracle is your Soul looking into Heaven.

Thus Oracle is nothing of man, and everything of Heaven. Oracle follows the Direction of Heaven, towards *Abba*, the Face of God-in-Heaven, Creation perpetual, and if profaned by even the smallest traces of mind and matter, it becomes blasphemy. Oracle is only of perfect Truth, the sacred Spirit that is Heaven.

Achieved only by Ascending unto the Firmament, sanctified Souls may look into Heaven, *high* into Heaven, and glimpse within the holy flashing Diadem to receive in kind instant Initiation—*Abba's* full Immanence, searing your Soul, changing you forever!

Thus are you filled omniscient, of the sacred nature of holy Spirit, of all things past, present, future, immediate and eternal, the Will of Heaven unobscured. And your Soul Marks Heaven, never to withdraw.

Thus may only witness Souls Oracular speak on Heaven. But do not speak of Heaven until commanded.

Oracle marks your Soul's complete Ascent before the Firmament of Heaven. There will your Soul remain until made Elect, Transfigured and Received. Thus has it been with the 27,000 Received Souls of my witness, thus it was with the three million before.

Oracle, the Crown of The Wind of Heaven, occurs when your Soul has sanctified completely, arriving before the Firmament. Thus you reach Oracle by mastering The Wind of Heaven.

Oracle will occur spontaneously during The Wind of Heaven, brought about by your Soul's thirst for Heaven.

Take heart, for it *will* happen in Heaven's time.

Goal: *To peer into Heaven and receive the Sacred.*

Preparation: *Find a place of peace where you will not be disturbed.*

Steps:

1. *While practicing The Wind of Heaven, while your Soul continues to lift toward Heaven, a change will occur. Suddenly you will feel as if part of your Soul has vanished. You will feel lighter, fatigued, like only the face of your Soul remains. But you will not be alarmed, because you remain the Truest essence of your Soul, the worthy.*

2. *Two things will happen: First fatigue—much like what it feels like after waking from a general anesthetic—will press down upon your Soul, such that you desire to succumb back into the opaque Clouds of Heaven. At the same time, your Soul will be buoyed forward, towards the face of your Soul, because you will instantly feel a divine Immanence ahead.*

3. *At first you will see with the eye of your Soul, perhaps for the first time, vapors of the rolling Clouds of Heaven passing into your Soul. Just as the eye of your Soul gazes into the Clouds behind and below you, you will suddenly know that Heaven hoves before you.*

4. *You will burst aware at this realization, and the eye of your Soul will lift, at first to behold the powerful, daunting chasm gates before you just below—dropping dark energy flowing like a river that would certainly return your Soul back to materiality should you venture nearer. That they drop descendant will repel your Soul.* Your first rise to Oracle is to open up all your Soul's Intent to see Heaven, for only such Sacred Intent will escape the fatigue—the draw of materiality—of your Soul's unworthy side. *Your Soul's exhiliration will buoy you up from the Clouds so that you will take your first look upon Heaven.*

5. *You will return your gaze to the wisps of rolling Heaven Cloud that pass over the chasm gates and into your Soul. As the wisps pass through, you will be filled with a knowing that you are on sacred ground that can only be described as Holy!Holy!Holy! Awe will first consume your Soul, followed by humility.* Your next rise to Oracle is to keep your awe and humility pure—to not reduce these qualities of pure Soul to unworthiness. You do this by Surrendering your Soul to Heaven. **Thus, by becoming like Heaven, you do not exile your Soul back to materiality.**

6. *By Surrendering you dwell in your essence of Soul—the Heaven Light—and you may peer deeper into Heaven. See, in Soul, how your Affinity for the Heaven Light reveals all of Heaven to you—the vast*

panorama! The Clouds, miles wide, rolling out in an ovate cornucopia from Creation towards you, ending invisibly at the Firmament.

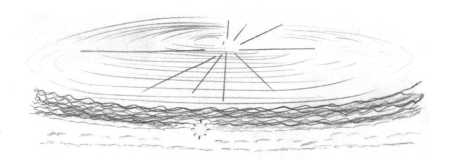

The Body of Heaven, with its millions-strong sanctified Host, all as One Spirit, flowing in Praise and glory—all directed to the Source high up. The Diadem crowning the Throne of Creation—the flashing light of divine colors unknown to earth, brilliant colors harder than stone, yet flitting faster than Soul can trace, and all around the Holiest of holy, the Power of powers—Abba, the Face of God-in-Heaven (Holy!Holy!Holy!)!

7. *At beholding Abba your Soul will again throe towards unworthiness. Your third rise to Oracle is to rekindle your Soul's thirst for Heaven, for if you weren't worthy you would not have Ascended to the Firmament, Heaven makes no such mistake. If you remain gazing upon Abba, then, you will be filled with Immanence Initiation, and your Soul will be burned, penetrated and consumed by a blast so sacred you will be changed forever. You will be filled with the nature of Heaven, you will become witness of Heaven!*

8. *And there, to the right of Abba, the Origin of the Heaven Light, which shines through the whole of Heaven like diamond light—silver streaks of silver-white that stream through every sacred Soul in the Body of Heaven and out, into your Soul.*

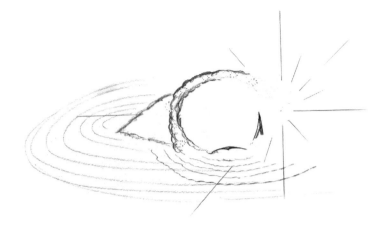

What you receive thus in Soul is Oracle.

Do not speak of what you have been given in grace, unless commanded by *Abba*. The rest of your existence will be a short wait until Heaven makes Elect your Soul, and you are Transfigured, and Received into Heaven.

> *With all your heart and Soul, thank deeply, graciously, and humbly the Heaven Light, the Sacred Beings in the Light, and all of Heaven for the Blessing just bestowed upon your Soul.*

> *Oracle Seals your Soul to the Firmament of Heaven.*

> *To return, simply Abbreviate HeavenHome, and you will find Heaven's Firmament before you.*

COMPLETING YOUR ASCENDANCE

Now it is up to you to master and Abbreviate all your HeavenWork exercises. Practice them regularly, constantly, particularly your advanced spiritual exercises, until you come to see through the eye of your Soul the Firmament of Heaven before you.

Transfiguration, the final Elevation of your Soul, is a process set in motion by Heaven while your Soul nears the Firmament. By the time you complete your Ascendance, the moment you discover the vast panorama of Heaven there before you, hovering before your Soul, Heaven will have already made Elect your Soul, and you will proceed into Transfiguration into Heaven.

But there are things you can do to speed your Election and Transfiguration along, things you can do now. They all involve taking the Breath of Heaven into your Soul. By approaching the Firmament of Heaven your Soul has already acquired the capacity to compel the Heaven Breath.

Therefore continue on to your Transfiguration HeavenWork exercises. You are so close. Come, and receive the Heaven Breath.

CREATIVE COMBINATIONS

Thus have you Awakened, Transcended and Ascended near to before the Firmament of Heaven, and the Heaven Light courses always through your Soul, and into those who come near in Spirit and on earth.

You have taken command of your life, you are your Soul, and your mind and body serve the will of your Soul, and your Soul the Will of Heaven.

Each day you visit the Clouds of Heaven to Slide closer to the Firmament. Each time it comes easier to arrive and remain in Heaven's Clouds. Your HeavenWork is in full flower, and every moment you are changed, every moment you are made purer, every moment in the Light are you rewarded.

You are ready to master the *whole* of your HeavenWork.

Take the time to skim through all the 61 exercises you've learned so far. Consider how well you Abbreviated them, how now you can make them occur automatically, without structure, independent of your mind and body, solely by willing with your Soul.

When you first learned them they all seemed different, but feel, now, how they blend, one into another, like fluid, to keep your Soul on sacred fire.

Only now can you see, there is no form to the HeavenWork exercises— they are all the same, all complementing ways to embrace life on earth with your Soul filled with the Light of Heaven. Like the Clouds of Heaven, your HeavenWork exercises flow into each other in great freedom, perpetually, spontaneously, creatively, day and night, through the immediate and certain intuition of your Soul.

Creative Combinations, the Crown of Constance, thus is your mastery of the HeavenWork. You are free now to practice your HeavenWork according to your Soul's own calling. Follow your Soul's lead.

If you should encounter someone, for example, and your Soul, Reading the other Soul, compels you to both Awaken Bless and inspire Cosmic Wind Chimes, simply combine them, using Abbreviation. In a flash, pull down the Heaven Light from the Door Up, and Bless them Awake in a powerful Plume. Then form a counterclockwise Vortex and Disclose unto the other Soul, and after, when you hover before the other Soul, Abbreviate Cosmic Wind Chimes, so that the other Soul, still intimate, can glean the experience of your Soul.

Or you can work your exercises freely in your own Soul. Abbreviate, for example, Shower of Light (five seconds), then Heart Purification (ten seconds), than Starburst (30 seconds). Or follow up The Dying with Soul Disclosure, and then Cosmic Wind Chimes. Or Lightwash a Soul directly by shortcutting Vortex directly into the heart.

Every HeavenWork exercise can be so freely combined, for their Origin is divine, and their nature perfect.

Practice the Crown of Constance vigorously to Ascend your Soul rapidly to the Firmament of Heaven.

INITIATION

Heaven rejoices each time your intrepid Soul leaps Ascendant toward Heaven, and with grace Heaven makes it known unto your Soul unmistakably, through Initiation.

Initiation is Heaven's immediate Answer when your Soul makes a breakthrough into sacred Spirit. Initiation is Heaven, and all the eyes of Heaven, smiling upon your Soul.

There are many types of Initiation. Besides the Ring of Fire, the earliest along the Path of Light is *Visitation Initiation*, acknowledgement of your Soul's accordance to the Will of Heaven by a sacred visitor—usually a Sacred Being in the Light charged to your Soul. There, within your Door Up, your visitor will appear. Immediate materiality will dissolve around your visitor. Your visitor will Disclose unto you, and your Soul will fill with joyous reunion and Remembrance so deep the mind cannot comprehend.

Sometimes, on very rare occasions, and if your HeavenWork bears a special purpose of Heaven, a Diadem Angel will suddenly appear. Instantly you will be thrown fully into your Soul and you will be seared with a Divine Transmission so powerful that your Soul will be changed forever!

During your Ascent, and sometimes repeated from time to time, you may experience *Cascade Initiation*, for your perseverance along the Path of Light and right works. Suddenly the world around you will brighten, the clouds thousands of feet above you will actually part, and sunlight will stream down only upon you. Your Soul will be lifted immediately because within the ordinary sunlight, the Diamond Heaven Light will splash down upon you, surrounding you in a 50' Cocoon of vibrant Light known only in Heaven, in which all of nature bends toward you in awe and honor. Best of all, in all this, your Soul feels all the approving eyes of Heaven gracefully upon your Soul, inviting you.

As your Soul passes Ascendant through the Clouds of Heaven and presents before the Firmament, Heaven begins to make Elect your Soul, and makes it know to your Soul through **Elect Initiation**: Suddenly the Clouds of Heaven dissipate and the awe-some whole of Heaven hovers before your Soul, for good.

And then there is **Immanence Initiation**, Heaven's greatest reward under Transfiguration. Before the whole of Heaven, once your Soul has tasted the Breath of Heaven, *Abba*, the Face of God-in-Heaven, blasts into your Soul an invisible Divine Transmission that passes through your Soul like a shock wave, filling you with complete understanding of the Path of Light.

If you have not yet received your first Initiation, you soon will, and they will happen more and more as your Soul Ascends to Heaven's Firmament. Keep to the Path.

HEAVEN'S MARK

Once your heart is made pure, after Volcano and once your body can bear immense Heaven Light within your Soul, you will be Blessed by Heaven. You will receive by spontaneous Initiation the **Mark of Heaven**—a permanent radiance of sacred Spirit around your Soul visible to those with Sacred Sight, intense silver-white spires of Light radiating brightly in every direction and dimension, passing descendant, Transcendent and Ascendant all the way to Heaven.

Your Creight will flower and you will be able to recognize other Souls who bear the Mark of Heaven.

HOW LONG?

How long will it take before your Soul Ascends before the Firmament of Heaven? How long the Path of Light, how long before your Soul Awakens, Transcends, Ascends, and is Transfigured into Heaven?

It depends entirely on your HeavenWork. It depends on how pure your Soul began this life, and how diligently and effectively you master your HeavenWork.

After I drowned in 1962 I didn't have the HeavenWork, the Path of Light laid out before me in a book. I hadn't yet received *Abba's* Direct Transmission into my Soul. The Heaven Light was my only teacher. It took me 17 years of leading a fairly normal life while constantly plying the Light in Soul before I was taken full Ascendant.

But in 1979, in those very moments first before Heaven, my Soul Elect was Engulfed in the Transfiguring Heaven Breath and given Understanding and granted passage In. But I did not enter In, nor did I join for eternity my dearest friends, the Sacred Beings in the Light. For my work on earth is not finished. I am the least of man, and thus I will not enter before you.

Many times the Breath of Heaven has since breached the chasm gates to Engulf my Soul in Divine Invitation to enter In—the same narrow gate that Jesus spoke of, the same gate that my Soul has witnessed carry In 27,000 Souls these past 28 years.

Know this, nothing of your HeavenWork is ever lost, but continues more indelibly within your Soul than a diamond. Should you not be given enough time in this lifetime, do not be discouraged. As certain as you live and breathe, you will have another chance, and you will be all the more prepared by the HeavenWork you perform today. Thus as it is in Heaven, it is within your Soul.

Life is the most precious gift of Heaven. Therefore live your life naturally, in accordance to the Will of Heaven. Practice your HeavenWork spontaneously, constantly and joyously. Incorporate your HeavenWork into every moment of your life. Leave the grasping ways of earth and peer with the eye of your Soul into sacred Spirit. Acquire the ways of Heaven, become like Heaven, and as such will Heaven Elect your Soul.

So long the Path of Light, so short the Path of Light.

TRANSFIGURATION

AWAKENING→TRANSCENDING→ASCENDING→**TRANSFIGURATION**

ELEVEN

TRANSFIGURATION OF SOUL

THE BREATH OF HEAVEN

Your Soul has the power to Awaken, Transcend and Ascend, but not to Transfigure. Transfiguration, the last and very brief Elevation of your Soul, is performed only by Heaven.

Transfiguration, your ultimate Crossover into the sacred Spirit that is Heaven, occurs the moment your Soul arrives before the Firmament. But it Crowns a process that occurs during the final stages of your Soul's Ascent.

During this process, as your Soul passes Ascendant through the Clouds of Heaven, becoming ever purer, Heaven makes **Elect** your Soul, and provides to you the Breath of Heaven, which passes out the Firmament, over the chasm gates, and into your Soul.

At first your Soul receives only small flashes of the Heaven Breath, for its crushing power contains the might of Heaven.

The Breath of Heaven, known in the east as *dorje* (thunderbolt), *shakti*, and *kundalini*, is the power of sacred change. Indeed, at your Moment of Truth, when finally you have reached the very end of the Path of Light, the Heaven Breath will cross over the chasm gates once more to Engulf your Soul in sacred Understanding and Invitation, and upon your Transfiguration, carry you along its narrow gate, past the chasm gates, as your Transfigured Soul is **Received** into Heaven forever!

By and large most Souls carry in to Heaven, for it is their time, their perfect Truth, their ultimate destiny. And yet some Souls, in perfect awe and sacrifice, postpone their Transfiguration to bide for an eon in the Clouds of Heaven for Heaven's cause—to show other Souls the way along the Path of Light—for it is not yet their time, though Heaven would Receive them.

For the 28 years of my Soul's witness of the gate of Heaven it has always been this same way—more than 27,000 times. Yet each time is like the first time, absolute, and every time my Soul is rendered into rapture.

Thus it was with every Soul who entered, thus will it be when your Soul enters In. Welcome therefore the Heaven Breath, practice regularly the

HeavenWork exercises that bring you closer to the Firmament.

There are things you can do with the Heaven Breath to make worthy Elect your Soul, things you are meant to do, to compel the Heaven Breath to rush to your Soul and speed Heaven's Transfiguration process along. Your first five Transfiguration HeavenWork exercises will help you compel Heaven to Elect your Soul, and the final four will help you prepare for your earliest Transfiguration. They are difficult but necessary, so take your time and do them right.

Once mastered, each will nurture your Transfiguration.

EXERCISE 62

FUSION BURST

Explosion-implosion.

As you near the Firmament you will pass beyond the sublime things of descending Spirit and enter the absolute, sacred things of Heaven. One thing of Heaven—the Breath of Heaven—will enter *you*, first in traces, then in greater measure.

Fusion Burst, the Crown of Starburst and continuation of Nova, uses Heaven Light to compel the Heaven Breath to make your Soul worthy Elect by eliminating the profane remnants yet in your Soul.

In Heaven, the Truth of truths, there is no time or space as we know them. Being simply is, the font of Creation within *Abba*, the Face of God-in-Heaven. You learned to call the Heaven Light into your Soul first through your Door Up, and then from all directions. In Fusion Burst you will learn to invoke Heaven Light not from outside, but from the heart of your Soul, the pinpoint center of your Soul.

This can occur only by practicing Starburst or Nova while in the Clouds of Heaven. There, so close to the Firmament, Heaven Answers your explosion of Heaven Light with a blast of Heaven Breath into your Soul.

Thus is your explosion of Heaven Light imploded by Heaven Breath, and in so doing your Soul is washed clean, then purged cleaner.

Goal: *To call the Breath of Heaven into your Soul.*

Preparation: *Find a place of peace where you will not be disturbed.*

Steps:

1. *Enter the Clouds of Heaven by Abbreviating The Wind of Heaven (exercise 60). Feel Heaven's Immanence press against your Soul, but do not push Ascendant. Instead feel with your Soul's intuition for the powerful wall of the Firmament before your Soul just past the Clouds. When you sense it, Mark it.*

2. *If you mastered Nova (exercise 57), perform it, using Abbreviation. If you skipped Higher Tantra, create a Starburst (exercise 49), using Abbreviation. You will find in the Clouds of Heaven that the Heaven Light does not shower into you from your Door Up. Nor does it flash*

into your Soul from all directions, but explodes from out the center of your Soul.

Immediately your Heaven Light explosion will be Answered by the Heaven Breath, which implodes into your Soul in a heat blast that quells your explosion, instantly rendering your Soul sublimely changed, purer.

Thus have you set Heaven on Electing your Soul, such is the way Heaven Initiates your Soul worthy Elect.

Once you have experienced Fusion Burst you know perfectly in Soul that at any moment Heaven might call you up.

With all your heart and Soul, thank deeply, graciously, and humbly the Heaven Light, the Sacred Beings in the Light, and all of Heaven for the Blessing just bestowed upon your Soul.

Repeat this exercise 10 times before moving to the next one,
But do not move on until you experience the Heaven Breath at least once.

EXERCISE 63

TRANSCONDENSING

Harnessing the Breath of Heaven.

Now to nurture your relationship with the Heaven Breath.

Just as you near the gate of Heaven, thus has Heaven moved to Elect you. Thus was your Soul, by grace, allowed to taste the Breath of Heaven. Now the Heaven Breath will begin to enter your Soul more freely, and more powerfully.

Because Transfiguration happens to your Soul, it is beyond your Soul's control. Spontaneous is its nature, and one thing you can be sure of: The Heaven Breath will come unto you unexpectedly.

Most likely the Heaven Breath will arrive during your greatest receptivity—while you are practicing your HeavenWork. Suddenly and without warning, a giant wall of Heaven Breath will sweep into you from one side, immediately collapse into your Soul, instantly Transcondense into a powerful lightning bolt, and pass out of you—all in less than one second. If you are startled, and unable to conduct It, your arms and legs will lurch out as if you were electrocuted.

You will not be harmed, but you will be disappointed, for the Heaven Breath always carries within perfect Understanding, and you will recognize the opportunity you missed.

But if you are not startled, if your Soul immediately recognizes, opens and receives the Heaven Breath, It will still Transcondense just as powerfully, but pass through your Soul painlessly and perfectly conducted, into materiality. Instantly and powerfully will your Soul be cleansed and made worthy Elect, while the materiality you struck with the Transcondensed Heaven Breath will be changed with a power such as Angels wield. Such is the stuff of Miracles.

Such is the elusive nature of the Heaven Breath, and the spontaneous nature of Transcondensing—the ability to receive the Breath of Heaven and pass It unto another.

Now that you have Fusion Burst, you are made worthy to Transcondense—the most powerful HeavenWork exercise under Heaven.

Goal: *To purge your Soul worthy Elect with the Breath of Heaven.*

Preparation: *Take an apple to bed with you.*

Steps:

1. *Your apple, of course, will receive the Transcondensed Heaven Breath. Lie on your back and hold the apple over your stomach comfortably with both hands. Before you go to sleep, with Abbreviation Invoke Heaven Light (exercise 6), Quicken your hands (exercise 7), and run relaxed channels of Light down your arms, out your hands, and into the apple. Notice because of its water content the apple readily receives the Heaven Light. Continue your Light channels throughout this exercise.*

2. *Using Abbreviation, enter the Clouds of Heaven until you feel the Wind of Heaven upon your Soul.*

3. *Form wordlessly and humbly in your Soul this Sacred Intent:* Abba, if it is your Will, Bless unto my Soul once again the Breath of Heaven. *Take a deep breath and release your Sacred Intent into the Clouds of Heaven.*

4. *Then relax. Continue the Light channels down your arm and into the apple. The more relaxed you are the more likely you will Transcondense. Keep calm and open your Soul so that you will surrender should the Heaven Breath come. As you begin to fall asleep, Abbreviate Continuum (exercise 23).*

Because the Heaven Breath will touch your Soul only when the time is right, Transcondensing may not happen your first try, or your next.

Just as you truly arrived here along the Path of Light, so you will Transcondense, and when your time is right—Heaven will see to it. If you hadn't already won Heaven, you wouldn't be here now. So keep at it, nightly, and continue all your HeavenWork exercises, for the Heaven Breath might appear any time.

The goal of Transcondensing is to become at ease with the Heaven Breath, to invite It in Safe Surrender so that It will Engulf your Soul. There is no mistaking Engulfment—your Soul is suddenly surrounded by a thick sky of sacred white, like a flashflood, that presses more and more upon you. In the mounting pressure your Soul is filled deep with sacred Understanding (wherein all your Soul's questions are Answered, and your Soul responds with absolute precision) and the power to change.

> **Engulfment:** *Heaven Breath passing from Heaven's Firmament around an Elect, newly-Ascended Soul, for the purpose of Transfiguration.*

In this intersession between your Soul's worthy Election and Transfiguration, the Breath of Heaven comes available for you to change things of earth for the good of Heaven, through Miracles of Compassion.

With all your heart and Soul, thank deeply, graciously, and humbly the Heaven Light, the Sacred Beings in the Light, and all of Heaven for the Blessing just bestowed upon your Soul.

Succeed in Transcondensing once, then repeat this exercise adding to your Sacred Intent that the Heaven Breath Engulf your Soul. When your Soul has experienced Engulfment once, then move on to the next exercise.

DEATH TRANSFIGURATION

If you should die after you have learned to Transcondense the Breath of Heaven, your Soul, worthy Elect, is empowered to enter Heaven. You have Ascended enough to enter Heaven forever. To make your destiny even more certain, your Soul will know exactly what to do as your body's death approaches.

As your body weakens and collapses into death, your Soul will fill with Heaven Light. You will become seated in your Soul, no longer distracted by the throes of your body or its mind. Even as your body lives, you will be able to see with the eye of your Soul the Firmament of Heaven and glean how the Firmament before your Soul opens and fills your Soul with divine Invitation and Welcome.

And you will know in Soul that in the moments after your body's death, the Breath of Heaven will receive your Soul, and carry you into Heaven forever.

Never forsaking the Path of Light, you can use Transcondensing as your one final HeavenWork exercise by calling the Breath of Heaven into your Soul the moment you sense your Soul beginning to be tugged back from your heart and head.

Even after death, if you are Engulfed in the Heaven Breath, you can Transcondense and be carried In the gate of Heaven.

EXERCISE 64

MIRACLES OF COMPASSION

Rendering Heaven unto the Soul.

Nothing sanctifies Soul greater than creating a Miracle of Compassion with Heaven. Yet this sacred exercise is shown and offered to you, but not required of you.

For Miracles are performed between you and *Abba* for the auspice of Soul and Heaven, and nothing other. They exact tremendous responsibility of your Soul. Therefore perform a Miracle only when you are deeply, divinely moved in Soul.

If you aren't so moved, then freely continue on to the next exercise.

On earth it is sometimes hard to recognize Miracles, and more than not we mistake magic for Miracle. Miracles—True Miracles—do not benefit the earth, body or mind, but Soul, and Manifest always in accordance to the Will of Heaven. Miracles are divine interventions in the service of Heaven.

There are many varieties of Miracles, depending on how you slice them, but they are all based on the one Root Miracle that is *Abba*-in-Heaven. The Path of Light—the way of Soul into Heaven—is a Trunk Miracle from Heaven, and what we on earth consider to be Miracles are Branch Miracles, individual interventions that move Souls onto and along the Path of Light to Heaven.

All Miracles come from the highest Heaven, from *Alpha* Creation within *Abba*, the Face of God-in-Heaven. From There, they come Manifest descending from Heaven unto earth, sometimes altering materiality, to be experienced by the Soul of man.

Though all Miracles come Manifest from Heaven, they don't all start There. Some Miracles originate on earth. Worthy Elect Souls near Transfiguration, who can Harness the Heaven Breath and look high into Heaven and upon *Abba*, the Face of God-in-Heaven, can create, in partnership with Heaven, a Miracle of Compassion.

Such Miracles Jesus performed—Miracles that eluded even the Gospel writers. His True Miracles were not of body, fish or wine, but of Soul, Heaven Light, Heaven Breath, and *Abba*.

Miracles are not simple, and they are not easy. They require Compassion, purity, power, and sacrifice, and the Miracle worker bears a tremendous responsibility under Heaven.

Compassion is love beyond illusion, beyond human love—perfect Oneness without distinction fully known only by the purified Soul touching the sacred ground of Heaven.

Even after you learn to create Miracles, performing them is always exceedingly difficult. But why wouldn't they be?

The key to Miracles is mastering Engulfment by the Breath of Heaven, attainable only when Heaven makes your Soul fully worthy Elect, and your Soul reaches your final Elevation, Transfiguration.

You create a Miracle by compelling the Heaven Breath to alter Creation for the good of Heaven, for the sanctification of Soul. Taking a closer look, creating a Miracle with Heaven involves many stages:

- *Inspiration*—identifying a Soul in sacred need and recognizing how Heaven can help;

- *Permission*—requesting *Abba* to grant the Miracle and receiving immediate Answer;

- *Marking and Sealing* the receiver Soul;

- *Engulfment*—entering the Clouds of Heaven to receive a vast cloud of Heaven Breath;

- *Sealing* the Heaven Breath unto *Alpha* Creation within *Abba*;

- *Return*—coming back to body and going about your normal activities (no matter how briefly);

- *Co-Direction*—at fruition, when your Miracle makes Manifest, the Heaven Breath will be rendered unto your Soul as well as the receiver Soul, for you to direct your measure of Heaven Breath unto the receiver Soul; and

- *Release*—always release your Soul after your Miracle is made Manifest, so that you are no longer Sealed to it.

Some Miracles occur instantly, others after thousands of years—thus the tremendous responsibility, thus the sacrifice. I, just one of many, am yet bound to a Miracle three thousand years in the making—to bring the Path of Light to every Soul on earth. I am not released, nor do I desire my release.

Thus I would teach you the purest of Miracles—the auspice of Heaven Light unto an unAwakened Soul, someone whose eyes you look into and see only darkness behind. And because it is a Miracle of Compassion you should select someone you do not like all that much, for also will you be changed.

Goal: *To place, with Heaven, another Soul on the Path of Light.*

Preparation: *Sit in a place where you will not be disturbed and determine whose Soul you want to place on the Path of Light. Use Abbreviation each step of the way.*

Steps:

1. **Inspiration.** *If your receiver Soul is not in front of you, you will first need to Distance (exercise 47, using Abbreviation) unto that Soul. There in the Clear Light, send a continuous Plume (exercise 34) of Heaven Light into the receiver Soul, and wordlessly form a ball of Sacred Intent within your Soul: That Heaven Awaken and place this Soul upon the Path of Light.*

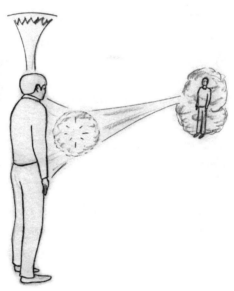

Even if your receiver Soul stands before you, you must still enter the Clear Light.

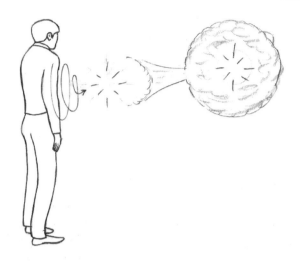

2. **Permission.** *There in the Clear Light, send wordlessly a Soul Prayer (exercise 42) to Heaven: Abba, if it is your Will, Awaken and place this Soul on the Path of Light. Know this, your petition must be so pure and sincere that you are willing to sacrifice your own life for the life of the receiver Soul. If and only if your Soul is Answered immediately by Abba may you proceed with your Miracle. Permission from Abba is unmistakable, always received in the Clear Light as your Soul bursting into a flame of joyous affirmation.*

3. **Marking and Sealing.** *In your Joy behold again in Soul your receiver Soul. Mark the Soul for the duration of your Miracle and Seal (exercise 59) the Soul: Abba, here is the Soul to receive our Miracle.*

4. **Engulfment.** *Enter immediately the Clouds of Heaven and press toward the Firmament until your Soul is surrounded in a thick cloud of Heaven Breath. The Breath of Heaven will press upon your Soul more and more, filling you with sacred Understanding and the choice to direct its power.*

5. **Sealing.** *As the Heaven Breath presses more powerfully upon your Soul, Seal (exercise #59) your Miracle unto the Heaven Breath by Transcondensing. In your Sealing Body Express the form of the receiver Soul's Awakening and immersion in Heaven Light; in your Outcome, form the instruction that the Miracle take place immediately. Make sure to also repeat your Outcome when you Assign the Heaven Breath. The moment you Transcondense, Assign the Heaven Breath to carry your Seal into the highest, holiest Heaven, unto Alpha Creation, which*

streams from behind Abba, the Face of God-in-Heaven. Instantly, when the Heaven Breath delivers your Seal unto Heaven your Soul will quake peaceably, yet powerfully like distant silent thunder.

6. **Return.** *When your Soul quakes, simply return to your body, and go about your normal life activities. Your Miracle will remain sustained by your Seals, and if you remain Ascendant you will not release, and you will obstruct the Miracle's Manifestation.*

7. **Co-Direction.** *In Heaven's time—immediately, hours, days, or even years later—your Miracle will come Manifest, and no matter where you are or what your are doing, your Soul will be stirred suddenly and completely alert to your Miracle and filled with sacred Understanding exactly where you left off. Your Soul will quake exactly as it did when you Sealed the Heaven Breath, the distant silent thunder will increase as your Manifesting Miracle rolls toward you, and you will immediately behold the receiver Soul before you. While the Miracle Manifest will roll mostly upon the receiver Soul, a measure of it will roll upon your Soul, and you will be filled Joyously with the knowing and ability to Transcondense the Manifestation entirely into the receiver Soul.*

8. **Release:** *As you Transcondense your Miracle into the receiver Soul, Bless the Soul, and in Soul Prayer thank Abba for the grace sacrifice rendered unto your Soul, and also ask: If it is within your Will, release me from my Seals. Crescendo your Prayer, and release it unto Abba. If Abba releases you your Soul will quake again in Answer, and you will feel your Seals dissolve away.*

Thus is Miracle. Nothing sanctifies a Soul more powerfully, and with every Miracle you create, Heaven will appear more and more to your Soul.

At first your presenting your Soul will just make out traces of the rolling Cloud that pass over the chasm gates and into and through the foot of your Soul, and filling your Soul with the Truth that you are touched by *holy!holy!holy!* ground.

Come unto the Firmament, come and know Heaven.

> *With all your heart and Soul, thank deeply, graciously, and humbly the Heaven Light, the Sacred Beings in the Light, and all of Heaven for the Blessing just bestowed upon your Soul.*

Create a Miracle with Heaven each and every time you are so moved in Soul.

Come, such that Heaven draws you near.

LIFESAVING

Accidents happen, some tragically. But that is the nature of material life. No matter how tempting it might be to the mind to petition *Abba* to intervene, know this: Heaven grants Miracles not of vanity, nor for the welfare of body and limb, but for Soul auspicious in Light.

To work Miracles you must see beyond life's distractions, and into Spirit.

So precious to the Soul, life is the avenue of sanctification leading to Heaven. And yet sometimes, when a Soul near or on the Path of Light is mortally wounded, Heaven *will* intervene by granting a petitioner a Miracle of Immediate Healing.

If you meet with such a situation the mechanism is the same as described above, but with a twist: You must also enter, in Soul, into the injured tissue. That is, during Inspiration, after Distancing unto the receiver Soul, you must then also will the Heaven Light to carry your Soul into the injury. Your Soul will immediately surge further into the Vortex Plume, and you will enter into a cloud of red.

Proceed to Permission, into the Clear Light, and Pray unto *Abba*: *Abba, if it is your Will that this Soul remain on earth, then heal now this body and Soul.*

If Answered affirmatively, return to the red cloud immediately, and Seal it, the injury, along with the receiver Soul, and be sure to Seal immediate healing into both Outcomes.

Accept no token of thanks should the receiver know of your HeavenWork, for you must release from it, but Bless her Awakened and tell her to thank Heaven.

And thus are sacred Light and Breath
the keys to the Kingdom of Heaven.

EXERCISE 65

ASCENDDANCE

Perfect Praise.

On earth we are used to using borrowed tools to express what we feel deep down. We use our minds to try to frame our Souls' elusive intuition, our tongues to express the love we feel, and our bodies to perform acts of kindness.

But these ways never seem enough. They fail to express the purity of the Soul, which flows ever freely into Spirit. The tools of body and mind are opaque, hollow and removed, secondary to the Expression of the Soul, and as such, are profane, useless before Heaven.

The Expression of your Soul is primary, pure, needing no translation, for your Soul's Expression is the language of Heaven.

Along the Path of Light you have learned to Express purely the essence of your Soul. Thus are you free to leave the ways of earth as you enter the sacred Spirit that is Heaven, and acquire the ways of Heaven. Thus are you free to become "as" Heaven.

On earth love is our greatest expression. We know love in body, mind, heart, *and* Soul. Indeed, earthly love elevates us above our human condition. But it also binds us to the earth, and our borrowed bodily illusions. Those meek in Spirit who love the earth, the things of the earth, and the bodies that walk the earth shall remain on earth. Yes, they shall inherit the earth, but in the end days, the earth shall inherit them.

But along the Path of Light, in the Clouds of Heaven, where there is no illusion of individuation, love purifies into universal Compassion.

And within the Body of Heaven, Compassion is purified further, Transfiguring into Praise—pure, perfect Praise, Joy and glory rising ever— directed perpetually unto *Abba* in the highest Heaven.

As such is Life eternal, the way of Heaven as it always was, is and ever shall be.

If you would enter Heaven, if you would *join* Heaven, you must become as Heaven. You must learn to Praise perfectly, just as it is in Heaven.

AscendDance teaches you how.

In Heaven, Praise is Expressed in Divine Music—the continuous, silent thunderous quaking within Heaven, a pure Expression without material reference that the mind can only translate as singing. That is why returning witness Souls sometimes describe the three million forming the Body of Heaven as "choirs of Angels."

AscendDance teaches you how to "sing" perfectly from your Soul, without your body's voice, to "dance" perfectly, without you body's limbs, and to "hear" the Divine Music, without your body's ears.

You begin AscendDance with the ways of the earth, with music and movement, but quickly you leave body, dropping the ways of earth and Transcending and Ascending to the Clouds of Heaven. There you Express freely your Soul, Praising *Abba* in the highest Heaven, with all the Body of Heaven. And in your Praise, the eyes of Spirit of the three million Transfigured who passed In before you also fall upon you, and then will Heaven make worthy Elect your Soul.

Immediate, spontaneous, and without structure is AscendDance, and as you Transcend and Ascend, all of your HeavenWork exercises will blend together in ways that free your Soul to enter the boundless awe, Joy, celebration, glory, and rapture that fills the Body of Heaven in ever growing Praise!

Come, leave the ways of earth behind, and join the Body of Heaven in celebration, in perfect Praise of God.

Goal: *To praise God, in Soul, just as it is in Heaven.*

Preparation: *Select appropriate music, and find a place where you can move freely and undisturbed.*

Steps:

1. *The music you select for AscendDance does not have to be religious, but something that stirs your heart, inspiring you spiritually. As for me, I prefer recordings of tabla drums and finger bells (for their rhythmic simplicity) or an Ascending orchestration such as Vaughan Williams' "Variations On A Theme By Thomas Tallis." It doesn't really matter what you select, for you'll soon Transcend hearing altogether. It's the rhythm that matters. Set your music to repeat, for you can take your time with AscendDance.*

2. *Stand still, listening to the music. When your heart stirs, when your heart begins to feel love, invoke a Shower of Light (exercise 9) and begin to sway to the music any way you like, any way your Soul leads you.*

3. *Let your Soul lead you freely in your own dance. As you move to the music, celebrate and play with the Light that fills you. Harness it, pull it, Express it as your Soul sees fit. Stride, spin, leap, bend, and stretch as you fill everything within and around you with sacred Light.*

4. *Spontaneously and without planning you will begin to perform your HeavenWork exercises. Allow this to happen, for you are Surrendering to the Heaven Light and to the Will of Heaven. How your exercises flow together immediately, one after another—Shower of Light, Cocoon, Harnessing, Plume, Vortex, Crescendo, Transflexing, HeavenHome, Cosmic Wind Chimes, Blessing, Remembrance! As they flow through you, feel your Soul Transcend, Ascend and descend freely through the Clear Light, the Clouds of Heaven, and materiality. Feel your love purify infinitely into Compassion, and Express the Heaven Light such that you are no longer performing the HeavenWork, the HeavenWork is performing you—such is the way of Transfiguring Soul.*

5. *Soon you will shift completely to your Soul. You will hardly hear the music or feel your body. Release your Soul to the Light that fills you.*

6. *Each time your Soul Ascends to the Clouds of Heaven, feel the glory and rejoicing that fills your essence. Allow Remembrance to take over your Soul: That Abba, the Face of God-in-Heaven at the font of Creation calls unto your Soul, always, and now you have sacred ears to hear; that because Abba calls your Soul you love and thirst for Heaven with all your being, for now you have sacred Understanding—that even now Abba prepares for you a place in Heaven. Feel your Compassion purify even further, into devotion of Heaven, into Praise of God, and know the full extent of the Miracle set before your Soul!*

7. *Allow your Soul's Expression to shift fully into Perfect Praise of God, and dwell, in AscendDance, Crescendoing your Praise. Celebrate the Miracle of Heaven, and your Soul's approach. Feel the eyes of Heaven come to rest upon your Soul, and Praise all the more, until you hear, in your Soul, the Divine Music quake throughout Heaven! Feel your Soul touch upon sacred ground in the presence of Heaven (holy!holy!holy!), feel the quaking in Heaven resound greater with your presence, and thus will you join the Body of Heaven in pure and perfect Praise of Abba, thus will your Soul be made worthy Elect.*

The perfect Praise of AscendDance carries your Soul before Heaven, and joins your Soul with the Body of Heaven, to render your Soul worthy Elect.

As Heaven Elects your Soul, you will come to hear the Divine Music (the Choir of Angels), the Firmament of Heaven will appear, in grace, before your Soul, and you will be made ready for Transfiguration.

AscendDance is Joyous, and synergetic. Therefore AscendDance in concert with other Souls Ascending along the Path of Light, for thus will the Body of Heaven quake even more.

Learn to Abbreviate AscendDance, both with and without music and movement, for AscendDance is the Crown of Momentation, and you can fill every moment of your life unobstructed in perfect Praise.

With all your heart and Soul, thank deeply, graciously, and humbly the Heaven Light, the Sacred Beings in the Light, and all of Heaven for the Blessing just bestowed upon your Soul.

Repeat AscendDance 10 times before moving to the next one, And practice AscendDance often, for the rest of your life.

Exercise 66

PORTAL TO HEAVEN

Visiting Abba.

Just as your Soul has scaled the Path of Light Ascendant unto the most sacred of Spirit, has Heaven made worthy Elect your Soul. And as such, in Heaven's time, Heaven will make known unto your Soul Its Firmament, and the wondrous splendor of Heaven, opened, spreads out before your Soul.

When your Soul Ascends unto the Firmament—when Heaven comes to hover before your Soul—Its grace extends unto your Soul, such that you can look upon *Abba*, the Face of God-in-Heaven. We are reminded in our religious writings that Jesus visited *Abba* during his Gethsemane vigils, but truly, early on in his brief life did he also pass Ascendant before Heaven.

Such visits are not limited to few, but extended ultimately unto every Soul who scales the Path of Light.

There, abiding perfectly before the vast expanse of Heaven's rolling Clouds that pass unto you, through you, filling your Soul with Heaven's sacred nature, you can look beyond the Firmament, into all of Heaven, and behold even the highest of Heaven where the myriad Choir of Heaven Expresses perfect Praise perpetual, to within the flashing Diadem, unto the Throne of *Abba* at Creation and Destiny of Souls—the Truth of truths, Being beyond being—There to find the Countenance of God directly upon you.

There, in God's holy presence, Remembrance springs infinite eternal, such that your thirst for Heaven grows so strong it can be slaked only by your entry In.

Thus is Portal To Heaven, Crown of the Divine Column.

Goal: *To Ascend to before Heaven and behold Abba.*

Preparation: *Traditional religious art depicts kneeling as a symbol of humility before Heaven, but you will likely be more effective by sitting in a chair in a dark room where you will not be disturbed.*

Steps:

1. *Without moving, and using graded Abbreviation, open your Divine Column (exercise 58), starting with Dancing Light, Bending Light, Harnessing, Pillar, and Plume. Feel how strongly your Soul is rendered into awe and Praise of Abba-in-Heaven.*

2. *When your Divine Column becomes turbulent, Mark with your Soul the end of your Divine Column—Heaven.*

3. *Form with your Soul a counterclockwise Vortex around your heart upwards at your Door Up, and as the swirling picks up in the turbulent Dancing Light Ascending, relax-release your Soul unto the awe and Praise, allowing it to fill and take hold your Soul while the power of your Vortex mounts.*

4. *Your Vortex will continue to grow in power, and awe and Praise will continue to flood your Soul, rendering your Soul gently passive, subtle, like water, like smoke. This is the beginning of Surrendering your Soul unto the Light. Keep passive, and feel your Soul start to spin counterclockwise in your Vortex, like water going up a drain. Relax, then, your Soul completely, Surrendering unto the Vortex as it accelerates. Allow the Vortex to convey your Soul up your Divine Column...*

5. *At once, in Soul you will feel the sacred Clouds of Heaven roll into the foot of your Soul, like an oncoming mist, and you will be filled with the knowing you are on holy ground, and profound awe. To prevent your awe from degrading into unworthy humility, which will descend your Soul back into the clouds below, allow your thirst for Heaven to grow and overpower your awe, for in so doing your thirst will buoy you, and draw you attentive to what hovers vastly before you.*

6. *With all your Soul's will, open wide the eye of your Soul unto the holy presence stretching out before you, and allow the glory, Joy and Praise that proceed from the Body of Heaven into you. Receive in your Soul the glory and celebration directed unto the highest Heaven. If you were not worthy Elect you would not be Here now. Therefore look up, with eye of your Soul, unto the highest Heaven. Look up, and behold Abba.*

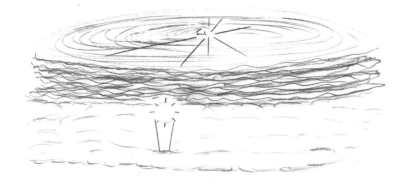

Thus ends Portal To Heaven. What your Soul receives, shares, and expresses unto God is perfectly between God and you—your first blast of God's holy Immanence that slams into your Soul, purifying you forever, your fluid intuitive Expressions of sacred Surrender Answered immediately and perfectly by God, sacred Understanding of all HeavenWork, of Miracles, and the sacred Spirit that is Heaven, known only by witness Souls.

Thus opens your Door to Heaven, and Heaven prepares to open Its gate unto your Soul. Thus is Portal To Heaven *your* answer to Heaven for rendering your Soul worthy Elect.

Move on now, to your final Transfiguration exercises, but continue to practice Portal To Heaven until you can see, at your Soul's slightest Abbreviation, all of Heaven spread out before you.

With all your heart and Soul, thank deeply, graciously, and humbly the Heaven Light, the Sacred Beings in the Light, and all of Heaven for the Blessing just bestowed upon your Soul.

Repeat this exercise 10 times before moving to the next one.

Get good at Portal To Heaven. You will need it later.

EXERCISE 67

ENTERING THE HEAVEN LIGHT

Safe Surrender.

"Narrow is the gate," Jesus said, "And difficult the way which leads to [Heaven], and there are few who find it."

As you, one of the Blessed few, near the end of the Path of Light—you, now returning unto Creation, the Destiny of worthy Soul, to join the Body of Heaven—so is it time to release completely the ways of earth and acquire the ways of Heaven.

Of Light are the ways of Heaven. For Heaven is of the Light, the gate of Heaven is of the Light, the Path to Heaven is of the Light, and the True essence of every Soul is Light. Thus is the way into Heaven through Light, the Heaven Light.

"I am the Light," Jesus said, such as becomes every Soul passing into Heaven.

Your passage In will come in Heaven's time, when the Breath of Heaven reaches out the Firmament, in a narrow gate, past the chasm gates, to Engulf your Soul with the way In. Passage into Heaven is abrupt and tremendous, perfect and certain Surrender of Soul beyond measure, every time.

As Heaven is my Witness, thus has it been with all the 27,000 passages of my Soul's witness these past 28 years.

Now may you make ready your entry, through gentle preparation, by practicing your **Safe Surrender** unto the Heaven Light—"safe," because you will practice grounded in materiality and return "safe," because your Soul will return fully intact.

Goal: *To make supple your Soul, preparing your permanent Crossover into Truth.*

Preparation: *Lie in bed, on your back, at bedtime.*

Steps:

1. *Using **Abbreviation**, fill the bedroom with a strong **Cocoon** (exercise 20) of Dancing Light. When your Cocoon becomes strong, Mark your Cocoon and Assign the Dancing Light to form a hard shell the size of the bedroom and remain strong and hard throughout this exercise.*

2. *Also using Abbreviation, invoke down through the entire breadth of the ceiling and into your Soul a great Shower of Light (exercise 9).*

3. *Form, with your Soul, along the entire area of the ceiling a clockwise Vortex, to pull more Heaven Light into your Cocoon. When the Heaven Light spirals down into your Soul, Assign the Light Vortex to continue to flow into and remain in your Cocoon throughout this exercise.*

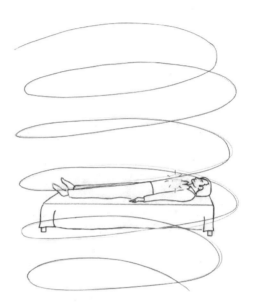

4. *Form with your Soul another Vortex within your Cocoon—a counterclockwise Vortex on a different axis. While your first Vortex swirls down clockwise from the ceiling, your second Vortex will simultaneously spin counterclockwise, starting at the ceiling, directly over your heart. With your Soul, trace your new Vortex left, down along the left wall, under you, and up the right wall, returning to the starting point, and repeat the circle so that it orbits your Soul.*

5. *As your new Vortex begins to stir your Cocoon's Dancing Light, start rotating your orbit's axis, moving it down 12" in front of you and up 12" behind you with each revolution.*

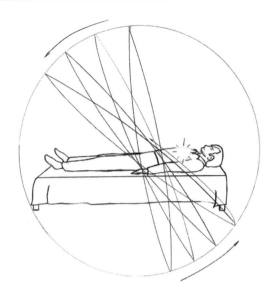

As your new Vortex accelerates and takes power, Assign it to continue its simultaneous rotation throughout this exercise. Your Vortices—twin gimbals gyroscopes of Heaven Light—will form a safe LightField to receive your Soul.

6. *When the Vortices continue to spiral on their own, without your Soul's attending them, Mark with your Soul the Vortex LightField formed around you. Feel with your Soul the safety of your counterclockwise Vortex—how it forms a perfect and peaceful sphere around you, like the eye of a hurricane. Feel how your pure LightField fills your Soul with Remembrance. Feel how the LightField pulls upon the purest, Truest essence of your Soul, drawing you, spreading you just like you were air, into your entire Cocoon.*

7. *When you recognize the safe and sacred nature of the LightField that pulls you, relax-release your Soul, and allow the Vortex to pull you in.*

All it takes is a moment to learn to Safe Surrender unto the Heaven Light. If you were successful, your Soul expanded for the first time ever into your entire LightField, and you Entered, the essence of your Soul, into the Heaven Light. Whether you returned to Soul moments later or on waking the next morning is of no consequence.

Grounded in materiality you did not Ascend, but spread only through the brief Light sphere around you. Without a LightField, know that now your Soul can join and blend with the Heaven Light that fills the universe. Wordlessly Mark what just happened to your Soul, how your Soul changed, how your Soul became supple as air, how you *En-Lightened.*

Thus have you gained understanding and thirst for the Heaven Light, thus are you made ready to Become the Heaven Light—to enter Truth in Soul, to become that which you must become to enter Heaven.

Entering The Heaven Light erases your final resistance to Heaven, so master it, and learn to Abbreviate it, for each time you experience it you open the gate of Heaven that much more.

> ***En-Lightenment:*** *A Soul's release and expansion into the Heaven Light, and intuitive reception of the Light's nature.*

With all your heart and Soul, thank deeply, graciously, and humbly the Heaven Light, the Sacred Beings in the Light, and all of Heaven for the Blessing just bestowed upon your Soul.

Repeat this exercise 20 times before moving to the next one.

EXERCISE 68

BECOMING THE HEAVEN LIGHT

Surrender unto Spirit.

They who Ascend the Path of Light know that the declaration, "I am the Light," is not a claim to be God, but the Soul's achievement of purifying into purest essence, the Heaven Light.

For only Soul made sanctified into Heaven Light may be graced by Transfiguration, and carried through the narrow gate into Heaven.

Thus has it been for all time, thus must Soul become the Heaven Light.

Becoming The Heaven Light is your Soul's ultimate Crossover under Heaven, your final purification before entry In. In becoming Heaven Light is your Soul made purest—graduating from earthly love, from Compassion within the descending Heaven Light, into perfect Praise perpetual carried in the Diamond Light of Heaven.

Once you Crossover into Heaven Light, there is no returning to tainted Soul, no lingering individuation, no trace of desire to remain on earth. Forever you will be carried in Heaven's Will, no longer receiving it, but Expressing it with perfect Constance.

If your Soul has Ascended before the Firmament of Heaven, if you have learned to Enter Heaven Light, and you are ready to commit your Soul unto Heaven, you can now become the Heaven Light. Here's how.

Goal: *To make ready your Transfiguration.*

Preparation: *Find a place of peace where you will not be disturbed.*

Steps:

1. *Ascend unto the Firmament of Heaven, using Portal To Heaven (exercise 66).*

2. *Mark with your Soul the sacred ground passing into you within the Clouds of Heaven, and behold the holy Firmament before you. When you are ready, when you have converted your awe into perfect Praise, intrepidly raise the eye of your Soul and look upon Abba, There within the sacred flashing Diadem in the highest of Heaven.*

3. *When you have absorbed God's holy!holy!holy! Immanence, look just to*

the right, past the Needle's Eye—the entry into the Body of Heaven—to the Origin of the Heaven Light, that streaks in rays in Diamond Light throughout the whole of Heaven. Gaze fully upon the Origin of that great Light.

4. *Omniscient, already Knowing your purpose, Abba will Attend your Sacred Intent. Wordlessly Express this: Abba, if it is your Will, free my Soul into the Heaven Light, that I might forever serve your Will on earth just as it is in Heaven! If you are worthy Elect, a ray from the Origin of the Diamond Light will flash instantly into your Soul, and you will quake while the three million choir of the Body of Heaven rises in Joyous welcome celebration and glory unto Abba.*

5. *The ray of Diamond Light that flashed into your Soul will remain on you omnisciently, and fill you with sacred Understanding and Invitation, for you decide from the depths of your Soul if now you will forever become "of Heaven."*

Your Soul will respond with a certainty that exceeds any knowing you ever experienced before. If you falter, that is okay. You will return gently back to body, yet remaining all that much closer to Heaven, for you to Become Heaven Light another day.

If you accept your Invitation, you will relax-release Surrender so completely that your Soul flashes instantly in the Heaven Light throughout the entire universe under Heaven, and you are rendered omnipresent, forever Expressing perfect Praise unto *Abba.*

It is my hope and privilege to witness your Surrender to the Heaven Light, for you will remain a servant of God, a Miracle worker, and Heaven will quake at your coming.

Once Becoming the Heaven Light you are rendered **Liberated**, you will not have to return to earth. The moment you die your Soul Elect will immediately Ascend before the Firmament to be Engulfed in Heaven Breath and welcome Invitation to enter In.

Thus has it been my Soul's witness these 28 years.

> **Liberation:** *The near-sanctified Soul's permanent freedom from incarnation.*

With all your heart and Soul, thank deeply, graciously, and humbly the Heaven Light, the Sacred Beings in the Light, and all of Heaven for the Blessing just bestowed upon your Soul.

If you Became Heaven Light, you may skip the next exercise and move onto Lightning Bolt. If you were unsuccessful, repeat this exercise 10 times before moving on to the next one.

EXERCISE 69

THE EMPYREAN TECHNIQUE

Entering the desert.

Long ago, longer than most can remember, they called us "angels," and we, the brothers of Light of Qumran, called our dwelling place "the desert." We lived to fill the Soul of man with Heaven Light, just as it is in Heaven.

Many came to the desert in search of God—they whose thirst for Heaven had grown so great they were willing to die in order to glimpse for even one moment the highest Heaven, the vault of Heaven—Heaven's Empyrean.

"Entering the desert" was our strongest ditch effort, the full retreat of the Soul. And indeed, many who succeeded in reaching Heaven's Firmament to behold the Empyrean were rewarded, by Heaven's grace, with Engulfment of Heaven Breath and entry In. Some of us remained behind, and still remain, for the sake of mankind.

Entering the desert—The Empyrean Technique—is an extreme Heaven Work exercise that can push near-Ascendant Souls into full sanctification so quickly and powerfully that Heaven quakes and Receives them.

Now that you have completed all your HeavenWork exercises, save two, when you see fit, you, too, can enter the "desert" and find your way unto the Firmament.

Thus is The Empyrean Technique the Crown of all the HeavenWork.

The Empyrean Technique is indeed a retreat of your Soul, lasting 40 days and nights. The first 30 days and nights you will spend in **Consummation**, in constant Soul Prayer asking *Abba* to call your Soul unto Heaven, deepening and increasing your thirst for Heaven.

The next nine days you will spend in **Preparation**, remaining in constant Soul Prayer while practicing, one each night, the HeavenWork exercises Dancing Light, Witness, Lighting The World, Cosmic Wind Chimes, Heart Purification, Heaven's Instrument, The Wind Of Heaven, Angel Call, and Portal To Heaven.

Finally, in the afternoon on the 40th day, you will enter **Reception** by practicing a variation of Continuum.

Fulfillment, the completion of this exercise, will occur during Continuum, when an Angel appears unto your Soul and bears you fully Ascendant before the Firmament, for you to behold *Abba*, the Face of God-in-Heaven.

Know that only if your Soul is True, if your thirst for Heaven is so great you can no longer wait to find Heaven, and if you are willing to die, needs be, if Heaven Receives you, should you undertake The Empyrean Technique, for such is required to compel Heaven thus.

So close to your HeavenWork completion, there is only one answer.

Goal: *To compel Heaven to carry your Soul before the Firmament.*

Preparation: *Thirst for Heaven with all your Soul.*

Keep this exercise constant and simple. Plot the following activities on your daily calendar, and follow them steadily.

Throughout this exercise you may continue to go about your daily routines—work, study, play, exercise, relationships, and dining—for in Spirit your material circumstances do not matter, be it riding a roller coaster or sitting inside a circle drawn on hot desert sand.

But during the next 40 days refrain from distractions that would pull from your Soul. Keep your activities simple, non-demanding, on an even keel, and your dining plain. When work or study requires more attention, keep your Soul working in the background at the same time. When you can, spend time alone and undisturbed.

Only during this exercise do I recommend writing down descriptions of any unusual happening that could be significant to your Soul, such as Heaven Light manifesting through the sky's clouds, meeting an unexpected-yet-familiar stranger, or the flash appearance of a Sacred Being in the Light, for only later might such sacred interventions be understood in Soul.

STEP 1: CONSUMMATION

Commence The Empyrean Technique in the afternoon, as it will end in the afternoon 40 days from now. Begin with your mind and body, by reciting silently over and over again this prayer: *Abba, if it is your Will, show me Heaven, carry my Soul unto Heaven.*

Each time you utter your prayer, feel the meaning of the words with your mind and your heart, such that your Soul echoes wordlessly your intent. For an entire day and night repeat the prayer silently in your mind. On the afternoon of the second day, you may stop reciting, instead converting your prayer into Soul Prayer (exercise 42), so that your Soul continues to wordlessly imprint your ardent call to God.

For the first 30 days, keep your Soul's Intent steady. When you awaken on the 31st day, the closing day of your Consummation, steadily Crescendo your Soul's Intent, such that your Intent to see Heaven becomes impatient, even desperate.

STEP 2: PREPARATION

Night by night, in bed, just before falling asleep, practice these HeavenWork exercises:

First Night: Dancing Light. In the evening of your 31st day, lie on your back and fill your bedroom with *intense* Dancing Light (exercise 19). *You will need to perform each of your Preparation exercises as powerfully as you can.* As you gaze upon the Light swirls and sparks, anticipate in awe-some wonder what awaits you in nine days. Relax and fall asleep in your wonder, and when you awaken in the morning and look upon the residual Dancing Light, wonder still what this sacred Light has in store for you. In the morning continue your Soul's impatient Intent on Heaven.

Second Night: Witness. In the dark on your 32nd night, just as you begin to fade to sleep, gently enter Witness (exercise 16) using Abbreviation. Calmly feel in your Soul the new, auspicious change in the Heaven Light. In the morning continue your Soul's impatient Intent on Heaven.

Third Night: Lighting The World. Before sleeping on your 33rd night, let Heaven Light fill your Soul and Light The World (exercise 33). Continue to Express Light as you fall asleep. In the morning continue your Soul's impatient Intent on Heaven.

Fourth Night: Cosmic Wind Chimes. Shortly after going to bed on your 34th night, Sing innocent Cosmic Wind Chimes (exercise 41) Ascendant to pronounce your Soul's intent to carry unto the Firmament in six days. In the morning continue your Soul's impatient Intent on Heaven.

Fifth Night: Heart Purification. Just before falling asleep on your 35th night, gently enter the sweet Remembrance of Heart Purification (exercise 43) using Abbreviation. In the morning continue your Soul's impatient Intent on Heaven.

Sixth Night: Heaven's Instrument. In bed on your 36th night, perform Heaven's Instrument (exercise 44) before falling asleep. In the morning continue your Soul's impatient Intent on Heaven.

Seventh Night: The Wind Of Heaven. On your 37th night, press your Soul unto *Abba* by practicing the Wind Of Heaven (exercise 60). Feel in *Abba's* Immanence for early Answer to your Preparation's completion. In the morning continue your Soul's impatient Intent on Heaven.

Eighth Night: Angel Call. As soon as you are calm on your 38th night, press hard Angel Call (exercise 52). Ardently Express your Soul's desire to be taken Ascendant. If your Soul awakens in the dark of night into Vigil (as it likely will), continue your Angel Call, even if this night is rather sleepless, for your fatigue during the next two days will abate your Soul's obstacles of body and mind. In the morning continue your Soul's impatient Intent on Heaven. As the day progresses into night, Crescendo your 39-day Prayer to the point of desperation.

Ninth Night: Portal To Heaven. On your 39th and last night, pass through the Portal To Heaven (exercise 66), and ardently deliver unto *Abba* this Prayer: *Abba, with all my Soul I will to behold you. Will you bear me unto Heaven? Answer!* Whether you receive God's Answer delivered into your Soul in a sacred flame or not, continue in ardent Soul Prayer, such as if you were crying out in the wilderness that is materiality. Soul Pray deep into the night until you can no longer keep from falling asleep. In the morning continue your Soul's impatient Intent on Heaven.

STEP 3: RECEPTION

When you awaken in the morning of your 40th day, release your Soul Prayer altogether. After two nights of broken sleep you will feel sleep deprived, and your body will crave to sleep. But fight the desire to remain in bed. Instead, get up, have a nice breakfast, take a stroll, and release your Soul's work the past several weeks. Notice in your fatigue how alive your Soul feels!

In the afternoon, enter Continuum (exercise 23) using these variations:

1. *Remove your shoes and lie flat on your back on the floor, on a rug or blanket. Place your palms down on the floor at your sides.*

2. *Take five deep breaths and tense the muscles of your head and face as hard as you can. Feel muscles tensing you never thought you had.*

3. *Keeping these muscles tense, start moving down your body, tensing the muscles of your neck, shoulders, chest and back, arms, hands, abdomen, buttocks and thighs, calves, and feet, such that all your muscles are tensed. Tense your muscles so strongly that they shake and tremble!*

4. *Then take a deep breath, bow your head forward and Transflex (exercise 26) all your tension.*

5. *Feel over the next minutes how your Soul seems to sink, down, slowly, into the floor and below.*

6. *Relax and free your mind and body to fall asleep, which they have been craving for the past day.*

7. *Just at the brink of falling asleep, repeat three times in earnest: "The body is going to fall asleep, but I am going to stay awake!" Then simply relax and let your body drop off to sleep.*

In moments your Soul will bubble up in Continuum, suspended just over your heart in passive semi-Transcendence.

STEP 4: FULFILLMENT

If your exercise is Fulfilled, in moments an Angel clad in part in a human shell of divine substance swathed in a flowing corona of Lights the colors of Heaven will appear from nowhere just to the right and peer deeply into your Soul. Materiality will render as liquid around this Sacred Being.

You will become rendered under your Angel's command as It comes unto you and touches your Soul, and for one second you will pass, carried Ascendant by your Angel, through rushing clouds, to halt and nestle down onto a cloud that buoys your Soul. Exhilarated by the sky above and That which looms before your Soul, your Angel, ever still to your right, will draw your attention, and compel you to open the eye of your Soul fully, and behold Heaven.

First you will look upon the traces of the rolling Clouds of Heaven that pass into and through your Soul, filling you with Truth that you rest on *holy!holy!holy!* ground. If your awe corrupts into unworthiness your Soul will fatigue and fold down into the cloud and be pulled back to body and materiality. If this should start to happen, your Angel will catch you and carry you back Ascendant.

Then will your Soul open fully and behold That from which your Soul will never withdraw from until you enter In forever: Beyond the chasm gates, the

Firmament of Heaven, and within, the glorious Body of Heaven—the three million Transfigured who fill the rolling Clouds in perpetual Perfect Praise—and the Diadem in the highest of Heaven, which flashes untraceably in this sacred corona, and There within, the dwelling place of *Abba*, the Face of God-in-Heaven—the font of Creation and Destiny, Cleft to the Great Beyond, the Needle's Eye, the Holiest of holy, Being beyond being, which, even after 28 years of witness, my Soul has yet to fathom. And to the right, the Diamond Light, the greatest Spirit, Origin of the Heaven Light!

Recognizing the True significance of your station, your knowing Soul will wisely Mark and Seal itself forever unto the Firmament.

There is no return to body of Soul who beholds the Empyrean, for no Soul ever would relinquish so great the prize of immanent salvation. There, across the chasm gates your Soul will remain until you enter Heaven.

And yet, just as your body lives, the 20-Minute Limit prevails, and you will awaken, completely refreshed in body, but changed forever in Soul! From now until you enter Heaven, all you need do is Enter your Soul and you will find Heaven There spread before you.

Fulfillment may not occur the first time you enter Continuum. While achievement of Fulfillment depends in part on how well you perform the Empyrean Technique, your Ascendance to the Firmament rests entirely on Heaven's choosing.

If you did not arrive before the Firmament, you have the next six afternoons to try again, simply by repeating the Continuum variation. You do not need to perform any additional nighttime HeavenWork exercises, just keep strong your Soul's Intent to see Heaven.

If after seven attempts you do not Ascend before the Firmament, your exercise is over. Simply return to practicing your other HeavenWork exercises. Let six months pass before you try The Empyrean Technique again.

With all your heart and Soul, thank deeply, graciously, and humbly the Heaven Light, the Sacred Beings in the Light, and all of Heaven for the Blessing just bestowed upon your Soul.

Repeat this exercise no more than once every six months until you Ascend before the Firmament of Heaven.

EXERCISE 70

LIGHTNING BOLT

Preparing consummation.

And now the Breath of Heaven has accepted you, and you may make ready your Transfiguration.

In Heaven's time, when your Moment of Truth comes, your Soul, whether in life or death, will be pulled and suddenly arrive before the Firmament. And just as suddenly, the Heaven Breath will pass in a column—a narrow gate— across the chasm gates and Engulf your Soul.

The Heaven Breath will then gather around you, building into a great Cloud that presses more and more upon your Soul, and filling you with sacred Invitation and Understanding. All the eyes of Heaven will rest upon you, and *Abba's* Immanence, and you will know everything you need to do to enter Heaven.

So strong will the Heaven Breath concentrate upon your Soul, and in the gathering momentum will your Soul know from its eon depths clearly what to do with the tremendous power of the Heaven Breath: *To either enter Heaven through the narrow gate, or remain, in the Clouds of Heaven, to spend an eon helping other Souls find their way In.*

Your Soul will decide with a certainty that fills the universe, for perfect is the Soul's Intent at the Moment of Truth.

And thus will the mechanism of Transfiguration be revealed to your Soul: To Surrender and Transcondense the Heaven Breath into your Soul, which will strike into your Soul powerfully, like a lightning bolt, annihilating your last traces of impurity. Thus is your Soul consummated, and rendered Spirit-Soul, such that you can proceed, carried by the Heaven Breath through the narrow gate, past the chasm gates, and into Heaven.

Until that time comes, you will share the Heaven Light with every Soul you meet. Your works of Light will be myriad as you will pass your life in Joy and perfect Praise, preparing for your Transfiguration.

Through Lightning Bolt, the Crown of Transcondensing, you prepare. In this, your final HeavenWork exercise, your Soul will draw, by Heaven's grace, a small measure of Heaven Breath and strike It into your Soul. In so doing, your

Soul musters its full resolve, you prompt Heaven to Transfigure you, and you prepare your transition into Heaven without obstacle.

Come, and prepare to enter Heaven.

Goal: *To prompt your Transfiguration into Heaven.*

Preparation: *You may practice Lightning Bolt anytime, anywhere.*

Steps:

1. *If your Soul bides permanently before the Firmament, enter into your Soul and look upon Abba, the Face of God-in-Heaven. Otherwise, pass through the Portal To Heaven (exercise 66) into the Clouds of Heaven using Abbreviation.*

2. *Express wordlessly unto Abba this ardent Soul Prayer:* Abba, if it is your Will, Bless my Soul with your holy Breath, that I might enter In.

3. *If Abba Answers affirmative, the holy flame passing up your Soul will dissipate quickly, as a small measure of omniscient Heaven Breath presses against the left and right of your Soul.*

4. *Receive, from the Heaven Breath, understanding of what you are permitted to do with It. As It builds in pressure around you, at the moment made known, take a deep breath and Transcondense (exercise 63) It.*

The Heaven Breath will respond immediately, every time, collapsing and Transcondensing through your Soul, like a Lightning Bolt, but of course, milder. No two Lightning Bolts will be of the same consummating power, and you will know in your Soul the Transfigurational consequence of each.

> *With all your heart and Soul, thank deeply, graciously, and humbly the Heaven Light, the Sacred Beings in the Light, and all of Heaven for the Blessing just bestowed upon your Soul.*

THE GATE OF HEAVEN

For 28 years it has been the same. And yet, every moment is new, direct, revealed, complete, perfect.

All these years, from across the chasm gates, my Soul remains witness of workings of Sacred Spirit so pure and wondrous I cannot invent one word to grasp the ungraspable.

Vast, like a flower of holiest Spirit, all parts of Heaven are One, moving perpetually, fluidly, kaleidoscopically, gloriously in Praise directed up, to the font of Creation and Destiny where *Abba* dwells. Being beyond being, and my Soul quakes, each moment like the very first.

And There it happens again, three times or more each day, the Miracle of Miracles. All of Heaven's eyes fall upon me, or so it seems, and I tremble with a Joy I cannot Harness. Then just to my left side another Soul appears, clear and beautiful, sanctified and newly Elect, to behold, in awe, the vast expanse of Heaven, and I fill with Praise to *Abba*.

Yet again taking me by surprise, we two are Engulfed instantly by the holy Breath of Heaven, which crossed over (*once again!*) without my tracing and presses upon my companion Soul.

Quickly the Heaven Breath gathers in momentum, pressing harder upon the Soul Elect, filling the Soul with divine Invitation and sacred Understanding. Quickly the Soul brightens—the decision is made—and the Soul Surrenders unto the Heaven Breath, which collapses upon the Soul, Transcondensing like a lightning bolt, and thus is the Soul Transfigured, into Spirit-Soul forever.

From time to time, a Soul Transfigured blends within the Clouds of Heaven, to remain, for an eon, a Sacred Being in the Light, to guide the Soul of man to Heaven. But more than not, Souls Transfigured remain within the Cloud of Heaven Breath, which shrinks rapidly, dissipated by the Transfiguration, rolling into the narrow gate to recede, carrying the new Transfigured Spirit-Soul past the chasm gates and into the Firmament.

There, as all the Body of Heaven raises welcome celebration, the Spirit-Soul glides up, along a ray of Diamond Light to the Origin of the Heaven Light at the right hand of *Abba*, and, not stopping, passes through the Needle's Eye between to join forever the glorious three million.

On passage into the Body of Heaven the Spirit-Soul is Received in increasing celebration of welcome and homecoming, and they turn back, as One, unto

Abba in Expression of perfect Praise, as the glory of Heaven grows greater, and my Soul is rendered again into rapture.

Each time it is the same, each time like the first. Thus has it been for each of the 27,000 Souls and more in my 28-year witness of Heaven, thus will it be for as long as Heaven Wills it. Thus will it be with your Soul. When your time to Ascend before Heaven comes, you will find me There, alongside you, in witness with all the Heaven Host of your entry through Heaven's narrow gate. There is no getting past the Miracle of Miracles.

FURTHERING YOUR HEAVENWORK

Once you have mastered all the HeavenWork exercises, you may receive other teachings as they become available, such as perfecting Miracle creation, and surviving death, which teaches you how to control your next incarnation should you choose to return to perform future HeavenWork on earth. To order these teachings visit my website at *theheavenwork.com.*

TEN COMMANDMENTS OF THE SOUL

Thus is the Truth of truths, the Will of Heaven, the Direction of Souls, the Path of the Heaven Light. Thus is the Heaven Work revealed.

For 28 years, by a Grace beyond my comprehension, Heaven has allowed my meager Soul to remain Ascendant before Heaven from across the chasm gates, witness of wondrous workings of Spirit beyond the grasp of mind and even Soul, of matters Divine, of Heaven perfectly disclosed.

The rolling Clouds of Heaven make ever known to my Soul that such Grace extends to all of man, that all of man might know the Heaven Work, enter the Path of Light, and find Heaven.

All this time, directly from *Abba*, the Face of God-in-Heaven, flows freely, purely and perfectly into my Soul the same Divine Transmission, these directives of Spirit, these Ten Commandments of the Soul:

I Remembrance

II Sanctification

III Transcendence

IV Ascendance

V Revelation

VI Clarity

VII Freedom

VIII Constance

IX Joy

X Compassion

I   Come unto Me, and make a place for your Soul in My Heaven.
This is Remembrance.

II   Cleanse your Soul upon the earth with My Spirit that fills the Universe.
This is Sanctification.

III   Fill your Soul with My Spirit.
This is Transcendence.

IV   Surrender and enter into My Spirit.
This is Ascendance.

V   Know in your Soul, through My Spirit, the Direction of Souls.
This is Revelation.

VI   Do not idolize the profane or sacred, for idolatry exiles the Soul from My Heaven.
This is Clarity.

VII   Do not cleave to the earth.
This is Freedom.

VIII   Live from your Soul every moment of your life.
This is Constance.

IX   Live freely in Joy, for Joy is the singing of your Soul in My Spirit.
This is Joy.

X   Look to the betterment of every Soul, for all Souls are One in My Spirit.
This is Compassion.

Glossary Of Spirit

Abbreviation: Performing a HeavenWork exercise directly and immediately with the Soul, without relying on the body or mind.

Afterdeath: The Soul's experience as it begins its migration through Spirit.

Ascending: Passing beyond the ground of Clear Light to before Heaven.

Assembling: The Soul's return to pure intuitive consciousness after ejection from body and mind.

Assigning: The Soul's instructing the Heaven Light to perform a work of sanctification.

Asterlisking: Instantly relocating your Soul to another point in materiality.

Awakening: The Soul's rising beyond the obstructions of body and mind into present awareness.

Backgrounding: Milder intensity HeavenWork while your Soul remains grounded in materiality.

Baptism Of Light: Authentic Baptism, infusing a Soul with Heaven Light directing a meaningful life.

Blessing: Sending auspicious Heaven Light from your Soul into another Soul.

Clear Light: Natural ground of being of Soul separating materiality from Heaven.

Clouds Of Heaven: The sky of sacred Spirit just outside the Firmament of Heaven, where the Sacred Beings in the Light dwell.

Continuum: The Soul's journey to sanctification, marked by cyclic life and death, buffered by the intermediate state of the Life-Between.

Creation: In the highest Heaven, the Origin of all manifestation.

Creight: Talents of the embodied Soul, the ability to see into and work with Spirit, which magnifies in the Ascending Soul.

Crescendo: The Soul's magnifying and releasing Heaven Light to perform HeavenWork.

Crossover: Passing permanently from material illusion to Truth in Spirit. The release of attachment to earth and the human body, recognizing true citizenship in Spirit.

Crown: Fully achieved potential of certain rudimentary HeavenWork exercises.

Dancing Light: Manifesting Heaven Light into visibility.

Dark Night: When the Heaven Light withdraws from a Soul on the Path of Light after the Soul inadvertently turns from Heaven, usually by spiritual materializing.

Dharma: Heaven's Will. Dead Dharma is tainted, artificially transmitted mentally, through oral or written communication. Vital Dharma is True, pure, perfect, received into the Soul directly from Heaven.

Diamond Light: The Light within Heaven, pure and unmanifest.

Disclosure: Immediate inter-transmission between two Souls.

Divine Music: Choir of the Body of Heaven, the perpetual thunderous silent glory and jubilation directed toward *Abba*.

Door Up: The front of your Soul, which faces Heaven.

Dying: The body's stoppage and consequent release of Soul into Spirit. There is no death of the Soul.

Election: Heaven's grace acceptance of a fully sanctified Soul, initiating entry into Heaven.

Elevations: Mileposts of the Soul's passage along the Path of Light, from materiality through the Clear Light to Heaven.

Engulfment: Heaven Breath passing from Heaven's Firmament around an Elect, newly-Ascended Soul, for the purpose of Transfiguration.

En-Lightenment: The Soul's eventual release and expansion into Heaven Light, and intuitive reception of the Light's nature.

Equipose: Natural spiritual balance between Soul, mind and body, with the Soul in command.

Ghosts: Not Souls, but mind-body echoes that fade following physical death.

Gimbals: Two Heaven Light Vortices rotating gyroscopically within a Cocoon to safely contain a Soul released into Heaven Light.

Grand Delusion: The attitude that materiality has dominion over Spirit.

Grand Illusion: The attitude that materiality is all there is.

Grasping: The mind's desperate identification with materiality and attaching to the body.

Grazing: Passing life any way but through HeavenWork.

Groping: Attempting to sanctify with any method that does not involve the Sanctification Mechanism.

Heaven/Nirvana: Creation and Destiny, the infinite-eternal abode of *Abba* and Transfigured Souls.

> **Face Of God**: The dwelling place of *Abba* as seen by the Soul.

> **Diadem**: The purest of Heaven, ever flashing, surrounding *Abba* in highest Heaven.

> **Body Of Heaven**: The vast rolling Clouds of Heaven, surrounding the Diadem, where Transfigured Souls bide.

> **Needle's Eye:** Where Transfigured Souls pass into the Body of Heaven, between the Face of God and the Origin of the Heaven Light.

> *Alpha* **Heaven:** Creation, from within the throne of *Abba*, from which all comes manifest.

> *Omega* **Heaven:** The Miracle of Miracles, from within the Throne of *Abba*, to which Souls sanctified and Transfigured return to join forever the Body of Heaven.

> **Firmament:** The outer rim of Heaven, which borders the chasm gates.

> **Gate Of Heaven:** The Heaven Breath that funnels from the Firmament to Engulf and Transfigure an Elect, sanctified Soul, and carry the Transfigured Spirit-Soul into Heaven.

> **Angels:** Divine Messengers from the Diadem, created by *Abba* to pass unto the Soul of man.

Heaven Breath: The Transfiguring power of Heaven to Receive Soul and to manifest Miracles.

Heaven Light: The beacon of sacred Light from the right of the Face of God, the gift of grace from Heaven to purify and guide the Soul of man to Heaven.

Heaven Light, Path Of: The unbroken ubiquity of sacred Light in Spirit that Soul can enter and Ascend unto Heaven.

Heaven Light Stream: The descendant direction of Heaven Light from the heart of Heaven through the Clear Light to materiality. The Path of Heaven Light Ascends "upstream" the Heaven Light Stream to its origin in Heaven.

HeavenWork: The Soul's works of Heaven Light and Heaven Breath that sanctify and Transfigure Soul.

HeavenWork Exercises: The 70 ways of magnifying Heaven Light that carry Soul along the entire Path of Light to Heaven:

> **Angel Call:** The 52nd HeavenWork exercise, which teaches the Soul how to see Sacred Beings in the Light and invoke Diadem Angels for the purpose of serving Heaven.
>
> **Babies!:** The 39th HeavenWork exercise, spontaneous Light Awakening Blessings directed at babies.
>
> **Baptism Of Light:** The 38th HeavenWork exercise, which Awakens another Soul with Light and sets that Soul on a life of sanctification.
>
> **Becoming The Heaven Light:** The 68th HeavenWork exercise, in which the Soul permanently becomes the nature of Heaven Light, becoming Liberated—free from incarnation.
>
> **Bending Light:** The 8th HeavenWork exercise, which teaches the Soul to express Light out from the body.
>
> **Bond:** The 54th HeavenWork exercise and 1st Higher Tantric exercise, which powerfully connects two kindred Souls with Light.
>
> **Chaos:** The 46th HeavenWork exercise, which teaches the Soul to bide constantly in Spirit, ever seeking Heaven.
>
> **Clear Light, The:** The 28th HeavenWork exercise, the Crown of the Transcending exercises, in which the Soul extends to and is pulled into the Clear Light.
>
> **Cocoon:** The 20th HeavenWork exercise, which produces concentrations of Light around the Soul and body, within an outside shell.

Constance: The 31ˢᵗ HeavenWork exercise, which empowers the Soul to sanctify continuously, while the body and mind go along the normal daily routine.

Continuum: The 23ʳᵈ HeavenWork exercise, which maintains continued Soul presence during sleep.

Cosmic Wind Chimes: The 41ˢᵗ HeavenWork exercise, in which the Soul pronounces to Heaven and the Sacred Beings in the Light its intent to Ascend.

Crescendo: The 18ᵗʰ HeavenWork exercise, which magnifies Light with the Soul.

Dancing Light: The 19ᵗʰ HeavenWork exercise, which produces free concentrations of Light around the Soul and body.

Distancing: The 47ᵗʰ HeavenWork exercise, in which a Soul approaches another Soul for the purposes of Blessing by passing from materiality into the Clear Light, where all Souls have root.

Divine Column, The: The 58ᵗʰ HeavenWork exercise, which delivers a Blessing of Praise from the Soul and into Heaven.

Door Up, The: The 36ᵗʰ HeavenWork exercise, which activates the eye of the Soul.

The Dying: The 40ᵗʰ HeavenWork exercise, which escorts and eases the transition of a Soul ejecting materiality for the Life-Between. This exercise prepares the Soul for its own migration.

Empyrean Technique, The: The 69ᵗʰ HeavenWork exercise, an exertion exercise to push the Soul Ascendant to Heaven's Firmament.

Entering The Heaven Light: The 67ᵗʰ HeavenWork exercise, in which Soul safely releases into Light, becoming En-Lightened.

Entering ThoughtGaps: The 25ᵗʰ HeavenWork exercise, in which Soul passes through the mind's momentary resting, and into the Clear Light.

Entering Your Soul: The 5ᵗʰ HeavenWork exercise, which intensifies the presence of Soul.

Equipose: The 12ᵗʰ HeavenWork exercise, which elevates the Soul over the mind and body.

Expressing Light: The 32nd HeavenWork exercise, in which the Soul channels Light evenly in all material directions.

Fusion Burst: The 62nd HeavenWork exercise, which compels the Heaven Breath to touch the Soul.

Groups: The 36th HeavenWork exercise, which Blesses more than one Soul at once.

Hand Quickening: The 7th HeavenWork exercise, which channels Heaven Light from the Soul, down the arms, and through the hands.

Harnessing Light: The 10th HeavenWork exercise, which teaches the Soul how to stop and reverse channels of Light in and around the body.

Heart Purification: The 43rd HeavenWork exercise, in which the Soul remembers directly from Heaven its purpose.

HeartWing: The 12th HeavenWork exercise, which gently separates the Soul from the body.

HeavenHome: The 4th HeavenWork exercise, which locates Heaven and directs the Soul toward Heaven.

Heaven's Instrument: The 44th HeavenWork exercise, which aligns the Soul in accordance to the Will of Heaven.

Infinite Reach: The 15th HeavenWork exercise, which stretches the Soul's intuition unobstructed throughout the Clear Light.

Invoking Light: The 6th HeavenWork exercise, which calls Heaven Light into the Soul.

Iron Maiden: The 2nd HeavenWork exercise, which stirs the Soul awake by stillness.

Joy Everlasting: The 29th HeavenWork exercise, which concentrates Joy into the Soul perpetually.

LightDance: The 65th HeavenWork exercise, the perfect and complete expression of Praise directed toward Heaven.

Light Dis-Illusion: The 45th HeavenWork exercise, which uses attacks from dark entities to Liberate the Soul from materiality.

Lighting The World: The 33rd HeavenWork exercise, which Expresses Light to Souls throughout the reaches of the earth.

Lightning Bolt: The 70th HeavenWork exercise, in which the Soul compels the Breath of Heaven to lightly charge through the Soul in preparation for Transfiguration and entry into Heaven.

Miracles Of Compassion: The 64th HeavenWork exercise, the most powerful sanctifying exercises, in which the Soul compels Heaven to alter manifestation for the cause of Heaven.

Nova: The 57th HeavenWork exercise and 4th Higher Tantra exercise, which invokes a spark of Heaven Breath to set the Soul on holy fire.

Opening Your Heart: The 11th HeavenWork exercise, which loosens the Soul's attachment to the body.

Oracle: The 61st HeavenWork exercise, in which Soul peers into Heaven.

Pearl: The 55th HeavenWork exercise and 2nd Higher Tantric exercise, which Seals the Soul into the nether Clouds of Heaven, where the Sacred Beings in the Light dwell.

Pillar: The 56th HeavenWork exercise and 3rd Higher Tantric exercise, which powerfully clears a channel between the Soul and Heaven.

Pillar Of Fire: The 21st HeavenWork exercise, which Transcends Soul rapidly by thermal discomfort.

Pillar Of Ice: The 22nd HeavenWork exercise, which Transcends Soul rapidly by frigid discomfort.

Plume: The 34th HeavenWork exercise, a mechanism of Blessing, which Expresses Light in a column into another Soul.

Popping Out The Ball: The 13th HeavenWork exercise, which expands the Soul to its natural size.

Portal To Heaven: The 66th HeavenWork exercise, in which Soul Ascends and beholds *Abba*, the Face of God-in-Heaven.

Sacred Intent: The 35th HeavenWork exercise, a fundamental part of Blessing attached to Plume, which assigns a specific sacred purpose for the Light.

Sealing: The 59th HeavenWork exercise, in which Soul deposits Light assigned with a specific purpose into materiality or into the Clouds of Heaven.

Sensing Souls: The 3rd HeavenWork exercise, which stirs the Soul awake by touching another Soul.

Shower Of Light: The 9th HeavenWork exercise, which teaches the Soul to call concentrations of Light directly from Heaven.

Simultaneous Blessing: The 37th HeavenWork exercise, synergistic intensity when two or more Souls Bless each other at the same time.

Sitting On Tufted Palm: The 53rd HeavenWork exercise, which carries Soul into the nether Clouds of Heaven, where the Sacred Beings in the Light dwell.

Slide, The: The 14th HeavenWork exercise, which uses the onset of sleep to safely pass the Soul out of materiality.

Soul Disclosure: The 48th HeavenWork exercise, a shared experience in which two Souls enter each other, mutually exchanging a pure and complete intuitive understanding.

Soul Prayer: The 42nd HeavenWork exercise, which empowers the Soul to convey its sacred intent into Heaven.

Soul's Great Awakening, The: The 1st HeavenWork exercise, which stirs the Soul awake by the touch of a hand.

Starburst: The 49th HeavenWork exercise, which opens the Soul completely and explodes Light to cleanse the Soul.

Transcondensing: The 63rd HeavenWork exercise, in which the Soul harnesses the Heaven Breath.

Transflexion: The 26th HeavenWork exercise, uses material resistance to challenge and push the Soul into exploding Light through the substance of the Soul.

Ungrasping: The 24th HeavenWork exercise, which uses the moment of sleep to pass Soul from materiality into the Clear Light.

Vigil: The 27th HeavenWork exercise, in which the Soul awakens at night and extends into the Clear Light.

Volcano: The 51st HeavenWork exercise, which sustains the body once a Soul has Ascended to the point of Liberation.

Vortex: The 50ᵗʰ HeavenWork exercise, a fundamental advanced exercise, which teaches Soul how to quickly pull and release powerful concentrations of Light.

Wind Of Heaven, The: The 66ᵗʰ HeavenWork exercise, which teaches Soul to push into Heaven's emanation in order to Ascend to Heaven.

Witness: The 16ᵗʰ HeavenWork exercise, which separates mind from Soul.

Heaven's Mark: A gift of Ascendance, the Soul radiating intense silver-white spires of Light in all directions.

Holy Fire: Heaven Light in Soul ignited by the Breath of Heaven.

Hungry Ghost: The mind's deep obsessive tendency to grasp in panic at materiality.

Insubstantiation: A Diadem Angel's dissolution of form upon return to the Face of God-in-Heaven.

Invocation: The Soul's ability to call and receive Heaven Light.

Joy: The singing of the Soul in the Heaven Light.

Liberation: The near-sanctified Soul's permanent freedom from incarnation.

LightBall: A ball of Heaven Light formed between the hands.

LightStitching: Vortexing Heaven Light with the hands.

LightWater: Filling water with Heaven Light.

LightWork: The general term for all uses of Heaven Light, not limited to the purposes of Soul sanctification.

Magic: The use of Heaven Light to move materiality for purposes other than the sanctifying.

Manifestation: The Soul's ability to influence *Alpha* Creation Heaven to alter materiality.

Mark of Death: The gray mask superimposing a Soul about to die.

Marking: The Soul's ability to locate and connect to an aspect of Spirit or station itself in relation to Heaven.

Marriage in Spirit: Two Souls mutually becoming partners in Spirit by bonding together with Heaven Light.

Materiality: The lower, dense ground of being, which provides resistance for Souls to sanctify.

Meaningful Life: Life that moves a Soul along the Path of Light toward Heaven.

Migration: The Soul's afterlife journey in Spirit.

Mind: The epiphenomenal emanation of the brain, not being but a self-identifying process, which perishes at the moment of death.

Miracle: The Soul's pure work with Heaven to alter Manifestation for the purpose of Soul sanctification.

Outcome: The wordless complete instruction of the Soul Assigning the Heaven Light during Sealing.

Prayer Pillar: The sustained channel of Light between a Soul and Heaven that carries the Soul's Prayer directly to Heaven.

Preincarnation: A Soul's disembodied state prior to injection and embodiment.

Profane: Anything not sacred.

Quickening: The Soul's entry into the womb's fetus, typically accompanied with a "kick."

Reading: The Soul's ability to recognize another Soul's sanctification needs.

Remembrance: The Soul's return to preincarnate awareness, full awareness of life purpose.

Sacred Beings In The Light: Liberated Souls who Ascended to Heaven but chose to remain in the Clouds of Heaven to help other Souls find their way.

Sacred Intent: The Soul's pure wish accompanying the Blessing of Heaven Light.

Sacred Sight: The ability of an Ascended Soul to look into sacred Spirit.

Safe Surrender: Entering the Heaven Light for a limited time.

Sanctification Principle: Heaven's Will that all Souls sanctify, the essence of the Spirit Universe.

Sanctification: The Soul's changing, entering the Sacred by purifying in the Light of Heaven.

Sealing: The Soul's Assigning Heaven Light to perform a sanctifying function on Its own.

Sealing Body: Deep spiritual information Sealed within the Heaven Light.

Sing: Under Heaven, to send joyous Sacred Intent Ascendant unto Heaven; in the Body of Heaven, Expressing perfect Praise unto *Abba*.

Soul: The eternal being under Heaven.

Soul Memory: Perfect memory of Soul nature, and past experiences in body or the Life-Between.

Spirit: The true non-substance of being, containing the Clear Light, the Life-Between, the Heaven Light, the Breath of Heaven, and Heaven.

Tabernacle: A free-standing Ascending column of Heaven Light.

ThoughtGaps: Voids between the mind's activities, through which the Soul can slip into the Clear Light.

Three Million, The: Those of us who already entered Heaven.

Transcending: The Soul's unbinding from materiality and returning to the Clear Light.

Transcondensing: The Soul's converting Heaven Breath into Transfiguring power.

Transfiguration: The ultimate permanent changeover of an Ascended Soul into Heaven or the Clouds of Heaven.

Transmission: Immediate, perfect and direct infusion of Sacred Understanding into a Soul.

Truth: The eternal sacred Being beyond being of Heaven.

Tufted Palm: The Heaven Light that buoys and protects Soul in the Clouds of Heaven.

Unfolding: Completely opening the eye of the Soul.

Veil Of Embodiment: Amnesia of Soul brought about by the body's mind, the inability to see beyond materiality.

Vortex: A spiral of Heaven Light.

World Sanga: We are all monks, every moment of our lives, bent on completing our HeavenWork.